Library of
Davidson College

BURT FRANKLIN: RESEARCH & SOURCE WORKS SERIES
Philosophy & Religious History Monographs 151

THEODORE OF STUDIUM
HIS LIFE AND TIMES

Western Facade of the Church of St. John of the Studium, Constantinople.
(Of the date of Studius, Fifth Century.)

THEODORE OF STUDIUM

HIS LIFE AND TIMES

BY

ALICE GARDNER

τῇ ἐντολῇ δεῖ παραμετρεῖν ἑαυτοὺς, ἀλλὰ μὴ τοῖς πέλας.
THEODORUS STUDITES. EP. II. 115.

WITH ILLUSTRATIONS

BURT FRANKLIN REPRINTS
New York, N. Y.

922.1
T388g

Published by LENOX HILL Pub. & Dist. Co. (Burt Franklin)
235 East 44th St., New York, N.Y. 10017
Reprinted: 1974
Printed in the U.S.A.

Burt Franklin: Research and Source Works Series
Philosophy and Religious History Monographs 151

Library of Congress Cataloging in Publication Data

Gardner, Alice, 1854-1927.   74-10035
   Theodore of Studium; his life and times.

   Reprint of the 1905 ed. published by E. Arnold, London.
   "The published works of Theodore": p.
   1. Theodorus Studita, Saint, 759?-826. 2. Byzantine Empire—Politics and government.
BR1720.T38G3 1974   281.9'092'4 (B)   72-82007
ISBN 0-8337-1280-2

TO

THOMAS HODGKIN, D.C.L.

IN GRATITUDE FOR THE SERVICES HE HAS RENDERED
TO ALL STUDENTS OF HISTORY, IN MAKING ITS
PATHS DELIGHTFUL, NOT BY AVOIDING
DIFFICULTIES, BUT BY GUIDING
TOWARDS THE ATTAIN-
MENT OF TRUTH

PREFACE

THE object of this book is to present a sketch of a notable man who lived in notable times. The author was attracted to the task not by the consciousness of possessing all the requisite qualifications, but rather by the belief that some work of the kind was wanted; in that Theodore of Studium is well worth knowing, and that very few English people have, as yet, had much opportunity of knowing him. It is earnestly hoped that those who read through this book will realise how, in this one life, were focussed many great historical tendencies which gave their character to the churches and the civil societies of the Middle Ages. But beyond this they will, it is hoped, profit by being brought nearer to one who, with all the faults over which no veil is here thrown, had in him the elements of real greatness. The fascination of Theodore's character has been felt by most of the historians of that period, even by some who have had the minimum of sympathy with his religious principles.

The sources are indicated in the footnotes. The chief original authorities are, of course, the works of Theodore himself and the Byzantine chroniclers, especially Theophanes[1] and his *Continuator*. Of the editions of Theodore's works some account is given in the Appendix at the end of the book.

---

[1] For convenience' sake, I give references to the Bonn edition of Theophanes rather than to the superior recent edition of De Boor.

With regard to the general history of the period, it is pleasant to be able to name three Englishmen whose works are of the highest value: Finlay, whose "History of Greece" has been re-edited by Mr. Tozer; Dr. Hodgkin, whose researches into this period chiefly relate to Western affairs, but who illuminates any branch of history which he has occasion to touch upon; and Professor J. B. Bury, who, in his "History of the Later Roman Empire," and still more in his invaluable notes to Gibbon, has done very much for those who desire to study both the times of Theodore and Theodore himself.

Of smaller monographs, those on Theodore by Dr. Carl Thomas and Dr. G. A. Schneider have been found very useful. Dr. K. Schwarzlose's *Bilderstreit* is a most luminous study of the whole iconoclastic controversy. Schlosser's *Bilderstürmende Kaiser* is still useful, but more valuable for the purposes of the present work has been the little treatise, *De Studio*, of Abbé Marin.

The writer has to thank Dr. Edwin Freshfield, of the Mint, Chipstead, for the beautiful photographs of portions of Studium as it now is, and of the Golden Gate, and also for the loan of some very helpful books; and Dr. Kenyon, of the British Museum, for permission to reproduce a part of a page of a Studite Psalter (facing p. 146). She has also to thank her brothers, Professor Percy Gardner of Oxford, and Professor Ernest Gardner of London, for help in revising the proofs.

CAMBRIDGE, *August* 1905.

CONTENTS

CHAPTER I

PAGE

Ruins of Studium—Character of the Monastery—Time of Theodore's Birth—England—Western Europe—The East—Isaurian Emperors—Beginnings of Iconoclastic Controversy—Civilisation of Eastern Empire 1

CHAPTER II

Earliest Biographies of Theodore — His Parentage — Character of his Mother—Education : Question of the Byzantine Academy—Did he learn the Classics?—Position in Byzantine Society—His Uncle, Plato—Changes in Imperial Policy as to Icons—Theodore and his Family retire from the World 14

NOTES: The two Lives of Theodore and the Brethren of Photinus 29

CHAPTER III

Life in or near Saccudio—Early Rule of Eastern Monasteries—Relations with Plato—Complications of East and West—Policy of Irene—Council Proposed—Difficulties and Tumult—Adjournment to Nicæa — Proceedings—Decree in Favour of Icons — Subsequent Difficulties—Italian War—Theodore ordained Priest —Assertion of Principle 31

CHAPTER IV

Monastic Revival—Theodore made Abbot of Saccudio—Intrigues of Irene—Constantine VI. sole Emperor—His Second Marriage —He tries to win the Studites—Unsuccessful Negotiations—Exile—Letter to Plato—Overthrow of Constantine—Restoration of the Monks 50

CONTENTS

CHAPTER V

Removal from Saccudio to Studium—Foundation and Early History of the Monastery—Theodore's Reforms—Letter to Nicolas on Monastic Discipline—Monastic Officials—Calligraphy—Regulation of Life—Spirit of Theodore's Rule—Catecheses . . . 66

APPENDIX : Translation of Two Catechetical Discourses . . 89

CHAPTER VI

Events leading to Coronation of Charles the Great—Position of Pope Leo III.—Relation of Events in East to those in West—Intentions of Charles, especially towards Eastern Emperors—Matrimonial Project—Irene's Difficulties—Her Deposition—Accession of Emperor Nicephorus—Question as to Non-intervention of Studites—Policy of Nicephorus: in West; as to Constantine VI.; as to the Patriarchate—Plato and Theodore as Champions of the Ecclesiastical Power—Appointment of Nicephorus to Patriarchate—Protest of Studites—Reconciliation . 93

NOTE on the Death of Constantine VI. 113

CHAPTER VII

Ecclesiastical Policy of Emperor Nicephorus—Restoration of the Priest Joseph, opposed by Theodore—Arguments—Negotiations—Second Exile of Theodore—He repels charge of Schism—Appeals to Pope—Nicephorus killed in Bulgarian War—Return of Studites—Death of Abbot Plato 115

CHAPTER VIII

Unfortunate Reign of Michael Rhangabe—Theodore's Influence—Charles acknowledged Emperor—Negotiations with Bulgarians—Their advance—Michael deposed and succeeded by Leo V.—Leo's Government—He renews the Iconoclastic Policy—His Supporters—John the Grammarian—Conference—The Patriarch Nicephorus deposed—Theodore's Palm-Sunday Demonstration—Third Exile. Letters 130

CONTENTS

CHAPTER IX

Theodore as Theologian—His Views as to Church Authority—Theological Importance of Iconoclastic Controversy—Theodore's Personal Attitude — Manichæism and Monophysitism — Distinction between *worship* and *honour*—Educational use of Pictures—Mystic View of Images—Nominalism—Superstitions—Three Elements in Controversy—Theodore's *Antirrhetici*—His Doctrinal Letters—Platonic View of the Universe—Studite Feeling as to the Humanity of Christ 148

CHAPTER X

Conflict between Church and State — Mitigations of Theodore's Sufferings — Changes of Prison — Scourging and Privation—His Letters to Studite Monks; to Communities and Private Persons; to the Pope and Patriarchs—The Pope's Letter to Leo V.—Murder of Leo—Theodore's Triumph . . 169

CHAPTER XI

Character and Accession of Michael II.—Theodore's Efforts for Restoration of Icons : Letters to Patriarch, Ministers, Emperor, &c.—Theodore approaches Constantinople—Change of Patriarchs — Michael gives Audience — Theodore withdraws to Crescentius—His Correspondence with Empress Maria—With Empress Theodosia, &c.—Rebellion of Thomas : Theodore recalled to Studium — Thomas put down—Saracen Wars — Michael's Negotiations with Emperor Lewis and the Pope—*Collatio* of Paris—Reference to it by Theodore ? Images in Frankish Church—Works of Dionysius brought to the West . 187

CHAPTER XII

Character of Theodore's Letters in General—Letters of Condolence—Of Advice—On Moral Questions—On Prayer—On Depression—To Irene and Euphrosyne, Abbesses—To Casia—On Christian Doctrine—For Reclamation of Theoctistus—His Testament—His Death and Burial—His Character 208

APPENDIX : Theodore's Correspondence with Casia . . . 226

CONTENTS

CHAPTER XIII

PAGE

Attention of Studites to copying of MSS.—Introduction of Minuscule Writing—Theodore's probable Share—Theodore's Iambics—His Hymns—Nature of Ecclesiastical Metres in the East—Their Growth—Pitra's Discovery—The Canon—Canons and other Verse attributed to Theodore 230

APPENDIX: Renderings into English of some of Theodore's Poems: (1) Iambics; (2) Church Hymns 247

CHAPTER XIV

Theodore's Influence on Posterity—Circumstances which led to the Restoration of the Icons—Orthodoxy Sunday—Loss of Hopes of Ecclesiastical Unity—Final Breach—Its Connection with Studium—With the Name of Theodore—Abbots and Monks of Studium after Theodore—Permanent Value of Eastern Monasticism 253

APPENDIX: THE PUBLISHED WORKS OF THEODORE . . . 271

INDEX 279

LIST OF ILLUSTRATIONS

WESTERN FAÇADE OF THE CHURCH OF ST. JOHN OF
THE STUDIUM, CONSTANTINOPLE . . . . . *Frontispiece*

SEVENTH CENTURY CAPITAL FROM THE CHURCH OF ST.
JOHN OF THE STUDIUM . . . . . . *To face page* 10

THE EAST END OF THE CHURCH OF ST. JOHN . . ,, ,, 68

SIXTH CENTURY CAPITAL OF THE CHURCH OF ST. JOHN
(FROM THE COURTYARD) . . . . . . ,, ,, 86

THE GOLDEN GATE (IN THEODOSIAN WALL OF CONSTAN-
TINOPLE), NEAR TO STUDIUM . . . . ,, ,, 138

PART OF A PAGE FROM A STUDITE PSALTER OF THE
ELEVENTH CENTURY: THEODORE AND NICEPHORUS
BEFORE THE EMPEROR . . . . . . ,, ,, 146

SEVENTH CENTURY CAPITAL FROM THE CHURCH OF ST.
JOHN (USED AS A TARGET FOR PISTOL SHOOTING
BY THE TURKS) . . . . ,, ,, 174

CRYPT AT THE SOUTH-WEST END OF THE CHURCH OF
ST. JOHN . . . . ,, ,, 220

THEODORE OF STUDIUM
HIS LIFE AND TIMES

CHAPTER I

INTRODUCTION—GENERAL OUTLOOK FROM CONSTANTINOPLE IN THE MIDDLE OF THE EIGHTH CENTURY

IN the south-west corner of the city of Constantinople, near to the Seven Towers and the Golden Gate, stands the Mosque called MirAchor Djami, formerly the basilica of St. John of the Studium. Few passing travellers know of its existence, and even archæological explorers, seeking, as a rule, either the purely classical or the purely oriental, have given it but little attention. The hour will soon be too late, as both the Church and the remains of the monastic buildings adjoining are speedily disappearing, and in the words of a recent traveller, "it seems certain to perish in a few years if nothing is done."[1] Yet those who have studied the beautiful early capitals, with the rich and delicate acanthus foliage and the crossing cornucopias, and have admired the proportions of the Church whence the marble pavement and the tasteful decorations have long since been removed,[2] cannot acquiesce readily in

[1] W. H. Hutton, "Constantinople," p. 234.
[2] A few beautiful capitals have been brought to England by Dr. Edwin Freshfield and placed by him in the Church of the Wisdom of God, Lower Kingswood, Surrey. See illustrations p. 10 and p. 174.

this loss to all lovers of early Christian art. To those who know even a little of the history of the Monastery and of those who dwelt in it, the desecration and neglect may seem matter for regret but hardly for surprise. For it only reflects the comparative indifference with which, at least till recent times, not only the reading public in general but the whole academic world has regarded the post-classical period of Greek history. Yet that period comprises the early developments of Christian doctrine and monastic discipline in regions which, after all, were near to their original home. And both from the point of view of the ecclesiastical investigator and of the more general historian, the part played by Studium is by no means contemptible. It has well been called " the Clugny of the East." Yet in some ways, Studium has rendered even greater services to the Church and the world than were accomplished by Clugny. Like Clugny it became the parent of many centres of religious life and arduous labour; like Clugny it maintained the cause of spiritual authority against material force; but it had a task greater from an intellectual standpoint than any which fell singly to any particular monastery of the West, in keeping alive the torch of ancient learning. If neither Clugny nor Studium escaped from exaggerations in the pursuit of their ideals, it is surely now time to estimate aright the services rendered by both and the constancy shown in both to the causes which claimed their devotion.

It is not, however, with the general history of Studium that we are at present concerned. That history had begun very long before the times during which the subject of this biography lived, nor did his connection with it begin early in his life—even in his active life. In fact, to his biographers it may seem an additional proof of his strongly-marked character that a place in which he spent comparatively little of his laborious life became afterwards so closely associated with his memory that the Studium of earlier days, great and rich as it must have been, has merged its historical interest in that of a community of which it was in no sense the parent. The origin and character of the Monastery will concern us when we come to the beginning of Theodore's rule and the influence of which it became the centre. At present we will attempt to discriminate the leading features of the period when Theodore first saw the light, and which made up the physical and social environment of his earlier days.

Theodore, commonly called the Studite, was born in Constantinople in 759 A.D. It may be allowed that the general indifference to the study of the early Middle Ages, especially to that of Eastern Europe, before the ninth century, if not justifiable, is more or less explicable. The reader is confused by wearisome spectacles of palace intrigues, monotonous wars, hair-splitting theological controversies seasoned by bitter personal venom, and he finds in the East few if any men of power to give interest and significance to the current of events. But, on the other hand, he finds after every time of unusual depression, a lifting of the clouds, the advent of a stronger dynasty or a new policy which wards off immediate dangers, and gives the Empire a new lease of life. For if in other things Byzantium was the daughter of Rome, she was pre-eminently so in that peculiar recuperative power which won for the City the title of "Eternal." Readers of Roman history are puzzled to account for the fact that so cumbersome a vessel, with so many defects in construction, should have weathered so many storms. But from early times onward, ever and anon, when foes without and dissensions within had seemed likely to bring about a final destruction, some able man or some fortunate conjunction of men and circumstances had effected, if not a regeneration of the state, a re-adaptation to altered conditions. So had it been more than once before the days of Augustus; so again in his time; in that of Diocletian and Constantine; in that of Justinian; later on, in the days of Heraclius and in those of Leo the Isaurian. Permanent success was granted to none of these re-organising emperors. Yet the work accomplished in each case was a service to human civilisation. For the Empire was through many ages the only guardian of Helleno-Roman culture against the untamed barbarism of the North and the organised fanaticism of the East.

The leading questions to be thought out, worked out, or fought out during the latter part of the eighth century and the succeeding period, and also the champions of rival causes, were on a larger scale and of more general interest than those of the two centuries preceding. This becomes manifest if we take a most cursory glance at the chief events happening about the time of Theodore's birth. England will not concern us in our present studies, but we may notice that England was coming more into the stream of European progress, since just then Offa of Mercia seemed to be attaining that superiority over the other kings in Britain which afterwards passed over to the West Saxons, and the same Offa, while doing something towards the creation of a united English nation, was also tightening the bonds between England and Rome. Again, it was about four years before Theodore's birth that the Englishman Boniface was slain in the midst of his missionary labours on the continent—labours that indicated an aspiration after a united Christendom, and helped to bring about a lasting result through temporary failure. In Western Europe, Pippin the Frank was at that moment fighting against the Saracens in Spain, and by his victories, in conjunction with the remains of the Visigothic people, wresting Narbonne from the Mohammedans, and thereby restricting their power to the regions south of the Pyrenees. Five years previously, in 754, Pippin, on receiving the rite of coronation at the hands of Pope Stephen II., had exchanged the title of Mayor of the Palace for that of King of the Franks, and two years later he had made that arrangement in Italy which was the beginning of the temporal power of the Papacy. For in the year, which, as Dr. Hodgkin[1] has pointed out, almost exactly corresponds with the date—on the other side of our era—of the foundation of Rome, the Power which, in spite of changes in situation and in constitution, still claimed to hold the undying authority of the "Respublica," had lost all hold on Italy by the fall of the exarchate of Ravenna into the hands of the Lombards (751 A.D.). The Lombards were speedily to be ousted by the Frank, who at first conquered not for himself but for the successor of St. Peter. But the emperors, especially those of the strong Isaurian dynasty that began with Leo III., were not likely to view so serious a loss with equanimity. Whether Italy and the Empire would be permanently loosened from the ties, both secular and spiritual, which had bound them

---

[1] "Italy and her Invaders," Vol. VII. book viii. ch. viii. p. 164.

together was still an open question in the early days of Theodore.

For these events in the West were closely connected with movements which began in Theodore's native city of Constantinople, and which largely determined the character both of his mind and of his fortunes. At this time, as we have already seen, the Empire was making successful resistance to external foes and to internal disorders. Constantine V. (Copronymus or Caballinus), who had been reigning for nineteen years when Theodore was born, was pursuing the general lines struck out by his father, Leo III., first of the Isaurian house. It was Leo who effected a brilliant repulse of the Saracens from the walls of Constantinople in 718 A.D. ("really an ecumenical date," as Professor Bury remarks),[1] since from this time forth the great Omeyyad dynasty declined in power, and Christendom was saved from immediate danger. Leo and Constantine were constantly carrying on war with the Saracens in Asia, and, speaking generally, they were successful. At the same time the Bulgarians were constantly invading Thrace; and in the year of Theodore's birth, Constantine suffered a defeat at their hands, which was adequately avenged a few years later.

We have again to reckon Leo and Constantine among the later Roman legislators or codifiers. The Ecloga, a compendium of the laws to be acknowledged in public and private life, was published in 740, and was accompanied by codes relating particularly to military, agricultural, and naval matters respectively. The Isaurians were careful administrators, and looked themselves into the financial details of the Empire with a view to accuracy and economy.

---

[1] "History of the Later Roman Empire," vol. ii. p. 405.

Strange indeed must it seem that men of such clear heads, with great organising faculties, patient in carrying out their designs, apparently conscientious in the discharge of their duties, free to all appearance from either petty scruple or misleading sentimentalism, should have superfluously embarked on an enterprise which well-nigh cost them their power in the ancient home of their empire, and which aroused an opposition to their policy among the ablest thinkers and most capable workers of those who owned their sway.

The bearings of the Iconoclastic Controversy on the whole life of the time, the conflicts which it involved among theological conceptions and practical principles, will concern us much in the course of our inquiries. The origin must remain obscure. Here we will merely point out a few of the most notable events in connection with it which occurred before the beginning of our narrative. It was most likely in the year 726 that the first edict against images was issued by Leo III. Whether or no the great volcanic disturbances which took place in 725, near to the island of Thera, had seemed a demonstration of Divine wrath against idolatry in the eyes of an Emperor whom his direst foes would not accuse of superstition; whether he was following the policy of the Caliph Yezid, who had begun operations against images a few years before; whether he was influenced by the injunctions of Jews, heretics, or renegade Catholics—are questions we must postpone for the present. The order was issued on the authority of the Emperor only. His attempt to obtain the assent and support of the Patriarch Germanus signally failed, as did apparently his efforts to win the approval of the heads of the Academy which represented and fostered higher education in Constantinople. The lower classes of the people were, as might naturally be supposed, violently averse to the proposed changes, and apparently the first actual sufferers in the conflict were the workmen employed in hewing to pieces a mosaic representing Christ which stood above the gate called Chalce.[1] Probably the measures which followed a State Council—oddly called a *Silentium*—in 739 were, no less than the previous ones, due to Leo's personal initiation and authority. The Patriarch Germanus was formally deposed, and a more pliant ecclesiastic, Anastasius by name, was set on his throne.

Meantime, a strong opposition had arisen in the West. Pope Gregory II., on receiving notice of the iconoclastic decrees, had at once protested in writing: "That the Emperor ought not to concern himself with matters of faith nor to change the ancient doctrines of the Church as taught[2] by the Holy Fathers." The subsequent action of the Pope is not easy to trace. Italy was in a seething state, and the iconoclastic decrees seem rather to have precipitated than originated a widespread revolt against the Emperor, to which heavy taxes had already given provocation. According to the principal Greek

---

[1] Or possibly it may have been an image in the stricter sense. According to one account, it was itself called Chalce; according to another, *Antiphonates*. See note in Hodgkin, *loc. cit.* p. 456. In any case, the image was in a lofty position, though some accounts represent the first edict as only directed against such pictures as were situated within reach of the worshipper, and thus liable to be physically saluted. For the whole controversy, see Theophanes (our chief authority) and Mansi, *Historia Conciliorum.*

[2] Theophanes, Bonn edition, p. 621. Observe that this opposition of Gregory II. to Leo does *not* rest on the probably spurious letters assigned to him.

authority, Gregory stimulated this resistance; according to the more probable accounts of the Latin writers, he tried to restrain it. Policy at that juncture might have prompted the same course of action as that which was prescribed by loyalty and desire for peace. In 731 Gregory III., having succeeded to the Papacy, called a synod of Italian bishops, which denounced the penalty of excommunication against all despisers of the holy images. The religious difference was now added to the earlier Italian complications. The Emperor withdrew both Illyricum and Southern Italy from obedience to the Roman See. When the Pope required outside help against the Lombards, Constantinople was the last quarter whence it might be hoped for. The result, most momentous for the whole course of European history, was, as we have seen, the armed intervention of the Franks, and the abeyance of imperial authority in the West, till it should be restored under very different auspices, with new duties and new supports.

The iconoclastic policy of Constantine V., who succeeded his father in 741, seems to have been more thorough-going and systematic than that of Leo. He attempted to gain support for his measures by means of a Church Council; but as none of the great patriarchs were present it is not counted except as the pseudo-council of Constantinople of 753.[1] It had been preceded by "Silentia," or councils, in various cities, was attended by three hundred and thirty-eight bishops, and was presided over by Theodosius, Bishop of Ephesus. In the iconoclastic decree

[1] 754 (?). For difficulties in the chronology of this period, see Bury L.R.E., ii. p. 425.

which it passed, the favourers of images were placed in the dilemma of choosing between Monophysitism or Nestorianism; either they must be endeavouring to represent the Divine Nature to the human senses, which would be blasphemous, or they must be dividing the nature of Christ, which would be heretical. As we shall see hereafter, this argument had as much force as most dilemmas on the minds of those who had learned to parry intellectual blows, and not much more on those who, if they could not lodge themselves between the horns of a dilemma, would have little standing-room for their religious opinions. What is of more immediate interest to us is the ceaseless warfare waged from this time forward between the iconoclastic emperors and the monks.

It is by no means easy to decide whether Constantine V. persecuted the monks because they upheld the icons, or whether icons and monks together provoked his detestation as maintaining a particular type of piety which he personally disliked, and which seemed to him undesirable for the public cause. He and his father, whether attracted or not by the simplicity of Mohammedan doctrine, had seen Mohammedanism at work, and they knew that a religion without asceticism, without external symbols, without saint-worship or religious orders, possessed a power in the field and on the march which enabled ordinary men to forego private inclinations and face imminent death.

For centuries there had been a recognised inconsistency in Christian lands between the ideal reverenced by the pious and the claims of the state on the services of the citizen. To practise celibacy when many countries were perishing for lack of men, to gather into separate communities at a time when the public

SEVENTH CENTURY CAPITAL FROM THE CHURCH OF
ST. JOHN OF THE STUDIUM.

service demanded a patriotic zeal of the most active kind—to love to dwell on hidden mysteries and to make much of fine points of metaphysical subtlety, when sound practical sense was the one thing needed to save the state—all this might move an irritable patriot to secularism and dispose an autocratic ruler to persecution. It was not only the monks, but also laymen whose religious practices and feelings resembled those of the monks who moved the ire of Constantine. The tendency to call on a sacred name—of Christ or of the Virgin—in a moment of unexpected peril, the habit of frequent church-going, the observance of vigils and fasts—became a crime in the eyes of one who had practically the power to decide what should constitute crime in a despotically ruled empire. To compel monks to give up their wealth might seem necessary for the threatened security of the state. To enforce the breach of monastic vows was undeniably intolerant, but not beyond the reach of justification under stress of circumstances. But to expose to public ridicule and to visit with severe penalties those practices which popular piety approved and clerical learning justified, was to throw down the glove to the religion of the people. Constantine was not an argumentative theologian, like some of his predecessors and followers. Yet he could form a telling argument, sharpened with a point of ridicule, as when, *à propos* of the worship of the Virgin, he asked an ecclesiastic what was the worth of a wooden box that had once held gold? But if the theological emperors had sometimes made themselves undignified, the persecuting emperors soon made themselves hated. It is difficult to give them credit, as some of their Protestant apologists would do, for a desire to reform religion and to make the people more rational in their piety. How much of a real reforming spirit is to be found among those who carried out the iconoclastic policy we shall have to inquire hereafter. Our present object is only to obtain a general view of the conflicting tendencies in Church and State at the time when our narrative begins.

One word more before we pass from this preliminary survey to the main subject of our study; we are apt, when we read of anarchy and of barbarian invasions, both in East and West; when we see the same kind of ecclesiastical discussions going on all over Europe; when we realise the deterioration of art and literature in the lands where, a few centuries before, they had reached so high a point of development—to fancy that by this time Græco-Roman civilisation was all played out, that the name "Roman Empire" was as inapplicable to the dominion of Constantine as to that which was founded half-a-century later by Charles. Yet such a view would be erroneous. In spite of decadence in many realms of culture, in spite of dangers which had robbed the Eastern Empire of its ancient security, and of disorders that hindered the ordinary course of civilised life, in spite of the loss of many treasures and traditions of ancient times, and the gradual drifting away of Constantinople from the yet more venerated home of culture and of order, yet after all the city where Theodore was born and bred was at that moment the focus of the best civilisation that existed, and contained within itself enough of the ancient world to vindicate it from any suspicion of encroaching barbarism. Remote indeed seems the Constantinople of the eighth century from all our modern ideas and ways, yet the London or the Paris of those days might perhaps seem still farther removed from us than that "queenly" city. For there men could still enjoy the delights and refinements of Greek life, and admire the masterpieces of Hellenic art, as they strolled from hippodrome and theatre to church and monastery, from the busy harbours of the Golden Horn to the secluded garden of the old foundation of Studium.

[The authorities for this introductory sketch are numerous, and many of them have been already cited. The principal original authorities are the Chronographia of Theophanes, and the documents in Mansi's *Concilia*. Among modern guides we have Bury's "Later Roman Empire," the last three volumes of Hodgkin's "Italy and her Invaders," Gibbon, with Professor Bury's notes, Hefele's "History of Church Councils" (last volume), and Schwarzlose's *Bilderstreit*.]

CHAPTER II

BIRTH AND EDUCATION OF THEODORE—FORMATIVE INFLUENCES OF HIS EARLY LIFE

IF the time of Theodore's early days was one of great agitation in matters political and ecclesiastical, he may be said to have grown to manhood in the very thick of the fray. For his native city, Constantinople, was the great centre of all the movements and contests of the time, and the family into which he was born was, on both sides, intimately connected with the administration of the imperial government and intensely susceptible to the religious influences around.

We have the advantage of possessing two "Lives" of Theodore,[1] one of which, at least, seems to have been the work of a follower and disciple, and the still more valuable records given by himself in his funeral discourses on his mother Theoctista[2] and his uncle Plato.[3] True, the "Lives" do not satisfy our curiosity on some points, and have the failings usually found in works written primarily for edification; while the Orations labour under the disadvantages which encumber all distinctly panegyrical discourses. Nor do the various sources always agree as to details. Nevertheless, they give us a good deal of material for forming, not only a fairly clear narrative, but also

---

[1] For these two lives, see note at the end of this chapter. I shall refer to the shorter one as *Vita B*, to the longer as *Vita A*.
[2] *Oratio* xiii.
[3] *Oratio* xi.

a vivid picture of the persons and events most important to Theodore during a great part of his life.

Theodore's father was a certain Photinus, who held a post in the imperial treasury—in Latin his position is called "regionum vectigalium quæstor"[1] —his mother, a lady of good birth, Theoctista, daughter of Sergius and Euphemia, "distinguished as to family and no less admirable in character." Biographers, of an age when word-play was considered elegant, liked to dwell on his "luminous" father and his "God-created" mother. But in fact the luminary only shines for them by a reflected light, and hardly anything is recorded of Photinus except his prudence, piety, and deference to his wife. It is even uncertain at what approximate age he died.[2] He seems to have had three brothers, like-minded with himself in religious disposition.[3] With Theoctista the case is otherwise. Her son—who seems to have been the eldest, at least of her boys—always cherished a sincere admiration and affection for her. In a letter, written while she was suffering from a dangerous illness, he extols her self-denying life, and expresses his grief that the cares of his office, more binding than iron chains, prevent him from coming to her. When she actually died— probably some time later, as he seems to have been actually present with her at the end—he pronounced to the monks under his care a discourse of great interest, as giving the portrait of a pious and wealthy lady in fashionable Byzantine society. Theoctista

[1] *Vita B*, 2. ταμίειας ἐχρημάτισε τῶν βασιλικῶν φόρων.
[2] He is not mentioned in Theodore's letter to his mother, among those of the family who are already departed (*Lib.* i. *Ep.* 6), but I have not found any mention of him as living.
[3] For the three brothers of Photinus, see note at end of this chapter.

had lost her parents in the great plague[1] which ravaged Constantinople in 749, and which was regarded by the orthodox as a judgment on iconoclasm. Her brother, Plato, was able to work his way up by diligence and industry, becoming first a notary, then a clerk of the imperial exchequer, fulfilling the functions of an office the honour—and probably the emolument—of which went to his negligent guardian. Theoctista, meanwhile, was allowed to grow up without education, till, with an energy equal to her brother's, she took the matter into her own hands. This does not seem to have been till after her marriage, which was probably an early one. Her ideas of matronly duty did not allow of her giving the daylight hours to literary occupation, but she found time for her studies late at night and early in the morning. Thus she taught herself letters γραμματίζει ἑαυτὴν ἡ σοφὴ καὶ συνετίζει, and being, even in early youth, of a religious turn of mind, committed the Psalter to memory. Meantime she adopted a severely ascetic life, wearing a dress like a widow's, eating little meat, fasting rigorously, especially in Lent, while making-believe to take part in necessary banquets, and keeping her eyes downcast when she attended improper spectacles. Her attention to her children and to her household duties was assiduous. She seems to have cared more for the comfort of her servants than for her own, since, besides their ordinary allowance of bread, wine and bacon, she always saw that from time to time, especially on feast days, they had some fresh meat, fish and other delicacies. Being a careful housekeeper and a strict

[1] See Theodore's "Life of Abbot Plato," 3, 4, and Theophanes, *cf.* 355. The accounts are ghastly and inexplicable. Both speak of coloured crosses appearing on *the clothes of the victims.*

BIRTH AND EDUCATION

disciplinarian, and naturally of a quick temper, it sometimes occurred that acts of theft or negligence would provoke her to exercise the prerogative of mistress over slave, and deal not only reprimands but sharp blows. On such occasions, however, penitence speedily followed. Retiring to her room, she would slap her own cheeks, to realise the pain she had given, and then would send for the injured servant and make humble apology. Hospitality and liberality to the poor and the sick were marked traits in her character, and her care for her own children was constant and watchful. She kept her daughter secluded from worldly follies, and instructed her in the Scriptures and in the care of the sick. Every night, after her children had gone to bed, she visited them and signed them with the cross, and in the morning, on arising from her scanty night's rest, she aroused them to join with her in early prayer.

These children seem to have been four in number, Theodore, Joseph, Euthymius, and a daughter whose name is not known.[1] They must have been closely attached to one another, and receptive of the same kind of impressions. At the age of seven Theodore was brought under outside influences, those of his instructors in letters.

The names of Theodore's teachers are not preserved for us. We do not even know whether the teaching that he received was private or shared by others. Grammarians and rhetoricians had always stood high in Constantinople. Special immunities and privileges had

---

[1] Some writers take the expression ἐξαδέλφη in *Vita B*, 15, to mean that the Empress Theodote was sister's daughter to Theodore, which would imply that there was another decidedly older sister in the family. But it seems more likely that Theodote was Theodore's cousin.

been granted to them by many successive emperors, and salaries were guaranteed to them by the state, though there is no ground for supposing that they were quite independent of the fees of their pupils. Besides teachers, books abounded and were probably easy of access. Here, however, we come upon a difficulty. We have already noticed a curious story, which hardly claims our acceptance, of an Academy at Constantinople burned down by Leo III., along with the professors who acted as librarians and refused to execute the iconoclastic decrees. This academy[1] is said to have been presided over by a Doctor, who bore the title "Œcumenical" and was supported by twelve colleagues. However this may have been, we know, on the testimony of Themistius, that Constantine the Great founded a library. It was later increased by Julian, and under Valens it was cared for by four Greeks and three Latin librarians. In the time of Basiliscus and of Zeno, it was wholly or partially burned and refounded, and its later station was in the Octagon, near to the part of the city called Chalche. Now if it was just in that region that the first removal of images was begun, we should find some reason for Leo's consultation of the doctors and for his displeasure at their unwillingness to remove the images, without resorting to the hypothesis of a permanent Council of Learned Men or the strange act of imperial incendiarism. Such speculations apart, however, we should like to be able to determine whether from the time of Leo to that of Bardas, as some historians say, there was really no first-rate public library in Constantinople,

[1] The *locus classicus* here is Zonaras, iii. 340. For Libraries and Librarians in Constantinople see discourse in *Constantinopolis Christiana*, by Ducange

since that would touch a question of importance for our present purpose: how far Theodore, during the years of his education, was familiarised with the chief works of classical antiquity. The silence of Theophanes would lead us to suppose that the great library was there, even if diminished in size. Books must have been easily procurable in Constantinople, or the ravages of fires could not thus have been redressed. One man at least who was Theodore's younger contemporary, Photius, afterwards Patriarch of Constantinople, was a scholar of encyclopædic learning, and yet the period of his education would, if the great fire is admitted, have fallen within the time during which the Library was in abeyance.[1]

It might be thought that such an important point as the acquaintance of Theodore with Greek literature ought to be easily decided from his biographies or from his own works. But here our biographer, in want of material, falls back on commonplace statements with moralising commentaries. He tells us how diligently and successfully Theodore prosecuted his studies in Grammar, Dialectic ("which those skilled in it call philosophy"), and Rhetoric, and dwells much on the good conduct and piety which marked his student life. "Grammar" should, of course, include general literature, but it was quite possible, then as now, for a student to acquire sufficient knowledge to pass muster in a crowd without going beyond compendia and books of extracts. The study of Dialectic was, of course, based on Aristotle, and it may be said that a belief in the power of argument was a legacy of the Pagan Greeks to the Eastern Church. Rhetoric was in the

[1] There was in Photius' time a college which had been founded by Bardas. But whence came its books?

same way an instrument for religious teaching which had to be acquired along the lines of secular instruction. The fact that Theodore became proficient in these subjects would not by itself prove that he received a broadly based Greek education.

Nor do his writings help us to decide the question. He does not make first-hand quotations from the classics, though this by no means proves that he was personally unacquainted with them. We might imagine that if he had read Plato, he could hardly have kept himself from quoting Platonic passages where they would evidently have been capable of interpretation on his side and against the iconoclasts. But after all, in quoting those of the Fathers most deeply imbued with Platonic philosophy,—particularly Basil—he may have thought that to go beyond a Christian Father to seek the origin of his principles in a heathen philosopher would have weakened rather than confirmed any cause. Yet there can be no doubt that in so far as Theodore and those of the same school were Platonists in mind, they preferred to take their Platonism, or at least to exhibit it, at second hand. Similarly, in our own days, many theologians acknowledge principles which have been ultimately derived from Kant and Hegel, while they may have as little actual familiarity with those philosophers as any of their readers or audience.

The facts remain, of course, that the Greek classics were to be read in the Byzantine libraries, that Theodore had a deep respect for books and learning, and that he did seriously devote himself to prolonged and arduous studies, both during his early youth and in later years. At the same time, we know that the accumulation of learning was not only a possible fact but one actually accomplished by some of his contemporaries. Yet even with some of the undoubtedly learned, the curious position of conscious intellectual indebtedness to a system and to persons whose authority had been repudiated, had involved a want of that sense of proportion which is essential to real literary culture.

Take for instance John of Damascus, an elder contemporary of Theodore, who had been, as his biographer tells us, well instructed in all Greek learning, and who wrote both an elaborate *Dialectica* and an account of One Hundred Sects or Heresies prevalent in his own or in earlier days. He actually confounds, or seems to confound, Pythagoreans with Peripatetics, and the chief mark of the Platonists seems to him to be the socialistic ideal of Plato's "Republic." If Theodore had ever wished to convert heathens, or even to demonstrate the superiority of Christianity to Paganism in any way, we should have known whether his knowledge as to pagan philosophy was clear or confused. But neither pagan philosophy nor ancient history was required to yield him arms for the dialectical contests of his life.

Theodore's zeal for knowledge, as he conceived it, and his familiarity with the Scriptures and with the Greek Fathers, is evident all through his writings. And no less clear is his appreciation of the need of clearness in terminology, and careful observance of logical forms, on the part of those who undertake to prove or disprove any controverted doctrine. In one of his letters, addressed to a young monk who seems to have been writing about what he did not understand,[1] he reproaches him bitterly for using technical terms—such as *relative*, *type*, and the like—without having

[1] *Lib.* ii. *Ep.* 151.

acquired the grammatical and philosophical skill that would have enabled him to use them accurately.

In rhetoric or eloquence Theodore certainly obtained a high place, all the more, perhaps, if, as his biographer says, he despised the empty verbiage which encumbered the study. His style can hardly be called simple, but when he was purposely aiming at a practical end and could afford to throw his oratorical flowers away, he could speak very vigorously and much to the point. He must have studied poetry with care, as far as the laws of versification are concerned. As to his readings in the poets, we have no evidence. But he learned to write elegant verse in the classical metres, and also to compose according to the new and elaborate ecclesiastical system of hymn or ode writing, in which accent was gradually beginning to supersede quantity.

What help he had at home in his studies, we are not able to say. In one of his letters[1] he mentions a commentary on St. John as *of* (which may mean either *belonging to* or *written by*) his father according to the flesh. But it hardly seems likely that Photinus, of whom we know so little, should have been a theological writer, though it is quite probable that he was a lover of books.

Theodore's quiet years of early study seem to have lasted till he was twenty-two years old. This fact suggests the question whether, in his studies, any practical objects were set before him,—whether he were preparing himself for any profession or calling. It might be supposed that his disposition and tastes would have inclined him towards the clerical profes-

---

[1] 31 of Cozza-Luzi Collection.

sion,—but we can hardly find any clear traces of such a profession at Constantinople just at this time. The leading ecclesiastics seem in many cases to have been promoted from the ranks of the laity—though this was, of course, against canonical rule—or else to have entered the Church through the cloister. It seems most probable that before Theodore definitely gave up his life in the world altogether for one of monastic seclusion, he was regarded as likely to follow some such lines as those of his father and uncle, and to rise gradually to a position of wealth and standing in the Imperial Service. This consideration brings us to the highly interesting question whether Theodore, and Plato before him, acquired in the Offices of the Government the neat and business-like handwriting for which they both became famous. We must return to this subject later.[1]

There was probably no actual need for Theodore to earn a livelihood, as his family had landed possessions, especially in Asia Minor, and his father's office must have been a lucrative one. Of one fact we may be sure—that he mixed in the upper society of Constantinople, and acquired that knowledge of men and manners, with habits of courtesy and social tact, which mark his correspondence, and entitle him all through life to the title of *gentleman*. Possibly to those who do not realise the excessive and scrupulous etiquette and ceremony which distinguish Byzantine society, his urbanity may seem to have a tinge of servility. In any case, it is an important fact that in early life he learned to know men and society, and that he was not an alien to the aristocratic world in which he was

---

[1] See chap. xiii.

obliged later to seek for partisans. And there seems to be something quite genuine in Theodore's appreciation of piety and purity as he discerned it among the religiously disposed of the members of the upper circles. To him the monastic life was always the highest. Any man or woman who had adopted and forsaken it was to be regarded as one who had put the hand to the plough and looked back. Yet the example of his mother and probably that of other members of his family had shown him that even in the world a good and pure life might be lived. He always seems to have felt tenderness for children, and to have admired conjugal affection and fidelity. He can never be accused of having such an exclusively monastic standard of excellence as to discourage efforts towards virtuous living under the ordinary conditions of society.

It may be remarked that the high and honoured position of Photinus and Theoctista, taken together with their recognised piety, would lead us to doubt whether the persecutions of Constantine Caballinus touched those of the laity who, while disapproving his anti-monastic and iconoclastic policy, did not incur suspicion by offending any of his strongest prejudices or feelings. After all, Constantine had a daughter who was notable for her piety and had a nun for her godmother.[1] If, during his reign, the family had shown any intentions of forsaking the world, the case might have been otherwise.

An interesting point in Theodore's account of his mother is her freedom from the superstition of her contemporaries,—the very trait which the iconoclasts were always holding up for opprobrium in their opponents.

---

[1] See Bury: "Later Roman Empire," bk. vi. ch. v., note at end.

She refused to allow in the case of her children the curious ceremonies practised on new-born babes. Possibly the view that such ceremonies were derived from the Devil may itself be regarded as savouring of superstition. But the prevalence of belief in magic and the resistance made to it in the name of Christianity is a fact to be taken account of in the controversies of the times. If almost everybody was credulous, the anti-iconoclasts had no monopoly.

The strenuous piety of Theoctista and her resistance to the worldly ideas and practices of her neighbours was encouraged by the reputation and influence of her brother Plato, although during the days of persecution he was not able to show himself openly in Constantinople. Plato had early conceived a desire to flee from the world, and he executed it in somewhat dramatic fashion. He left Constantinople with one servant, crossed the straits, and wandered away to a desolate region till he came to a cavern into which he entered. He then gave his head to be shorn by his attendant, put on a vile garment, and sent the man back with his ordinary clothes to the city. The servant departed weeping, and Plato went on his way till he came to the monastery of Symboli, in Bithynia, over which a holy man Theoctistus presided as abbot.[1] Plato was admitted to the abbot's presence, and replied satisfactorily to the questions put to him. Nevertheless Theoctistus feared that a man of gentle birth and good social position would find such a life as that which he contemplated too severe for his endurance. But Plato would take no repulse. "Father," he exclaimed, "I give up all to you, mind and will and body; treat

---

[1] The name suggests kinship to the family of Plato and Theoctista, and we are told that the family had possessions in Bithynia.

your servant as you will; he will obey you in everything." Thus Plato began his life as monk. As time went on, he never relaxed either in active labours or in private discipline. In course of time his reputation grew, and on the death of Theoctistus he succeeded to his office.

These were the years of persecution. But better times were at hand. In 775, Constantine Caballinus died, and was succeeded by his son, Leo IV., commonly called, from his mother's race, the Khazar. Leo did not at once reverse nor did he actually continue the ecclesiastical policy of his father. He does not seem to have been a strong man, and he was in a very difficult position, as he had several grown-up brothers of doubtful loyalty, a young son, whose succession he wished to secure, a very ambitious wife, and probably a feeble physical constitution which made a long tenure of power improbable. Irene, the Empress, was an Athenian, a devoted venerator of images, and from inclination or policy inclined to favour the monks. At first it seemed as if a compromise would be made. Leo showed himself "a friend of the God-bearer and of the monks,"—not, however, of the icons. On the death of the iconoclastic Patriarch, a man of learning and good reputation was appointed to succeed him, Paul of Cyprus, who had attained the ecclesiastical grade of Lector. Paul seems to have hoped for a restoration of the old state of things, but Leo, urged perhaps by the fear of a faction which had risen in insurrection under some of his brothers, began after a time to use strong measures against the opponents of iconoclasm. What kind of policy he would ultimately have adopted is uncertain, as he died in 780, after a troubled reign of five years, leaving his throne to his son Constantine,

BIRTH AND EDUCATION

aged ten, and under the guardianship of his mother Irene.

The Empress had now a fair field for carrying out her own ideas. Whatever her moral character may have been, she was certainly a woman of capacity. She proved herself more than a match for the recalcitrant uncles, and her respect for the monastic state was rather oddly shown in her orders for the tonsure of the most illustrious rebels. The patriarch Paul, penitent and miserable, desired to retire from an office in which he had not acted up to his convictions. Happily, death saved him from any such humiliation. His last request,—that the question of the icons should be decided by a General Council—was accepted as an obligation by his successor. This was Tarasius, a layman of distinction, whose political experience was likely to stand the Empress in good stead. He did not in the subsequent history prove himself a very strong champion of the monastic cause, but his influence, when freely exercised, was in favour of the monks and of the icons.

There was now no need for Plato to absent himself from Constantinople. His vows had not been such as to preclude him from exercising social influence, and when he returned to his old surroundings, the spell of his strong character was first felt by his sister and her children, and especially by Theodore. This influence brought about a renunciation of all secular life on the part of the whole family. It was not a difficult matter to accomplish, as they possessed estates in Bithynia, a province where ascetics and ascetic communities seem to have flourished. In the late troubles, the religious houses for women had become disorganised, but Theoctista would be able to live "cellular fashion" with her little daughter, while her husband and his three brothers, her son Theodore and his brothers, Joseph and Euthymius, could probably be accommodated in suitable places of retirement, possibly all of them under the direct supervision of Plato himself.

Theodore gives a pathetic account of the parting of mother and sons. The wave of enthusiasm seems to have carried away the whole family, yet at the last moment the youngest boy, Euthymius, felt his heart fail, and clung around his mother's neck, imploring that he might remain with her. But her answer was inexorable: "If you do not go willingly, my child, I with my own hand will drag you on board the ship." This seems an inhuman speech, but in point of fact there seems to have been quite free consent to the breaking up of the family on the part of all its members, and in the case of Theoctista, the ties of family affection were not snapped by the adoption of a new life.

If Theodore himself felt any weakness, he is not likely to have expressed it. It seems to have been a good deal by his persuasion that the final step was taken, and he had found a hero-model as well as a spiritual father in his uncle, with whose fortunes his own were hereafter to be very closely linked.

If, from this critical moment, we look back on Theodore's early life and training, we see how fitly it had prepared him for the part he was to play in life, as religious controversialist, as monastic reformer, and as party leader. Family surroundings had fostered his natural tendency to emphasise the religious side of life and thought, and his reading had been in great part theological. Yet he had learned to look at religious questions, not perhaps in what we should call a philosophic aspect, but at least as a genuine Greek must look at all matters which are to be discussed according to logical principles, and contemplated under the forms of the old philosophies. The practices which he had observed in his mother, the example of asceticism shown in his uncle, their utter disregard of all worldly considerations where higher interests were at stake, had helped to form in his mind a type of the devout and self-denying life which was to serve as the model of many influential communities. And his intercourse with men and women of various characters and modes of life had given him a certain power of discerning character and of appealing to responsive feelings, which was essential to his success as champion of a fluctuating cause. At the same time, apart from any such evident advantages as a youth of his great capacity might derive from friends, teachers, and society, there was nourished in him one quality in which so many of his contemporaries were notably deficient;—a single-heartedness in all his efforts, and an entire loyalty to duty, sustained by a firm belief in his own vocation to serve the cause of righteousness and truth, the cause oppressed by all the forces of an autocratic government and an unsympathetic world.

NOTES ON CHAPTER II

I. "The two Lives of Theodore." These are printed *in extenso* in vol. xcix. of the *Patrologia*. The second is the shorter, and is now acknowledged to be the work of Michael the Monk, a Studite and younger contemporary of Theodore. The other and longer biography is evidently based on the shorter one, but contains some additional matter, especially concerning the earliest stage of Theodore's monastic life. It was formerly attributed to

Michael, whose name it bears in two early codices, but since that authorship has been assigned to the other life, this one has been regarded as the work of a certain John, or of Theodorus Daphnopates.

II. " Brethren of Photinus." The three converts of Plato have, in interpretation of the documents, been regarded as three brothers of Plato (*Vita B*), or as brothers or sisters or brothers and sister of Theodore (*Vita A*). *Or.* xiii. 6, would seem to be conclusive in favour of the view that they were brothers of Photinus. But it seems strange that we hear no more of them.

CHAPTER III

FIRST YEARS OF THEODORE'S MONASTIC LIFE—DISCIPLINE—THE SECOND COUNCIL OF NICÆA AND ITS CONSEQUENCES—THEODORE ORDAINED PRIEST

THE time at which Theodore forsook the world was one of great disorganisation in Eastern monachism. There was, however, much zeal for asceticism and a strong desire for a regulated common life evident in many quarters, and wanting only the call of a leader and the skill of an organiser to reconstruct the tottering fabric and make it far more stable than it had been before. It was, perhaps, well for Theodore that the first years of his profession were for him a period of quiet and seclusion. The place to which he and his family had retired was a country estate called Boscytium, not far from Saccudio, where Plato was abbot. It was in the form of a crescent, well planted and breezy, with pleasant flowing water.[1] Either here or at Saccudio, under the direction of his uncle, Theodore superintended the building or rebuilding of a church dedicated to St. John the Evangelist, both the floor and the walls of which were adorned with rich mosaics. For a task of this kind, his familiarity with the noble buildings of Constantinople must have well fitted him. In the zeal for his newly adopted vocation, he was eager to accomplish the very lowliest of monastic

[1] The description of Boscytium in *Vita A*, is almost identical with that of Saccudio in *Vita B*.

duties, such as digging in the garden, helping the sick brethren in their labours, and cleaning out the domestic buildings.[1] But this work was not incompatible with serious study, and in fact it was through reading the ascetic works of Basil that Theodore became so active in both practising and enforcing the rules as to labour, seclusion, and regularity in prayer and in work, which were held to be binding on all monks.

This brings us to the difficult question : under what kind of rule did the monks of the Eastern monasteries live towards the end of the eighth century? If they had been asked, they would doubtless have replied : "under that of the great Basil." Yet in the genuine works of Basil, and even in the spurious ones[2] which were accepted as his by Plato and Theodore, we fail to see anything like a rule such as those of the great Western orders or like that which Theodore subsequently drew up for Studium, and which, as we shall see, was copied by many other communities. What Basil gave was mostly in the form of answers to questions, directions as to the application of the fundamental principles of monachism to the needs of social life. The principles are in great part taken as set forth in Scripture, especially in the Gospels, and a large portion of his exhortations are equally suitable to the laity and to professed monks. They are not delivered on authority, but deduced from Scripture and reason, yet the principle of authority is uttered with no uncertain sound. In fact, it might seem to some devotees that

[1] *Vita A*, vii. and *B*, 6. It is not quite clear whether in *Vita A* this work was carried out in Boscytium or in Saccudio. It would seem more probable, according to *Vita B*, that it was in Saccudio.

[2] In the Migne edition of Basil, there is a scholium, purporting to be by Theodore, defending the genuineness of the *Constitutiones Asceticæ*, *Patr. Gr.*, xxxi. p. 1319.

the principles of authority and of asceticism were often at variance, since excessive fasting, or the indulgence of individual leanings to one or another kind of work or of discipline, was tightly controlled by the application of the maxim that "We ought not to please ourselves." The Basilian writings generally, though austere in parts, breathe a spirit of what has been called "sanctified common sense," and allow scope in a wise leader to consider all the circumstances in cases where he has to decide in apportioning works and penalties. Obedience, poverty, labour, devotion, and abstinence, except under strict limitations, from female society, are rigorously insisted upon. But the rules laid down are not very minute, and often allow for variety in following them out.

Nevertheless this "rule of Basil" was, and was rightly, regarded by the Eastern monks as their chief, almost their sole authority. The other important sources of monastic law were the decrees of Councils, necessarily varying in range and purport, and the imperial legislation,[1] especially that of Justinian. In the "Novels" we find rules as to the appointment of abbots, the length of the novitiate, the dealing with runaways, and similar matters which, as we have abundant evidence, were not always scrupulously observed, but which helped to form the basis of subsequent legislation. The matter need not be discussed further, till we come to Theodore's reforms and regulations in his later post as abbot of Studium. Here we need only note that he was acting on received authority, when he either stimulated or supported Plato

---

[1] On early monastic rules in the East, see the admirable monographs: Meyer, *Die Haupturkunden für die Geschichte der Athos-klöster*; and Nissen, *Die Regelung des Klosterwesens*.

in bringing the monks of Saccudio to consent to a far more stringent rule than they had hitherto followed. Their asceticism, be it observed, is of an active and social kind. Solitary life, however lofty in its possibilities, had come to be regarded as so liable to abuse as to be only tolerable in rare cases. Such a case, probably, was that of Theoctista, whom Plato desired to live "cellular fashion," probably because there was just then no well-managed nunnery at hand.

Meantime, the united bonds of affection and respect between uncle and nephew were ever becoming stronger. They seem to have lived in constant intercourse, and Theodore must before long have taken up his abode in Saccudio, for we hear no more of Boscytium after the first. Here, however, a chronological difficulty meets us: in the Lives of Theodore, it would seem as if he did not take up the monastic profession till after the Second Council of Nicæa, and it would also seem that Plato became abbot of Saccudio at the time of the family migration. We need not concern ourselves to ask what had become of his previous monastery, that of the Symbols. In those days, a small community of the kind might easily dwindle and vanish. But the one statement we have as to Theodore's age—that he was made abbot at the age of thirty-five, having followed the life of a monk for thirteen years [1]—is difficult to reconcile with the supposition that he entered monasticism only in 787. And again, in Theodore's own Life of Plato, we are told of Plato's choice as abbot (though Saccudio is not named) before the Council, of his refusal to take higher ecclesiastical offers subsequently made to him, and of his return to

---

[1] *Vita A*, xvi.

FIRST YEARS OF MONASTIC LIFE

his monastery after the Council. Again, among the signatories to the resolutions passed at Nicæa, his name appears as Plato, monk and abbot of Saccudio.[1] Either hypothesis has its difficulties. According to the generally received chronology, the family renunciation and migration followed the return of Plato to Constantinople soon after the death of Leo, and he must have left his little flock, probably under the superintendence of Theodore, during his attendance at the Council of Nicæa. But whether Theodore heard of the deliberations and resolutions of that Council before he left his paternal home at Constantinople, or while he was undergoing his novitiate at Saccudio, there is no doubt that he followed them with a deep interest, and welcomed with delight the triumph of the icons and of the cause of the monks.

To us, looking back on the struggle of conflicting forces during that critical period, it seems that another and greater cause was at stake than either that of mosaics or that of monasteries, that if Irene and Tarasius had known how to make the most of their position, the breach between East and West might have been healed, and the supremacy of one Empire and one Church established for the Middle Ages and possibly for Modern Europe. For, as we have seen, it was the ecclesiastical policy of the Isaurian Emperors that had served as pretext and as goad, if not as original motive, for the successive acts of unfriendliness between Rome and the East which were speedily ripening into hostility, and which bore the seeds of permanent alienation. If then this Council, œcumenic or universal in reality as in profession, had sought not only to assert the same standard

[1] Mansi, *Hist. Conc.*, vol. xviii.

of faith and ritual for East and West, but also to adjust the rival claims of patriarchal powers, and particularly to establish a *modus vivendi* with the Papacy in Rome, and if at the same time the Imperial Court at Byzantium had drawn nearer to the other great Court of Christendom, that of the Frankish champions of Papal power, then we may fairly say that the unity of Christendom would have been secured in ways passing the dreams of the most visionary catholics and cosmopolitans, Charles the Great would never have been crowned in Rome, the Crusades would not have failed for want of unity and a policy in militant Christendom, Greece would have continued to dominate the barbarian world, and there would have been no Renaissance needed, for there would have been no death or trance of ancient culture. But neither Empress nor Patriarch was equal to the emergency—perhaps neither of them in any way discerned the greatness of the issues of the moment. It seems hardly too much to say that if Theodore the Studite had been ten years older at this time, in which case he would doubtless have taken a leading part in what was done, the cause of unity, at least in the ecclesiastical sphere, might have triumphed, since Theodore, as we shall see hereafter, had no scruple against acknowledging the far-reaching claims of Old Rome, and felt no remarkable deference to the See of Constantinople. And if ecclesiastical unity had prevailed in East and West, imperial unity would have had a longer and more vigorous life, there would have been no "Holy Roman Empire" as a separate and Western institution, and the whole course of European progress would have taken a different direction.

But after all, amid the great complications of Eastern and Western affairs, it would have required breadth of view, tenacity of purpose, and diplomatic skill in an unusually happy combination to avert the great cleavage. In Italy, at that time, there were at least three great powers or interests, besides many minor ones, the conflicts and combinations among which claimed the attention of the Eastern Church and Court. First there was Pope Hadrian I., irritated at the withdrawal of ecclesiastical provinces formerly under his sway, and at the reduction of power and revenues which he had suffered at the hands of the Greeks, or subjects of the Empire, whom, till they had purged themselves of heresy, he might vituperate as "unutterable."[1] He declared that they were in league with the Lombards of the coast to carry off slaves, and he suspected them of various machinations among the doubtfully loyal dukes and princes who ought to have acknowledged the Papal authority. Then there was the great King of the Franks himself, Charles, now also King of the Lombards, who had received, along with the Lombard crown, a weight of cares in those Italian regions which had been imperial, or ruled by semi-independent dukes or princes, and endless opportunities of friction with the Papal power. For though Hadrian was far too wise to be anything but polite —not to say adulatory—in addressing his powerful protector, there was a pardonable querulousness in the appeals he made for help in Italy to the hard-worked warrior who had to provide against Saxons, Avars, and Saracens, not only against recalcitrant bishops

[1] "*Nec dicendi Græci.*" Letter of Hadrian to Charles, probably of date 778. No. 63 in *Codex Carolinus*, Migne's *Patr.*, vol. 98. The relations of Byzantium and Italy in these years have been worked out from Frankish, Papal, and Greek sources by Dr. Hodgkin and Professor Bury; (*Cf.* Gasquet, *L'Empire Byzantin et la Monarchie Franque;*) also by Otto Harnack.

of Ravenna or an intriguing Duke of Spoleto. Again there were those lesser powers, Lombard in origin, but never effectually controlled by the Lombard kings, of which the most important just now was that of Beneventum under Arichis. This Prince was an enlightened man, favourable to letters and to building. He was not very loyal to Pope or King, and had been in communication with the late emperors. His wife, Adelperga, was a daughter of the last Lombard King, Desiderius, and her brother, Adelchis, had fled to the Byzantine Court. But the policy of the Beneventines was not altogether philhellene if, as the Pope believed, they were intriguing with a disloyal governor of Sicily, whom Irene had to recall, but who subsequently found refuge with the Saracens.

The wisest and broadest policy for the Byzantine court, so far as we can judge, would have been first to make sure of Charles, and secure such an amicable and intimate union with him that the North-Italian question, as between the two great sovereigns of the civilised world, might have been permanently settled; next, to obtain the hearty co-operation of the Pope in the Conciliar Action now to be taken for the restoration of the icons; and finally, to have mediated an agreement between the Beneventines and their spiritual and secular superiors. Unfortunately none of these lines of policy was effectually pursued. An abortive attempt at an alliance with Charles proved worse than nugatory. The attempt to win over the Pope was not sufficiently respectful of his dignity to make him a cordial friend, however much he may have sympathised with the religious policy of the Empress; and the Beneventines were allowed to slip away from Greek influence, so that the later attempt to reinstate the Lombard prince was defeated by his nearest kinsfolk.

At first, however, Irene conceived a wise and bold project. This was to unite her son Constantine in marriage with Rothrud, the eldest daughter of Charles and of his best-beloved wife, Hildegard. The embassy sent with this object from Constantinople reached Charles during his second visit to Rome, in 781. The arrangement was made and confirmed by oath. We do not know the political conditions, but we are told that a certain Greek eunuch named Eliseus was sent to the Frankish Court to instruct Rothrud, or Eruthro, as the Greeks called her, in Greek letters and speech, and in the ways of the Roman Empire. It would be interesting to know how Eliseus fared. At the Court of Charles he would probably have found other pupils besides Rothrud anxious for instruction in Greek, and if he had been a powerful man, he would undoubtedly have made his mark. As the engagement lasted for six years, Rothrud and probably her sisters and companions (for Charles cared much for the education both of his sons and of his daughters) may have acquired considerable knowledge of Greek literature, though probably it was in matters of ceremonial ($\mathring{\eta}\theta\eta$) that the courtier chiefly sought to instruct her. But at the end of that time, the contract was broken off by Irene herself. Her motives are not clear. It can hardly have been that she now felt so secure of the Pope as to consider it safe to dispense with the King,—for the Papal assent to the Council of Nicæa had not yet been obtained. Her action has with great probability been attributed to mere personal jealousy. The advent of a daughter-in-law so strangely connected and so differently brought up from the ladies of the Court might have introduced a new and dangerous element into the Palace, and have lessened the influence of the Queen-mother, whose love of power was undoubtedly great. Be this as it may, Irene broke off the marriage alliance, and sought as bride for Constantine an Armenian lady, Maria by name, a pious woman,[1] but not attractive to the young bridegroom, who seems to have set his heart on marrying the Frankish princess. Charles was able to console himself so far as Rothrud herself was concerned. He always preferred to keep his daughters with him, he used to say. They followed him on horseback when he rode abroad, and studied under his directions at home. But the rebuff which he had received from Irene coloured his views of the Eastern Court generally, and prevented him from acknowledging the orthodoxy of the Greeks, even after it had been recognised by the Pope himself.

Meanwhile Tarasius and Irene had both written to Hadrian I. announcing the change in the patriarchate and in the attitude taken up by the Court towards the images; also their intention of holding a Council for the purpose of correcting past errors. In Irene's letter[2] (that of Tarasius has not survived) the Pope was asked either to come himself or to send representatives, the charge both of mission and of prospective arrangements being entrusted to the Governor of Sicily. The answers sent by the Pope were friendly in the main, but cautious and not too yielding. He approved the religious objects of the new rulers, but touched on sundry grievances:

[1] Theodore wrote to her, *Ep.* 81 in bk. ii. and 218 in Cozza-Luzi Collection.
[2] The substance of these letters is given in the full epitome of Hefele ("Hist. Ch. Councils"), English translation. For unabridged account see Mansi, vol. xviii.

the uncanonical appointment of a layman, in the person of Tarasius, to the Patriarchate of Constantinople; the retention by the Patriarch of the title *œcumenical* or *universal*, which had caused offence since the days of John the Faster of Constantinople and Gregory I. of Rome, and which, even if softened in meaning, seemed to trench on the prerogatives of the successor of St. Peter; and the provinces withdrawn from Roman jurisdiction by Leo the Isaurian. The last point was naturally the most important, and the only one, perhaps, that could effectually postpone a good understanding. He sent with his letter to Irene two ecclesiastics, both named Peter, an arch-presbyter and an abbot respectively. They were received as mandatories sent by the Pope to represent him in the Council. But it was by no means clear that they were technically authorised to assume any such position, and at a later time, when, for a short period of his life, Theodore wished to minimise the authority of the Seventh Council,[1] he could say that Rome had not sanctioned its acts, since the messengers who had come thence and had taken part in its deliberations and decisions, had really been sent for quite a different purpose.

But there was a second difficulty in the way of assembling a council. To be general, or œcumenical, a council must be attended, personally or representatively, by the five Patriarchs of Old and New Rome, Alexandria, Antioch, and Jerusalem. New Rome was on the spot; Old Rome might be regarded as present in the person of the two Peters; but Egypt, Syria,

[1] *Lib.* i. *Ep.* 38. Even if, as Baronius supposes, this part of the letter is not by Theodore, we see that such an objection could plausibly be made.

and Palestine were so hopelessly cut off from Christendom and so entirely within the power of the Mohammedans, that even the summons of Tarasius could not reach them. But the Court and Church were equal to the emergency. The Patriarch of Jerusalem had lately declared himself in favour of the icons. Antioch and Egypt were held to be represented by a certain John and Thomas respectively, who were sent by certain oriental monks (? ἀρχιερεῖς) with letters of credence to Tarasius and the Fathers in Council. Their names accordingly appear among the first in all the lists of signatures to the decrees of the Council.

But there was a third and yet more dangerous hindrance in the way. We have seen that the iconoclastic emperors possessed the confidence of the army. It does not seem probable that the soldiery was more free from superstition than any other part of the nation, but it was distinctly anti-clerical, and perhaps also opposed to female rule. The first meeting of the assembled Fathers was to be held in the Church of the Apostles at Constantinople. It was to be a solemn occasion; the Patriarch, and the orthodox and unorthodox bishops, with abbots and priests, were assembled in the main part of the building, while the Empress and her son were in the portion usually assigned to the catechumens. Suddenly there was a rush of armed men into the church; the life of the Patriarch and of his partisans was threatened. The household troops were called in, but could effect nothing. The iconoclastic captains prevailed, and the bishops of that party raised a shout of triumph. The Patriarch and the orthodox escaped by flight, and the Synod was temporarily dissolved. But Irene again

SECOND COUNCIL OF NICÆA

showed herself not easily to be beaten. She devised means by which, on pretence of a necessary expedition against the Arabs, the recalcitrant troops were withdrawn from the city and replaced by others, drawn from the East, in whom she could trust. Her chief agent in this matter was Stauracius, "patrician and logothete," a correspondent of Theodore's in later times. When the Court had also withdrawn and the loyal troops had obtained possession of Constantinople, the tumultuary bands were disarmed and dismissed.

The way was at last clear. But it seemed desirable that some other city should be chosen for the meeting place of the Council. The place selected, from its convenient situation and its halo of orthodox sanctity, was Nicæa in Bithynia. Here the Fathers met again, under the presidency of Tarasius, rather more than a year after the abortive attempt made at Constantinople.

The proceedings of this Synod have been chronicled at great length. Only the more important of them need concern us here. In the very first session, three notable iconoclastic bishops read their recantation, and were not only pardoned but allowed to take part in the Synod. When seven more followed their example, some remonstrance was raised on behalf of ecclesiastical order, but whether from charity or from fear, leniency prevailed, though the penitents were not allowed straightway to resume their places. The question of image-worship was taken up and discussed during several sessions. The letters from the Pope and from the East, already referred to, were read, though the portion of Hadrian's letter to Irene which brought forward the Papal grievances was prudently omitted. Arguments from the Scriptures and from the Fathers relating to images were read, with a summary of the arguments used on the other side, and a lengthy refutation. These arguments may be left till we come to consider the controversial works of Theodore. Here we need only say that if, as is most probable, Plato had some hand in drawing up the arguments and counter-arguments by order of Tarasius, it is not unlikely that his nephew had a share in the work. Or if Theodore had not yet embarked on polemics, he must have now become familiar with the theoretical ground of the controversy, and with the authoritative passages of Scripture and of Patristic literature which served as watchwords on either side.

Far the most important work of the Council was done in its seventh session, when a decree was passed that holy pictures, of Christ, the Virgin, angels, and saints, were to be portrayed on vessels, garments, and walls, for salutation and honour. This *honour*, however, was distinguished from the *worship* due to the Divinity only, in words that cannot adequately be rendered in English, though perhaps *adoration* corresponds loosely to λατρεία, *reverence* to προσκύνησις. Such as it was, however, the distinction was already familiar, and it was to be used a good deal hereafter. It need hardly be pointed out that no representation of the Deity, in other form than that of the human Christ, was in any way sanctioned or approved. We may observe in passing that as yet there was no difference made between painting and sculpture, or representation in two or three dimensions, such as came afterwards to be recognised in the Eastern Church.

After the chief dogmatic declarations of the Council had been made, with the customary anathemas of the heretics on the other side, certain canons were passed, mostly relating to monastic discipline. The last session was held at Constantinople. The Empress and the young Emperor signed the decrees, the Fathers departed, and the work of restoration, as regards cult and discipline, seemed to have been accomplished.

But there were threatening clouds, some near at hand, others in the distant West. Certain of the most zealous and uncompromising of the monks were disgusted at the lenity with which former iconoclasts had received not merely absolution, but restoration to their priestly functions. Chief of the recalcitrants were a certain Theoctistus, and Sabas, whom we may probably identify with the abbot of Studium of that name. Tarasius was in a difficult position. On the one hand, the Empress was urgent for a policy of pacification. On the other, amid so much shiftiness and want of principle, he could ill afford to offend the most zealous of his allies. Then again the circumstances of his own consecration were not such that he could pose as a consistent supporter of the canons; while the charge of simony brought against his colleagues and even against himself might be difficult to refute. Any hitch would cause an alarm cry against the validity and the œcumenical character of the Council. Tarasius seems to have hedged, to have denied his knowledge of inconvenient facts and his responsibility for the very light penances inflicted. He is not greatly to be blamed if there was, after all, no great principle at stake, and if his diplomatic action prevented a schism. True, Sabas and Theoctistus continued to be alienated, but they seem to have been in a very small minority. Even Plato continued on good terms, for the present, with the Patriarch. Still, if Tarasius had been able to keep turncoats out of office, he might have made a reactionary policy less easy than it proved in the sequel. Meantime he professed great zeal in his efforts against simony, and on this side he hoped for the support both of Pope and of monks.¹

Pope Hadrian, meantime, withheld his sanction. He seems to have been ready to acknowledge the assembly as a lawfully constituted local synod, but not as an œcumenical council. Tarasius had made no concession about the withdrawn dioceses and "patrimonies of St. Peter," and again, if the Eastern Church had become orthodox as to images, it still omitted the *filioque* clause in the Nicene Creed. Hadrian seems to have hesitated till his death, which occurred in 795. Towards the East he was critical, perhaps querulous. But towards the West he became almost an apologist for the policy of the Empire.

These curious fluctuations and combinations are seen in the correspondence of Hadrian with Charles, King of the Franks. In 790, a remarkable document was drawn up by the learned men of Charles's Court² treating of the whole subject of the images and of the behaviour of the Byzantine rulers. Certain survivals of the theocratic idea,—expressions of very exalted character applied to the Emperor and all that emanated from the imperial person—were severely reprobated by that authority which, within twelve years, was to assume distinctly theocratic pretensions on its own behalf. The images were justified on what may be called common-sense grounds, in virtue of their educa-

---

¹ The account of these affairs is in the histories of the Council, but it is treated more at length by Hergenröther, in his Introduction to "Life of Photius," than by most modern writers. Among the chief sources are two letters of Theodore, 38 and 53 in book i., which offer many problems.

² *Libri Carolini;* published, as is Hadrian's reply, in vol. xcviii. of Migne's *Patrologia*.

SECOND COUNCIL OF NICÆA

tive and stimulating effect on Christian devotion, not by reason of intrinsic claims to adoration. This does not seem fundamentally different from the distinction between προσκύνησις and λατρεία, but the difference between a policy of tolerated diversity and one of compulsion goes much deeper. Four years after, a Council was held at Frankfort, which passed a decree the exact significance of which is very difficult to determine. It condemned the action of the late Council *held at Constantinople*, in that it had declared that honour and worship were to be paid to the icons just as to the Holy Trinity.

Overlooking the mistake as to place, we can hardly say that the theological misrepresentation was the result of the density of the Western mind compared with the subtlety of the Eastern. It shows, not a failure to understand, but a culpable and voluntary misunderstanding; not a confused impression of truth, but a clear statement of its contrary. It is not too much to say that this has often been the attitude of West to East.

Meantime, it may be that the clash of arms, which has often drowned the voice of the laws, had also extinguished that of theology. In 788,[1] the Byzantine Court had actually taken the field on behalf of the Lombard Pretender. The year before, Arichis of Beneventum had been obliged to submit to Charles, after an invasion of his principality, and a young Beneventine prince, who, on the death of his elder brother, became his father's heir, had been carried off as hostage. Soon after, Arichis himself died, and Charles

---

[1] This was before the sending of the *Libri Carolini*, and may partly account for the irritation shown by Franks for Greeks. But it does not explain the want of understanding as to the main points at issue, which distinguishes the writings of 794.

adopted the magnanimous and bold policy of sending young Grimwald back to rule over the Lombards in Beneventum. Grimwald, for a time, remained loyal to his powerful patron, so that when his uncle (on the mother's side) Adelchis, with troops under the command of imperial officials, landed in Calabria, they found no support, and were defeated in a decisive battle. Adelchis returned to Constantinople, and Charles ruled as undisputed King of the Lombards.[1]

Meantime Theodore had rejoiced in the triumph of the icons and was not, as yet, inclined to side with the disaffected party of Sabas. His uncle was anxious that he should receive priestly ordination at the hands of Tarasius, probably with the view to his subsequent promotion, either as abbot or as bishop. In later days, Theodore pleaded the duty of canonical obedience to justify his action on this occasion, since Tarasius seemed to some of the monks to be still under a cloud. But in all probability he felt no compunction at the time, and looked forward to an active career in a church now restored to Catholic orthodoxy, in intimate alliance with the secular authority, and in course, at least, of justifying herself in the eyes of the whole world.

The study is a confusing one. The most abstract of speculations on the relations of spirit and matter, the most subtle distinctions in the possible attitudes of the human mind towards the Divinity, were complicated with territorial disputes in distant lands and palace intrigues at home. But for the present these were

[1] In Hergenröther's account of these affairs it is assumed that the breaking off of Constantine's betrothal to Rothrud was consequence, not (as it may have been) cause of Charles's expedition against Beneventum. Also the relations between Hadrian and Charles seem to have been represented as more cordial than we should gather from their correspondence. *Cf.* Hodgkin.

nothing to Plato and Theodore, for the cause of the icons was, to them, the cause of God. If questions of ecclesiastical policy and of the supreme political authorities had been adequately considered at the time ;—if " the letters of the Greeks and the usages of the Roman Empire," in which Eliseus instructed the Princess Rothrud, had, broadly understood, served as a basis for the required harmony, possibly a more permanent settlement might have been achieved. However, something had been done, in that thought and devotion had, in some quarters at least, prevailed over physical force. And if the assertion of principle against power should again be' required, certain decisions had been authoritatively affirmed that would justify resistance even unto death.

CHAPTER IV

PALACE REVOLUTIONS—THEODORE'S FIRST CONFLICT WITH THE CIVIL POWER

THE eight years following the Council of Nicæa, stormy and disastrous for the Empire, were probably the most quietly fruitful and entirely satisfactory of Theodore's life. Not that he and the community to which he belonged were so remote from the Court as to be kept in ignorance of the party distractions by which it was constantly agitated. Nor yet that the external foes who were ever threatening even the provinces nearest to the "queenly city" herself could be regarded from Bithynia with indifference or contempt. But rather that the opportunities now enjoyed by Plato and Theodore for defining the rules of their monastery and increasing its numbers and its influence seemed to them to justify the suggestive name of the lady to whom they owed this peace and leisure,—a name which has a strangely ironical sound in the ear of the historian. Possibly the restoration of the Church seemed to them the great work to be accomplished, whether the ruling authority was to be designated as Irene and Constantine, as Constantine, as Constantine and Irene, or as Irene alone. And the restoration of the Church was to be achieved by means of the monks. If their view was limited we shall see hereafter that it was not entirely fallacious. Here we may notice that, in the course of a few years, the community of

Saccudio had reached the number of one hundred monks, living together in order and loyalty.

It was towards the end of this period of repose that a decisive change was made in Theodore's position. Up to the age of thirty-five, for thirteen years since his first religious profession, he had worked in all things with and under his uncle, the abbot Plato. It is quite possible, as his biographers would have it, and as his own writings suggest, that Plato was much more ambitious for him than he was for himself. It was Plato who had insisted on his consecration as priest, and later, in the year 794, it was Plato who brought about his appointment as abbot of Saccudio, while he who had practically created the position, vacated it, and became a private monk.[1] The story of the transaction is not without difficulties. One historian[2] believes that Plato's retirement from office was the work of Irene, who wished for a more pliable person to support her schemes, and who proved—not for the only time in her life—deficient in judgment of character. Nor does the abdication seem to have involved anything like diminution of dignity in the eyes of the world. To the chronicler Theophanes, Plato is, after this date, still abbot of Saccudio. And to Theodore he is still the Father,—not in a mere personal sense only, but as shepherd of the flock. The most probable suggestion is that discerning troubles to come, Plato wished to be assured of his successor, and followed the example of those Emperors who had their sons crowned during their own lifetime. He had sufficient confidence in the reverence and affection of

---

[1] I fail to see the grounds on which Auvray concludes that Plato withdrew, for a time, to Constantinople after Theodore's elevation.

[2] Gfrörer, *Kirchengeschichte*, ii. 177.

his nephew to rest assured that should he himself recover from the illness under which he suffered—and of which he did not minimise the symptoms—the life restored would not be one of lessened influence and prestige. Under these circumstances he summoned the brethren around what he would have them believe to be his dying bed, and obtained a unanimous declaration in favour of Theodore. The manner of choice can hardly be called strictly legal or regular, especially as we have no mention of any episcopal intervention or sanction, such as the legislation of Justinian demanded. But it was not a time to wait for formalities, even if it had not been the case—as we know it to have been from many contemporary documents—that the wishes of a dying abbot had a good deal of weight in determining the choice of his successor. In point of fact, Plato recovered, and for a period of eighteen years uncle and nephew lived together as practically joint abbots, first of Saccudio, later of Studium, in such harmonious co-operation that it is difficult to see which was the prime mover in the several actions of their common life. In the older man, the frank acceptance of technical subordination did not imply any shrinking from responsibility. In the younger, a bold and independent course of action was compatible with most dutiful reverence towards the spiritual father from whom the most potent influences of his younger days had been received. The spectacle they afford of mutual deference with conjoint authority forms a striking contrast to the miserable strife for power between the two imperial rulers.

The enterprises of Irene against Lombards and Franks in the West had, as we have seen, met with nothing but disaster, nor had her troops which encountered the Bulgarians to the North obtained much better success. These facts, rather than wicked envy aroused by a spectacle of superior piety—as an orthodox chronicler suggests—may account for the state of friction in Court and army which favoured an attempt on the part of the young Emperor to emancipate himself from maternal control. He was now, in 790, twenty years old, and he had come of a capable and warlike stock. His mother had consistently kept him in the background; she had broken off a matrimonial alliance flattering to his imagination and his hopes; she had bound him in wedlock to a woman for whom he felt no affection; of late she had committed all affairs to her minister Stauracius, patrician and logothete, whose authority completely overshadowed, even in appearance, that of young Constantine. Finally, misled, as it was reported, by soothsayers, she was trying to secure the whole imperial power for herself. But now at length her son showed some spirit. He formed a design, along with some men of high birth and office, to capture the Empress and send her away to Sicily. If they had succeeded, it is curious to think what new webs of intrigue might have been spun. But Irene was beforehand with them, as she had been with the uncles. An earthquake gave occasion for a migration from the city, and this movement seems to have facilitated the capture of the conspirators. They were seized, scourged, shorn, and exiled or confined. The Emperor himself was beaten like a perverse child and kept in solitude at home. Meanwhile the Empress continued to intrigue with the soldiers, and to impose an oath that they would not acknowledge the authority of the Emperor so long as Irene lived. But not all the military leaders had sunk to so low a point. The decisive opposition came from the Theme of Armenia. There the demands of the Empress were flatly refused, and the troops declared their loyalty to the Emperor, and their determination to acknowledge the dignity of his mother only in the second place. A certain Alexius, bearing the curious surname of Moslem, was sent to pacify them, but instead of doing so, he allowed himself to be placed at their head, while they imprisoned their previous governor and proclaimed Constantine sole Emperor. They were speedily joined by other troops. Constantine was restored to liberty and established on the throne. His partisans were apparently recalled, and those of Irene, especially Stauracius, degraded and exiled. Irene herself met with the mildest possible treatment, being suffered to retire, with abundant wealth, to a palace which she had herself built. This is reckoned the first year of Constantine VI.

If only Constantine had at this juncture achieved some decided military success, his power might have been permanently established. An expedition which he led against Cardom, King of the Bulgarians, seems to have ended in panic and flight on both sides. He next turned his arms against the Saracens who had attacked Cyprus the year before, and were now threatening or ravaging Cilicia. But here again he met with no success. Very soon after he showed his weak if amiable character by yielding to the persuasions of his mother and her followers, and restoring her to liberty and to some measure of authority, so that henceforth *Constantine and Irene* became the objects of the people's acclamations. A wretched time followed. Alexius, the governor of the Armenian Theme, was suspected of ambitious aims, scourged and degraded. An expedition against the Bulgarians ended in failure and

FIRST CONFLICT WITH CIVIL POWER 55

the loss of some valuable lives, as well as of much wealth. Another insurrection in favour of the unhappy "uncles" was suppressed, but with such barbarity as to do more harm than good to the reigning sovereigns. Tonsured before, they were now subjected, one to blinding, the rest to the loss of their tongues. Strange to say, a few years after they are again in rebellion, and again captured, this time exiled. Five melancholy spectres they flit across the stage, with fresh loss of dignity and some added disability after every failure, cleaving apparently to one another as companions in misfortune. But probably a yet more disastrous step was that by which the Emperor brought himself into conflict with the more respectable and independent of the churchmen, in his repudiation of his wife Maria, and his union with the lady of his choice, Theodote.

This step, we are told by Theophanes, was taken by the express advice of Irene, who was desirous of acquiring popularity by bringing her son into general hatred. If this were her motive, she succeeded admirably, so far at least as the monks were concerned. Certainly they do not seem to have suspected her of any share in the mischief. Yet to Theophanes himself, after all her intrigues, treacheries, and unnatural cruelties, she is still "pious and beloved of God," and hence we can hardly suspect him of maligning her. Constantine desired his wishes to be carried out in a lawful manner. The unhappy Empress Maria was shorn and sent to a cloister, and the Patriarch Tarasius was asked to perform the nuptial ceremony for the Emperor and the court lady whom he was openly acknowledging as her successor.

Tarasius was again in a difficult position, and like

most weak characters, he endeavoured to make a compromise which brought him little favour in either quarter, though it enabled him to retain his Patriarchate. He is said to have opposed the immoral and illegal demand of the Emperor, but finding that his words were unavailing, to have refused personally the performance of any marriage rite, though he gave a passive sanction to the solemnisation of Constantine's second marriage, with the nuptial crowning, by a certain ecclesiastic named Joseph, abbot of the monastery of the Kathari, and holding also the rank of steward— possibly to the Patriarch. The coronation of Theodote[1] as Augusta was soon after performed by Constantine himself. In time she bore him a son who received the name of Leo.

With the endeavour of Constantine to obtain the blessing of the Church on his illegal union with Theodote, we are again brought into connection with the history of Theodore. It is not quite clear why the Emperor was anxious to be approved in Saccudio. The relation (probably cousinship) of Theodote to Theodore may have counted for something; or the somewhat strained relations between Tarasius and Plato owing to the disaffection promoted by Sabas may have led the Emperor to think whether it might be possible to obtain one clerical influence in counterpoise to another. Or again there is the possibility, suggested by Theophanes, that Irene was working underground to arouse a monastic opposition to her son. Or Constantine may have wished to clear himself from

---

[1] The mention of "crowning" in the sense of marrying is confusing to readers who do not know that the placing and interchanging of crowns on heads of bride and bridegroom is an important part of the marriage ceremony in the Greek Church.

FIRST CONFLICT WITH CIVIL POWER

any imputation of a return to iconoclasm, with which he seems to have threatened Tarasius, in order to ensure his pliancy. In any case, Constantine tried hard to secure the support of Theodore and Plato. But they had already broken off and separated themselves from communion with Tarasius and Joseph, nor were any efforts, whether of persuasion or force, of the slightest avail to turn them from their resolution.

The communications of the Court with Theodore were made first through another abbot, Nicephorus by name, one of Theodore's kinsmen, and later by an imperial secretary, Stephen.[1] The beginnings of the negotiations with Nicephorus are not known, but we have a letter of Theodore's written in reply to one sent to him from Nicephorus through a certain deacon. In it he deprecates any censoriousness or bitter animosity, he only desires that he and those with him may be left in their penitential seclusion, though he intimates that it is impossible for him to trangress the law. He calls Heaven to witness that this controversy is not of his own seeking. But his judgment is not rashly formed. He is but adhering to the precepts of Scripture and the Fathers, and he dare not approve what is contrary to their authority. "These things I have dared to open to you as to a father and friend; since we,[2] as God, who readeth the heart, knows, are making no declaration—we are not in a position so to do—nor are we indulging in hatred. But we cherish affection for the most pious Emperor, and for all my kinsfolk [including Theodote?] as one who loves his own people, as you know,

---

[1] *Th. St. Ep.* i. 4, 5. We have now the great advantage of Theodore's correspondence to guide us. The chronology is reasonably determined by Thomas, *Th. v. St.* p. 51, note 3.

[2] The *we* is official—Theodore slides from plural to singular and back.

and we make mention of him in the holy liturgy and pray for him in public and in private. And we are in communion with the Church. May we never be separated from her! Have pity upon me, a sinner and no more. I desired to mourn my offences in this corner, not to be mixed up with the things of the world. What evil is there in that? Allow me this boon, dearest kinsman; you can, I know. And let me dwell in peace, apart from human affairs. By your kindness and skill straighten what is crooked, and make the rough places plain. And be our mediator of peace, and our champion for quiet; so that whatsoever is profitable for us in this matter may be settled according to justice and reason."

If Nicephorus undertook any such mediatorial office he was not successful. In his letter to the next negotiator, Stephen,[1] Theodore feels called upon to justify his position of critic or opponent of the higher powers by references to instances in Scripture (David, Joab, Moses) and to maxims from Basil. The Emperor and Empress were not unwilling to pardon, and would even have consented to bribe, but the fact of the ecclesiastical separation had become real, and the uncanonical act of Joseph had not been punished. Harsh means were accordingly employed. Plato was summoned to Constantinople, and confined in a cell within the Palace, under the oversight of the offender Joseph himself. The monks of Saccudio were scattered; those highest in dignity and position, after an ignominious scourging, were sent into exile in Thessalonica, Theodore himself being of the number.

To his uncle in prison, Theodore wrote several

---

[1] I do not feel at all sure that this letter belongs to this juncture.

letters, to keep up the old man's courage and cheerfulness and to describe his own fortunes. They are just what one might expect from a younger to an elder, a man almost *in loco filii* to a parent, and at the same time from a superior to a subordinate. Along with the superabundant expression of deferential affection, there runs through them a vein of exhortation,—as he tries to counteract any tendency to weakness or despondency that might have come over the sufferer in his present confinement and loneliness. The letters bear testimony to the strong interest which the monks and their persecutions excited among the people with whom they came in contact. A portion of one of them may be roughly translated here.[1]

"Since you ask me to relate everything to you minutely, from the day of our sad separation,—our journey, and all our fortunes—though unequal to the task, I must not hesitate to do as you bid. On the day when you departed, Father, willing to follow even the way of death, we also set forth on the way of exile, mounted on such beasts as were to be procured. And at first, being unaccustomed to such experiences, we felt somewhat uneasy. When we came to certain villages, we found that while those in charge of us were loosing the beasts, resting, and procuring necessaries, we were a spectacle to all sorts and conditions of men. Our ears were besieged with noise and shoutings. This kind of inconvenience became less troublesome when we were used to it. We were more distressed by the sickness of our Father the Lord Deacon. Thus, in anxiety and fatigue, we continued our way. Our course, with halting-places, was as

[1] *Lib.* i. *Ep.* 3.

follows: from Cathara to Liviana; thence to Leucas; and so on to Phyræum. There we had a sad adventure, which is worth relating: there came upon us unawares nine of the foremost of our Brethren, surrounding us all in tears,—a sight to break the heart. Our leader would not permit any conversation. We looked sadly at one another, exchanged greetings, wept and parted. When we stopped at Paula, we met your much honoured sister [Theoctista] with my lord Sabas [abbot of Studium?] and held a secret meeting with them, which lasted the whole night, with such talk as you might expect, for we saluted one another as about to die, and parted in sighs and sorrow. There was much strain and anguish, though nature was finally overcome. Thence proceeding we halted at Lupadium, where we were kindly received by the inn-keeper, who provided a bath to relieve our blisters, some of which had become very troublesome. Thence we came to Tilis, where the abbot Zacharias and Pionius received us with warm sympathy, desiring to accompany us on our journey, though that was not allowed. Thence to Alceriza, on to Anagegrammeni, Perperina, Parium. There we held communication with the bishops,[1] and modestly reminded them of their oaths. On to Hercus and Lampsacus, where we picked up some people from Heraclea, and waited three days without being able to sail. Taking ship thence, we stopped at Abydos, and were received with piety and compassion by the Governor; we stayed for a week, and then sailed to Eleuntes. There we waited another week, since the wind was contrary, and when it became favourable we reached Lemnos after a nine hours' sail.

[1] Or communicated in the ecclesiastical and technical sense?

I cannot sufficiently praise the goodness of the bishop of these parts, who received us with greater hospitality than had yet been shown to us, cheered our spirits, and gave us supplies for our journey.

"Thence sailing in some fear, for we mistrusted the natives of that shore, and the north wind was blowing and whistling, in twelve hours we measured a course of a hundred and fifty (Roman) miles, and anchored at Canastrum in the neighbourhood of Thessalonica. Thence to Pallene, which lies near the Gulf; and on into the Port. Mounting our beasts again, we entered, at the third hour, into the City, it being Saturday, and the Feast of the Annunciation. And what an entry we made! This too must not be omitted. The Præfect had despatched a Captain of the chief regiments with a military contingent to await us at the East Gate, where they received us in silence, drawn up in line. And when we had entered, having shut the gates, they led us through the market-place, escorting us in sight of those who had come together for the purpose of seeing us, to the presence of the Governor. What an excellent man was he! He showed us a friendly countenance, and having made reverent salutation, spoke to us with kindly words. When we had prayed in the Church of the Holy Wisdom, he sent us on to the Archbishop. He, again, after prayer in his oratory, being a very holy man, received and saluted us, conversed agreeably, and provided us with baths and food. The next day we were led on, and taking us, as if to prayers, to the Church of St. Demetrius, they separated us from one another, amid prayers and embraces. Taking us two brothers [Theodore and Joseph?] to the place where I am now, they separated us, in tears and embracings such as moved the bystanders to pity. Thus are things with me, Father. And now I wear on my sighing and sorrowful life. I have received the Sacred Bread from your hand, as having in it the strength of the Holy Trinity. I keep it as a safeguard against evil, and feast my eyes on it, as if I were kissing your right hand. Again I weep, and my heart sinks within me. . . . But what has come over me? I call to witness both men and heavenly powers that it is the law of God which has separated you from me. His command is one and is eternal. Let it resound under Heaven. I will rejoice and send forth the praises of God. . . . And you, thrice-blessed Father, rejoice and be of good cheer. . . . Even the enemy, as the great Gregory says, knows how to admire the courage of a good man; when wrath shall cease, good deeds shall shine by their own light. Angels applaud you, men call you blessed, Christ has received you and has opened to you for ever the gates of the Kingdom of Heaven."

One may find some overstrain in the general tone of this letter. The persecution had evidently been comparatively light, the sympathy shown almost excessive. But we must remember that the break-up of Saccudio must have seemed to Theodore and to Plato to give the death-blow to their dearest hopes, that seclusion was hard to a nature like Theodore's, at once powerful and tender, and that Plato was growing old and infirm. But what strikes us most is the futility of Constantine's attempt to stop the spread of the schism. Not firm or not cruel enough to strike with a merciless hand, he persecuted the monks just enough to give them great consideration in the eyes of people generally, not with a sternness sufficient to deter others from following in

FIRST CONFLICT WITH CIVIL POWER 63

their steps. He gave to Theodore that love of martyrdom which became almost a ruling passion in his life, and stimulated all the recalcitrant elements that had already shown themselves in Plato.

Nor did this persecution make up by duration what it lacked in intensity. Irene, helped by her ally Stauracius, again plotted against her son, and this time with final success. While Constantine was in Constantinople, rejoicing in the advent of his son and heir, his mother, whom he had quitted at Brousa, began once more to tamper with the soldiers. In the spring of the next year (797), Constantine again took the field against the Saracens. But the campaign was rendered nugatory by a false report, spread by Stauracius, that the Saracens had fled. The ignominy which his failure brought upon him, with the death of his young son shortly after, made Constantine's prospects dark, and probably encouraged the inertia which hung upon him like a fate. About midsummer, the final blow came. The conspiracy broke out while the Emperor was staying in one of the suburbs. He tried to fly to Asia Minor. But there was now no Alexius to take his part. With a refinement of treachery, Irene negotiated with the few supporters of her son, offering to retire into private life, and then threatened to betray these negotiations if her son were not speedily delivered into her hands. She had her will. Constantine was captured, and in August 797 he was blinded by Irene's orders in the Purple Chamber in which he had been born. He survived the mutilation but a few years.[1]

There is hardly a more pathetic figure in history

---

[1] For the date of the death of Constantine VI. see note to chap. vi.

than this of the last acknowledged ruler of the Græco-Roman world. It is he, rather than Romulus Augustulus, whom we naturally set up as a pendant to contrast with the greatness of the Restorer of the Empire in the West. Constantine was not without estimable qualities. He was strong in his affections, moderate even in acts of resentment, soft-hearted to a fault. He seems, from his fitful military enterprises, to have realised his responsibilities as defender of the Empire against barbarism. But he was altogether wanting in determination, and he did not know how to make the most of his opportunities. It is hard to see that he inherited anything either from his Isaurian grandfather, or from his Athenian mother. Had he been made of harder stuff, or had he acquired the delicate art of intrigue, he might have acted a notable part, and the course of the world's history would have been different. Little pity has been wasted on his wretched fate, which, after all, he had mainly brought upon himself. Yet such pity as is due to unaggressive natures, all through life the prey of jealous and malicious persons who ought to have been their guardians and protectors, should be bestowed before all others on this unhappy prince, the last of the great Isaurian dynasty.

With the triumph of Irene came a monastic reaction, the liberation of Plato and the recall of Theodore, first to Constantinople, then to his post as abbot of Saccudio. Those who feel interested in Theodore may experience some regret that they find in his writings no word to condemn the iniquitous acts which brought about his restoration. How did he really feel towards Irene? Can it be that with his readiness to suffer all things for conscience' sake, to reprove wickedness in high quarters, and to uphold at all costs the dignity of the moral law, he should on this occasion have sunk to the position of a time-serving courtier, and have lavished praises on the head of one whom he inwardly despised? Or is it possible that, like some of his biographers, he should have been ignorant as to Irene's part in the palace tragedy? Or did he so completely identify his protectress with the cause he had at heart that he regarded her crimes as something almost external to herself, a kind of Nemesis by which she fulfilled the designs of Providence against wicked doers? Some such attitude seems to have been taken by the chronicler Theophanes, himself a sufferer for his faith, who acknowledged the horrors that had been accomplished, and the share in them which was to be assigned to Irene herself,—who tells of a seventeen days' darkness after the event in the Purple Chamber—yet to whom the Empress is God-beloved and pious to the end of the story. Let those who feel sure that their own moral judgment—their sense of ethical proportion in matters that closely concern their personal predilections or convictions,—is never warped nor fluctuating, be the first to cast stones against these suffering monks who saw in their persecution a temporary triumph of evil over good, and in their restoration the beginnings of happier times.

CHAPTER V

FIRST YEARS AS ABBOT OF STUDIUM

IT was shortly after the return of Theodore from exile that the events occurred which, at first seemingly destructive to his work, led to his promotion to a sphere of larger scope. In the year 799, there was an inroad of Saracens,[1] under the leader whom Theophanes calls Abimelech, into the country already known as Romania, where the monastery of Saccudio was situated. They ravaged as far as Mangana, and carried off the horses of Stauracius, who was quite taken at unawares, as well as one reserved for the use of the Empress herself. Thence they swept on into Lydia. Saccudio was not, apparently, destroyed, nor even deprived of its monastic character, for we find it frequently referred to later on, but for the time it was an undesirable residence for a defenceless community. At the same time, Theodore's friends and followers would naturally wish that he should be in a position close to the headquarters of imperial and patriarchal authority. Consequently we find that in 799, Theodore migrated from Saccudio, accompanied of course by Plato and most likely by all the monks who had formerly been under his rule, and was established as abbot of the great monastery of Studium, within the walls of Constantinople.

---

[1] Theophanes, p. 734 ; *cf.* Karl Thomas, chap. iv.

We have spoken, at the outset of this biography, of the fine position and the magnificent buildings of the Monastery of Studium. Those buildings, especially the large church, and also the antiquity of the institution, gave it a certain prestige. Yet outwardly it was at this moment anything but prosperous. The community had dwindled down to the number of ten monks. And changes in circumstances, no less than diminution of numbers, had made it possible for the monastery to take a totally new departure, under a rule not only more vigorous than the former, but in many respects totally different.

A glance at the earlier history of Studium will make this point clearer, and enable us to discern the nature of the scope now given to the organising powers of Theodore. According to a good many authorities, the founder was a certain Studius, who came from Rome, where he was Consul, along with Aëtius, in the year 454. It was most likely in 462 or 463 that he founded the church,[1] dedicating it to St. John the Baptist. He had formerly built a church dedicated to St. Michael at Nacolia. He had not originally intended to make St. John's a monastic foundation, but that step was taken soon after, and

[1] Our best authority is the lexicographer Suidas, whose exact words are worth quoting (Suidas, Ed. Gaisford, ii.) :—

Στούδιος, δυνάστης ὃς καὶ τὴν περιβόητην μονὴν ἔκτισεν. ['Η τῶν Στουδιτῶν μονὴ πρότερον καθολικῆς ἐκκλησίας ἦν [Em. τῶν καθ. ἐκ.], ὕστερον δὲ μετῆλθεν εἰς μονήν].
'Ο αὐτὸς Στούδιος δυνάστης κτίζει τὸν ναὸν τοῦ ἀρχιστρατήγου Νακωλείας ἐν ᾧ φέρονται καὶ στίχοι ἡρωϊκοί:

Στούδιος ἀγλαὸν οἶκον ἐδείματο · καρπαλίμως δὲ
ὧν κάμεν, εὕρατο μισθόν, ἑλὼν ὑπατηΐδα ῥάβδον.

According to Nicephorus Callistus, these lines were inscribed at Studium, and if so, the date of foundation would be earlier than that given by Theophanes, Cedrenus, and others. But probably Suidas is to be preferred. For reference to authorities on the foundation and early history of Studium, see Eugène Marin : *De Studio* (Paris, 1897.).

the buildings were occupied by monks of the order called Acoemeti.

This name signifies "the sleepless ones,"[1] not that the individual members of the community took no rest, but that they were divided into choirs in such fashion that in their houses the voice of psalmody never ceased. The order was founded early in the fifth century by a certain Alexander, a man of noble birth who had fled to the desert, first to escape the world, later to avoid the office of Bishop of Edessa, which would have been forced on him. He founded a monastery on the Euphrates, enforced strict poverty among the monks, and formed seventy of them into a band of preachers. Later on he came to Constantinople, where his rule was further developed by his successor, Marcellus, and where the monks, not generally popular, are said to have gained the goodwill of the wealthy Studius, who established them in his new foundation.[2] These early monks were like the later Studites in their uncompromising zeal in matters theological, but they differed in at least one important particular: they were not all obliged to work.[3] On two occasions they made themselves conspicuous in theological controversies. In 484 occurred the first breach between the Churches of the East and the West which threatened permanent schism. The Patriarch of Constantinople, Acacius, was formally deposed by the Pope of Rome, and it was an Acoemetic monk, most probably a Studite, who undertook the dangerous office of bearing

---

[1] The name is applied in the Greek Church to a candle kept perpetually burning.

[2] For Alexander and the Acoemeti see, *inter alia*, Helyot, *Hist. des Ordres Monastiques*, i. p. 238 *seq.*

[3] A good deal of manuscript copying seems to have been done by the Acoemeti.

THE EAST END OF THE CHURCH OF ST. JOHN.

THEODORE AS ABBOT OF STUDIUM

the decree to Constantinople. The grievance against the Patriarch was a supposed inclination to the doctrine of the Monophysites (believers in the "One Nature" of Christ) which had been condemned by the Council of Chalcedon. So zealous were the Studites for the decisions of that Council, that they refused to admit a new abbot except on condition that the consecrating bishop anathematised the opponents of the Chalcedonian decrees.

The Acoemeti thus helped to keep alive the Christological controversies which the statesmanlike Emperor Zeno was endeavouring to mitigate. But shortly after, their eagerness in the same or a very similar cause brought them up to the verge of the heretical swamp, or possibly even beyond it. Anastasius, the successor of Zeno, almost lost his throne in consequence of the violent disputes in Constantinople which followed the addition to the hymn *Trisagion* (Holy, Holy, Holy) of the words "who was crucified for us." The doctrine that one of the Trinity had suffered was indignantly rejected by the Acoemeti. It seemed a natural consequence of their theological attitude that they should go on to denounce, with the Nestorians, the term God-bearer, τὴν θεοτόκον, as applied to the Virgin Mary. However, before long they came to the compromise which ended the temporary schism. Their abbots figure in various synods, but they are not conspicuous again till the time of the Iconoclastic Controversy. Like the other monks, the Acoemeti of Studium were exiled by Constantine Copronymus, and we have seen that their abbot, Sabas, was among the most uncompromising of the ecclesiastics at the Second Council of Nicæa, and on the side of Plato and Theodore in the affair of the marriage of Constantine VI.

Studium, then, when Theodore became its head, had already traditions of uncompromising and even protesting zeal. This kind of zeal is sufficiently conspicuous in the later history of the Monastery. Yet there seems no reason for regarding the history of Studium as continuous. As already mentioned, the earlier Studites had but little of that respect for labour which was such a marked feature in Theodore's rule. On the other hand, I do not find in Theodore's arrangements any provision for the perpetual psalmody which was the essential characteristic of the earlier regulations. One point—which we may call a happy accident—forms a connecting link between the old and the new: the Church at Studium was dedicated to St. John the Baptist, and it was always a joy to Theodore to draw a parallel between the ascetic monks who opposed the unlawful marriage of the Emperor, and the ascetic prophet who had maintained the cause of domestic morality at the court of the Herods.

We may conceive, then, that as soon as they were settled in Studium, Theodore and his uncle began to systematise and to develop the rules and mode of life which they had begun at Saccudio. We are told by Theodore's biographers a good many details as to his monastic life and regulations, and we have also a considerable part of the Constitutions which afterwards went under his name and were borrowed or copied by other communities.[1] We have also the penalties he is said to have affixed to the various offences committed in the monastery. It is quite possible that a good part of these documents was only reduced to quite definite form under his successors. More interesting

---

[1] Ὑποτύπωσις καταστασέως τῆς μονῆς τῶν Στουδίου.—Migne, 99, p. 1703 seq.

as being almost undoubtedly his own composition, are the iambic verses in which he sets forth the duties and privileges of all the members of the community, from the abbot down to the cook. His general idea of what monastic life, and especially the life of an abbot, should be, is, perhaps, most clearly expounded by him in a letter to a pupil, of which I give here a general translation [1]:—

"To my Pupil Nicolas.

"Since, by the good pleasure of God, you have been promoted, my spiritual child Nicolas, to the dignity of abbot, it is needful for you to keep all the injunctions in this letter. Do not alter without necessity the type and rule that you have received from your spiritual home, the monastery. Do not acquire any of this world's goods, nor hoard up privately for yourself to the value of one piece of silver. Be without distraction in heart and soul in your care and your thought for those who have been entrusted to you by God, and have become your spiritual sons and brothers;—and do not look aside to those formerly belonging to you according to the flesh, whether kinsfolk, or friends, or companions. Do not spend the property of your monastery, in life or death, by way of gift or of legacy, to any such kinsfolk or friends. For you are not of the world, neither have you part in the world. Except that if any of your people come out of ordinary life to join our rule, you must care for them according to the example of the Holy Fathers. Do not obtain any slave, nor use

[1] *Lib.* i. 10. This is in parts almost identical with the "Testament of Theodore," said to have been delivered to his chosen successor.

in your private service or in that of the monastery over which you preside, or in the fields, man who was made in the image of God. For such an indulgence is only for those who live in the world. For you should yourself be as a servant to the brethren like-minded with you, at least in intention, even if in outward appearance you are reckoned to be master and teacher. Have no animal of the female sex in domestic use, seeing that you have renounced the female sex altogether, whether in house or fields, since none of the Holy Fathers had such, nor does nature require them. Do not be driven by horses and mules without necessity, but go on foot in imitation of Christ. But if there is need, let your beast be the foal of an ass. Use all care that all things in the brotherhood be common and not distributed, and let nothing, not even a needle, belong to any one in particular. Let your body and your spirit, to say nothing of your goods, be ever divided in equality of love among all your spiritual children and brethren. Use no authority over the two brothers of yours who are my sons. Do nothing, by way of command or of ordination, beyond the injunctions of the Fathers. Do not join in brotherhood or close relation with secular persons, seeing that you have fled from the world and from marriage. Such relations are not found in the Fathers, or but here and there, and not according to rule. Do not sit at a feast with women, except with your mother according to the flesh, and your sister, or possibly with others in case of necessity, as the Holy Fathers enjoin. Do not go out often, nor range around, leaving your fold without necessity. For even if you remain always there, it is hard to keep safe your human sheep, so apt are they to stray and wander. By all means keep to the instruction three times a week in the evening, since that is traditional and salutary. Do not give what they call the little habit [of novice or postulant?] and then, some time later, another as the larger. For there is one habit, as there is one baptism, and this is the practice of the Holy Fathers. Depart not from the rules and canons of the Fathers, especially of the Holy Father Basil; but whatever you do or say, be as one who has his witness in the Holy Scriptures, or in the custom of the Fathers, so as not to transgress the commandments of God. Do not leave your fold or remove to another, or ascend to any higher dignity, except by the paternal decision. Do not make friends with any canoness, nor enter any women's monastery, nor have any private conversation with a nun, or with a secular woman, except in case of necessity; and then let it be so that two are present on either side. For one, as they say, is cause of offence. Do not open the door of the sheepfold to any manner of woman, without great necessity; if it is possible to receive such in silence, it is all the better. Do not procure a lodging for yourself, or a secular house for your spiritual children, in which there are women, for that were to run great risks; but provide yourself with what is necessary for journeys and other occasions from men of piety. Do not take as pupil into your cell a youth for whom you have a fancy; but use the services of some one above suspicion, and of various brothers. Do not have any choice or costly garment, except for priestly functions. But follow the Fathers in being shod and clad in humility. Be not delicate in food, in private expenditure, or in hospitality; for this belongs to the portion of those who take their joy in the present life. Do not lay up money in your monastery; but things of all kinds, beyond what is needed, give to the poor at the entrance of your court; for so did the Holy Fathers. Do not keep a safe place, nor have a care for wealth. But let all your care be the guardianship of souls. As to the money, and various necessaries, entrust them to the steward, the cellarer, or to whosoever charge it falls; but so that you keep for yourself the whole authority, and change offices among persons from time to time as you see fit, receiving account as you may demand, of the tasks entrusted to each. Do nothing, carry out nothing, according to your own judgment, in any matter whatever, in journeying, buying or selling, receiving or rejecting a brother, or in any change of office or in anything material, or in regard to spiritual failings, without the counsel of those who stand first in knowledge and in piety, one, two, three or more, according to circumstances, as the Fathers have directed. These commands, and all others that you have received, keep and maintain, that it may be well with you, and that you may have prosperity in the Lord all the days of your life. But let anything to the contrary be far from you in speech and in thought."

This letter shows sufficiently what was Theodore's ideal of an abbot's life, with its privileges and responsibilities, and as it represents accurately his own practice and that of all those sent forth from Studium to preside over similar communities elsewhere, it enables us to grasp the principles on which the great monastery was founded. We may generally divide these principles under three heads: the establishment of a hierarchy of officials, each having his special work, for which he was responsible to the Abbot; the minute regulation (or rather a regulation which was made more minute as time went on) of all the duties and practices of the monks, both for worship and for labour; and the constant and diligent instruction of all members of the community in the fundamental ideas of the monastic life, that their minds might be quite clear as to their position and responsibilities, and their hearts warmed with enthusiasm for the high vocation to which they had been called.

I. The officials of the monastic community comprised the second in command ($\tau\grave{o}\nu$ $\tau\grave{a}$ $\delta\epsilon\acute{u}\tau\epsilon\rho a$ $\phi\acute{\epsilon}\rho o \nu \tau a$) to the abbot, a steward, a substeward, *epistemonarchs* to settle disputes among the monks, *epitactae* (or *observatores*—I fear an Englishman would call them spies) to take note of the behaviour of the brethren on all occasions, a *canonarch* to superintend the church music, a *taxiarch* to maintain order in processions and other ritual, and sundry caretakers of larder, table, and wardrobe, down to the porter who opened the door and the *excitatores* who aroused slumbering brethren to their religious duties. In a completely communistic and self-sufficing establishment, which came to comprise as many as a thousand members, all the numerous craftsmen, builders, tailors, gardeners and others, were in a sense public officials. How their several tasks were allotted to them is not quite clear, but the ultimate responsibility for every man's position must have lain with the abbot. When the choice was exercised by Theodore himself, who evidently had the power of keeping in close touch with a large number of widely differing persons, and who could use the information supplied by the *observatores* as to the habits of each man, it was probably satisfactory, and if not, it could at any time be changed. If only the monks imbibed, as many of them undoubtedly did, the principles which he had himself received from Basil as to the duty and privilege of obedience and of "pleasing not themselves," they would not be likely to quarrel with their appointed tasks, at least while Theodore was personally present with them. In the verses to which we have referred, he made suggestions which gave a halo of dignity to the meanest kind of labour. Thus those who sewed skins together were to remember that they practised the trade of St. Paul. The servant who laid the table was to regard it as the table of Christ, at which His Apostles were to feast.

Certainly Studium had one of the requisites for keeping up *esprit de corps* and loyalty to the Community in the large number of office-bearers both temporary and occasional. The smaller offices must have been very numerous. Thus in Lent there was a special brother appointed to go round to all kitchens and workshops at nine in the morning, and say: "Fathers and Brothers: we die, we die, we die. Let us remember the Kingdom of Heaven."[1] The elaborate psalmody must have demanded attention from a good many trained people. Further, there was an officer set over the young, who was specially bound to treat them with tenderness. These young people were probably novices or incipient monks, since we have, I think, no trace of a school for secular pupils at this time in Studium, though from biographies and letters we see how eagerly Theodore promoted the teaching of "grammar" and the other liberal arts.

---

[1] *Constitutiones Studianæ*, 23. In the rule of Athanasius of Athos the exhortation ran: "Let us remember the everlasting punishment."—See Meyer's *Athosklöster*, p. 135.

Care for the sick formed the occupation of at least one official, but the sick, as the young, seem to have been members of the community. Strangers were received, but exhorted not to bring gossip from outside into the monastery. Preparation and subsequent cleansing of the guest-chamber was entrusted to a selected brother. A severe task must have been that of the wardrobe-keeper, as according to Studite rules, communism extended even to clothes.[1] Every Saturday the clothes were brought together—probably to be cleaned and mended—and redistributed. Theodore himself set the example of indifference to clothing by taking particularly shabby garments for himself.[2] There was a special monastic penalty against giving away an old coat. Of course the ecclesiastical vestments were regarded differently, and were to be decent and even splendid.

But the most interesting, and perhaps for posterity the most important of the functions entrusted to any of the Studite monks was that of copying manuscripts. The services which Studium and its daughter communities rendered to calligraphy will be considered later.[3] Here we may notice that among monastic penalties are several awarded to copyists who are careless and slovenly in their work, and that Theodore especially eulogises in his uncle, Plato, the beauty of his handwriting and his great industry in copying,[4] while the biographers of Theodore represent him as a most industrious and skilful calligraphist.

[1] It may be doubted whether the weekly circulation of clothes was more than a counsel of perfection. The clothes allowed by *Const. Stud.* to each monk can hardly have all been worn at once.

[2] On the dress of the Studite monks, see Helyot, *Hist. des Ordres Monastiques*, i. p. 242. He represents the later Studites as wearing green cloth with a double cross of red on the chest. But his information is not very exact.

[3] See chap. xiii.   [4] Theodore's Oration, xi. 17.

II. The regulation of the daily life of so large and so heterogeneously occupied a community was no light task. In general, the framework of the monastic life was determined by the cycle of ecclesiastical festivals and fasts. The fasts were always rigorously kept at Studium. Abstinence from flesh was enforced at all seasons, but not from wine, though of drink the number of cups allowed was always determined. Besides Lent and the "Feast of St. Philip," which roughly corresponds to Advent in the West, the Greek Church keeps "The Fast of the Holy Apostles" from All Saints' Sunday (our Trinity Sunday) to the Feast of St. Peter and St. Paul on June 29.[1] Besides these seasons, Friday in every week, and perhaps also Wednesday,[2] was a fast day. On the other hand, the long fasts were lightened by sundry holy days, and not only Sunday but Saturday were regarded as days on which fasting was unsuitable. Fasting with the Studites generally meant one meal a day, and abstinence from fish, cheese, and eggs; also from wine, which was replaced by hot peppermint-water. The strictest fast involved abstinence from apples and figs. To the slavish modern digestion, the paucity of the food would probably be less trying than the constant changes of meal times. Thus during fasts the one meal of the day was taken at three in the afternoon, the brothers having been occupied at their various kinds of work since Prime (about six). At times when there was no fast but hours were sung, work was done till midday, when a meal was taken, and liberty was then allowed till two, after which work went on again

---

[1] For the Greek feasts and fasts, see ‘Η 'Εκκλησία μας by Μᾶνος.

[2] So Marin interprets *Catechesis Chronica*, 15. I am not certain about the Wednesday.

till lamp-lighting. There was no specially cooked evening meal, but the remains of dinner, with bread, served for supper. The time of the first meal during seasons when hours were not sung was after the liturgy, which began at nine. Apparently during days of labour, the monks were not all present at the mass, but were summoned after its conclusion to a service of song, followed by the benediction, after which they went to table.[1]

Of direct philanthropic work, besides doles to the poor, we have not much indication in the Rules. But from Theodore's letters it is clear that some of the monks visited the sick and those in prison and especially that they were assiduous in performing the last rites for the dead.[2]

The leisure time allowed to the monks was not supposed to be spent in idleness, though a midday siesta was probably the custom. The proper alternative to corporal or manual industry was intellectual occupation. "Is it work time?" said Theodore, "To your labour. Is it leisure time? To your studies."[3] On days when there was no manual labour, the monks were summoned together by the wooden clapper, which figures largely in the Studite rules, to the Library, where each received a book for his private reading. These books must, under penalty, be restored at the appointed time in the evening. There was a special custodian of the Library, whose business was to see

---

[1] I gather this from *Const. Stud.* 27 and 33, but confess that the two passages are not quite clear to me. Dr. Karl Thomas says (*Th. v. St.* p. 63): "Die Arbeit der Mönche war nicht besonders anstrengend." But would the learned doctor find it a light task to work metal or to copy manuscripts from seven to three, or even from six to nine and two to six?

[2] *Lib.* i. *Ep.* 13.   [3] *Cat.* 118.

that the books were there and to keep them clean. Unfortunately we have no means by which to ascertain what these books were. From Theodore's own range of reading as indicated by his citations one would suppose that they consisted mostly of patristic theology, though there may have been some secular works, especially such as could be brought under the head of "grammar."

Mediæval asceticism was, of course, never favourable to personal cleanliness. Infrequency of washing is mentioned by Theodore as one of the hardships they were bound to endure.[1] From the fact, however, that there was a special rule against the use of oil in the bath, we may infer that a non-luxurious bath in pure water was not prohibited.

There were, either in Theodore's time or soon afterwards, many rules affixing penalties to unpunctuality or slovenliness in chapel or refectory. If a brother broke a dish, he had to stand and hold out the pieces, while the abbot drew down his cowl[2] [in sign of ignoring the offence?]. The singing of psalms did not go on only in the church. This would have been inconsistent with the industrial character of the community. But the brethren were instructed to sing certain psalms while engaged in their several occupations, an obligation from which the copyists were not unreasonably exempt.

Although there seems to have been a daily celebration of the Eucharist, there were special "liturgical days" on which monks were supposed to communicate or to show good reason to the contrary, and any who neglected to communicate for forty days was excluded from the church for a year.[3] Theodore himself seems to have desired to leave the question of

---

[1] *Cat.* 128.   [2] *Const. Stud.* 35.   [3] *Const. Stud.* 62.

frequent or less frequent communion to each man's discretion, though he strongly exhorted his correspondents or hearers to communicate as often as they could do so with a clear conscience.[1]

Confessions were heard every day by the Abbot, but here again frequency or infrequency was apparently at first more or less optional. Theodore was often obliged to exhort his monks to have more constant recourse to the healing art of the confessor. According to the scheme of penances, confession must at least be weekly. The penalties imposed for offences were, in minor cases, certain prostrations or bows, and restrictions in food and drink; for serious sins, temporary segregation from the community. Besides the penalties for purely monastic offences, we have, in the Studite rules, penance prescribed for each of the sins which were becoming recognised as deadly, but had not yet been reduced to the number of seven. Each sin is defined, so that the work forms a short ethical treatise.

A comparison of the rules with the discourses and letters of Theodore suggests that, however clearly laid down on paper, the Constitutions of Studium cannot have been always strictly kept. It would, for example, have been superfluous to inveigh against avarice before men who were incapable of holding any kind of property—even the clothes on their back—as their own, or to warn against sexual impropriety those who had no intercourse with women of any kind. But it is quite possible, as we have suggested, that the system was not solidified during Theodore's lifetime. Certainly the asceticism of the life practised did not keep the number of applicants for admission within very narrow

[1] Cf. *Lib.* ii. *Ep.* 220, with *Cat. Or.* 107.

limits. In general Theodore is said to have adopted the maxim: "Him that cometh unto me I will in no wise cast out." But it became necessary to have certain rules of entrance. All candidates had to stay for two or three weeks in the guest chambers till they had been made thoroughly to understand what the Studite life involved, at the end of which time the abbot received them into the community. Knowledge of the rules and willingness to abide by them seems to have been the only criterion. But surely it was no slight one.

III. But neither the binding together of the brethren by an organised hierarchy, nor the guiding and restricting of their whole life by a network of rules, could have made the Community into a living organism, animated by the same spirit and striving after the same ideas. As Aristotle had seen that no form of government can be secure unless the citizens are educated in the spirit of the polity, so it was by incessant training, through habits of life and exposition of principles, that Theodore created the most influential monastic establishment of the East. And this exposition of principles, not in the cold light of reason, but aglow with the fiery enthusiasm of a prophet, is to be found in catechetical discourses which the "fathers and brothers" received from the abbot himself.

Of these we possess one hundred and thirty-four, probably selected by one of his successors for reading in church, called collectively the *Parva Catechesis*, and a smaller number from the *Magna Catechesis*.[1] They

[1] In the Migne edition of "Theodore" these discourses are, for the most part, only given in a Latin translation, and that not first-rate. But there is a far better edition, in Greek (with Latin translation, and a very appreciative introduction), by M. Auvray, published in Paris, 1891. The discourses belonging to the *Magna Catechesis* are to be found in the *Novem Patrum Bibliotheca*, vol. ix.

were delivered over a long period of time, and they certainly are not, as we have them, in strict chronological order. But they have a common character, and enable us to understand how Theodore acquired and kept a hold over his own monks, as his letters explain to us his influence with persons outside. They are all short and strictly to the point, without the verbosity which is found in some of Theodore's letters and in most of the longer discourses.[1] They can hardly have occupied more than ten minutes in delivery, and were preached in the evenings three times a week, and more frequently in Lent. Theodore was one of those preachers, more often to be found, perhaps, in societies where an ornate style is prevalent, than in days like ours when simplicity, not to say slovenliness, is generally preferred, in that his sermons are best when unpremeditated and too short to allow of much rhetoric. What chiefly distinguishes them is the ring of profound conviction, of intense earnestness which is not to be mistaken. He speaks under a sense of deep responsibility, for he believes that he will have to give account for the souls of all those over whom he presides. He has no time to beat about the bush for illustrations or motives, no need, as a rule, for argumentative disquisition. Sometimes he may dwell for a few minutes on the nature of the heresies against which, during the later part of his office, he and his community were continually protesting. But more often he is able to rely entirely on the orthodoxy of his hearers, and what he feels himself bound to inculcate is the observance of the duties obligatory on all Christians and more especially on those who have chosen the monastic profession

[1] But, as we shall see, the genuineness of some of the longer discourses is not beyond question.

and thereby cut themselves off from the world. The antithesis between the Church and the World is more strikingly expressed in his addresses to the monks than in his letters to other people. Elsewhere he may say that a devout life is possible for a layman, but in his own church, addressing his spiritual "fathers and brothers," he speaks as if the strict observance of the precepts of Christ were only possible to those who had completely renounced the world. Two institutions are constantly mentioned together, as being tolerated for those in the world, but entirely inadmissible for any who really aimed at the higher life,—matrimony and slavery. Yet the argument against the latter,—that man is "made in the image of God," does not seem less forcible for the laity than for the clergy and recluses. Obedience and poverty are, in a somewhat similar way, regarded as matters to be insisted on for a religious community without being incumbent on the laity. But in general, it is Christian morality, interpreted in the strictest sense, that Theodore is endeavouring to promote in his monks, or rather, to inspire them to cultivate in themselves.

Ethics and theology, with Theodore, are alike austere. The transitoriness of life and the nullity both of earthly joys and of earthly sufferings are ever before his eyes. The approach of death is dwelt upon at all seasons. The possibility of a lapse into evil living on the part of the most virtuous is always held up in warning, though the equal possibility of recovery after any number of lapses is also insisted upon. The terrors of the law are always there, though the promises of the Gospel may sometimes counterbalance them. The joy of a festival prompts a warning against the abuse of any relaxation. The life to which

Theodore calls his sons is a perpetual Lent of which the Easter is to be hereafter. His most comforting exhortations are mixed with warnings as to the craft and subtlety of the Devil. If he begins his discourse with the text, "Sic Deus dilexit mundum," he reaches Sodom and Gomorrah before the end.

Yet above the tone of sternness and sadness there sounds a peal of triumph. The self-denying and sometimes persecuted monks are, after all, the victors in the end. They have overcome the fear of death, and their persecutions are welcome as giving them a share in the sufferings of their Lord. "What shall separate us from the love of Christ?" and "Eye hath not seen nor ear heard . . . the things that God hath prepared for them that love Him." These are the words that seem naturally to occur to Theodore whenever he compares the struggles of earthly life with the blessedness of that which is to come.

If there is more of the fire of Gehenna in these discourses than seems natural to a man of sound mind and trustful heart, we may notice that the materialism which is, perhaps, necessarily associated with suffering does not intrude into his conceptions of heavenly joy. The glories of the world to come are spiritual only. Of purgatorial fire we seem to have no trace. Of course, Theodore and his brethren commemorated the departed and prayed for them. But it is evident that by this time no systematised belief in Purgatory had been established in the East.

Amid his religious exaltation, there is always a vein of tenderness in Theodore's character. It is evident how intense an interest he took in the monks individually, how he delighted in their progress, and mourned when they fell away from virtuous living.

Forbearance and brotherly kindness were virtues that he was earnest in inculcating, equally with those of a sterner kind. His moral exhortations show a comprehensiveness of mind and a large experience. Thus he never forgets the great diversity of character among the men with whom he has to deal, leading to a diversity in temptation and need for discipline.

The style of the discourses is terse, pointed, and expressive, occasionally rising to eloquence when the sufferings of martyrs or some similar theme has presented itself. They abound in quotations from Scripture, especially from the Gospels and the Epistles, and these quotations are generally relevant and natural, without any forced interpretation. The dignity of Scriptural thought and language seems to have been imparted to the discourses themselves.

There is a good deal of local colour about them which adds to their interest. The Feast of the Assumption, apparently used as a market day, gives occasion for a comparison between spiritual and temporal traffic. The vintage and the harvest, depicted in words that show a real feeling for nature, furnish illustrations for moral lessons. Events that have been happening at the monastery are turned to a like end. A threatened invasion of the Abgareni suggests the thought that spiritual foes are worse. The appearance of a messenger from Court at a time when the relations between Court and monastery are strained leads to a comparison between the welcome and the unwelcome arrival of death. The decease of any one of the brethren is dwelt upon, for comfort and admonition. Even a slight ailment in the foot, from which Theodore had suffered and been healed by medical treatment, is used to point a moral: that

SIXTH CENTURY CAPITAL OF THE CHURCH OF ST. JOHN.
(FROM THE COURT YARD.)

of submitting to a spiritual doctor in the diseases of the soul. The hideous and barbarous punishments inflicted by the Byzantine emperors are cited to illustrate the judgments to be passed on rebels against the King of Kings, and may suggest a question how far the notions, even of educated people, on the character of the divine government, may be generally coloured by the various manifestations of political power to which they have been accustomed.

One feels throughout that the speaker is entirely identifying himself with his audience. If he exhorts to fidelity and watchfulness, he is warning himself with the others. If they may fall, so may he, and there is provision for recovery in all cases. The labour of all in the monastery, however different in kind, is directed to the same end and is a form of divine service. All have been called to the highest vocation. Their common sufferings are the earnest of common joys to come. Their life is a school, and like schoolboys they live in hope of the holidays. Or it is a seed-time of which the harvest is to be hereafter. Their hardships are joyfully accepted as the chastisement of God, and in all their toils they are following the footsteps of Christ. That a belief in the Divine Government which involves terrors and unending sufferings may yet, fundamentally, be a religion of ecstatic faith and love, has been proved by many great souls of mediæval and even modern times. The seeming incongruity was practically reconciled in Theodore the Studite, and in the whole community which was animated by his spirit. Like all religious leaders, he felt his religion to be the most real thing of his life, and his life and influence would be quite unintelligible apart from an intensity of conviction which may have sometimes worn the garb of fanaticism, which may have left scope for many unamiable or even unworthy traits of character, but which made him a power in the Church and in society. He could strengthen others because he was strong himself, in the strength which comes of singleness of purpose and entire assurance of ultimate success.

APPENDIX TO CHAPTER V

TWO OF THEODORE'S CATECHETICAL DISCOURSES

DISCOURSE LXI. (*From the "Magna Catechesis."*)

THE abundant cornfield delights the heart of the husbandman on his approach. Much more is the ruler of souls gladdened by the spiritual fruitfulness of those under his charge. Thus do you bring joy to me, my children, you who are the field of my labours and a plantation of God, by the increase, and as it were the blossoming forth of your virtues. And I rejoice to see the zeal of each one about his business, the industry and care of each in working out his salvation;—the gentleness of one; the laborious industry, even beyond measure, of another; the reverence and caution of a third; the skill of a fourth in replying to the attacks of adversaries, without cessation or weariness; the peaceable character of a fifth, unmoved by passions—result of peace and calm within, not of outward forcing; in another, confidence in me, for all my unworthiness, and the disposition to regard me as better than I am; in yet another, a disposition untouched by earthly longings or any love of the world; in a word, I delight to see the growth and fruitfulness in the spirit as shown by all of you in all divers ways. Are we not thus all walking together and knit together by our heavenly impulse, and by the holy prayers of my father [Abbot Plato?]. I wonder not a little, and surely this is worthy of wonder. Yet I tremble above measure every day. For what if God, seeing how idle and unprofitable is my service, and waxing wroth against my sins, were to withdraw His favourable hand from the midst of us? For then there might come upon us what to speak were unfitting, or even to think, such a thing as discord, or slackness of soul, or a falling away, whether secret or manifest.

To the end, therefore, that you may confirm me—unworthy as I am—and yourselves, in the lot of the saints and the inheritance of the righteous, and in all good repute, keep to these same things, my children, or rather press on further still, in discipline and in zeal, from glory to glory, from knowledge to knowledge, from our citizenship to a citizenship meet for God; swerving not from what you have resolved and agreed upon in the presence of God and of the angels, and of my humble self. Let us not become slack, nor lose heart if the time seems long—though in truth it is not long—for our life is but a dream and a shadow. And since we should become yet more humble and obedient by the study of the inspired Scriptures, let us beware lest we be puffed up in the vanity of our mind, so as to make our knowledge an occasion of evil, and likewise also our power in speech and argument, our experience, our skill, our correctness in framing and uttering our words; our good reading, or maybe our subtlety, our skill of hand, our psalmody, our learning, our skill in music, our culture, and the like. But let the gift of these things be to us rather a cause of fear and of self-abasement before God who has given them. For thus we shall find God merciful,—or rather bountiful, and ready to give us yet more, that we may be filled with good things. And we shall be a holy temple to God, beautified with gifts upon gifts. But if we shall become presumptuous towards God, and seek to lord it over our brethren, stretching up, as it were, the neck of our souls, and raising our eyebrows and hoisting our shoulders and walking boastfully, seeking this or that, judging others in our pride and foolishness:—asking ever "why are not things otherwise?" or "why have not I the charge of this matter?" or "why should this man have the management of that business?" if we act thus, we are indeed vain and foolish, and are like those in the proverb who pour water into leaky vessels.

Not so, my brethren, not so. Let us not make our opportunities a cause of destruction or the day of work a day of loss; nor, when we may mount the walls of virtue, slip down into vice. Our opportunity is great, our days are delightful. For they are spent in following the commandments of God, in attaining everlasting wealth, in purchasing the kingdom of Heaven. Let us run, let us hasten. I exhort you, I beseech you. I would kneel before you and implore you as my inmost life and all my joy, my boasting and my crown, my glory and praise. Those who have affirmed and those who have denied; those who have followed the way for long and those who are new to it; those from distant folds and those bred among us; all now of one herd and one flock, of one fold and one charge, nurslings of one shepherd! Let us think no more of evil that might come. May you live thus and strive thus and be perfected thus in Christ Jesus our Lord, to whom be the glory and the power with the Father and the Holy Spirit now and for ever. Amen.

DISCOURSE XXVII. (*From the "Parva Catechesis."*)

THE time has come for the sowing of earthly seed, of corn and of other things. We see men going forth to work from the end to the beginning of the night, taking all care that they may sow what is best and most productive, that the needs of the body may be supplied. And shall we, the husbandmen of spiritual seed, sleep our time away, and neglect to sow what we should? How then should we bear everlasting hunger? What excuse can we give for our idleness? Let us awake, then, and sow more zealously and more plentifully than the sowers of natural seed! For he that soweth sparingly shall reap sparingly, and he that soweth in blessing shall reap blessings. What do we sow! Petitions, prayer, supplications, thanksgivings, faith, hope, love. These are the seed of piety, and by them the soul is nourished. With the natural seed the husbandman can only be patient, awaiting the early and the latter rain. But of our seed we are the masters to cause rain and dew—our weeping and contrition—at our will, and as much as pleases us. Since this is within our choice, I beseech you, brethren, let us also sow much and let us water very much, and let us increase the fruits of righteousness that when the spiritual harvest of the unseen world shall come, we may fill our hands and our laps with sheaves, and may cry aloud: "The blessing of the Lord is upon us. We have blessed you out of the house of the Lord. Thou shalt eat the labours of thy hands. Thou art blessed, and it shall be well with thee."

So far about these things. I wish to remind you, brethren, that the nights swell out as the days diminish. And as by watchings the body declines, so by much sleep does the flesh grow in fatness. And as the flesh becomes fat, the passions increase along with it. What shall we say then? Each of you has a psalm, an exercise, a prayer. Let all things be attended to in order, all for the edification of the soul, for the strengthening of the spirit, that Satan may not tempt you by intemperance. But I say this not as to sleep alone, but also as to food and drink, and it may be as to other things. To keep to a fixed order without deviation is the best means to keep ourselves whole and uninjured. Now that the Emperor is returning from his campaign,[1] thoughts arise in our hearts, as we ask "how will it go with the things of the Church? that is to say, with our own affairs?" But it is written: "Cast thy care upon the Lord, and He shall bring it to pass." And "If God be for us, who can be against us." He cared for our lives in former years, drawing us out of manifold temptations and afflictions. So again may He care for us in days to come. Only let us walk worthy of the Gospel, having our citizenship in heaven. For we are strangers and sojourners upon earth. We have no part nor lot therein. For who, coming from eternity, has remained in the world, that he might inherit anything? Have not all who have come in gone out as from a strange land? For this is but a place of sojourning. Our true home and heritage and abiding place is in the world to come. May we come thither and be accounted worthy to inherit with all the saints the kingdom of Heaven in Christ Jesus our Lord, to whom be the glory and the power with the Father and the Holy Spirit now and for ever. Amen.

[1] Auvray thinks this refers to the expedition of Michael Balbus in 823. If so, this is one of Theodore's last discourses in the monastery.

CHAPTER VI

IRENE—CHARLES—NICEPHORUS—THE DISPUTE ABOUT
THE ELECTION TO THE PATRIARCHATE.

THE years occupied by the quiet, constructive work of Theodore and by the sole monarchy of Irene are memorable in universal history, since by studying them we can attain some comprehension, as to causes and immediate results, of the most portentous event of the Middle Ages, the Coronation of Charles the Great as Emperor at Rome. Strange to say, this event is one of which no hint could be gathered from Theodore's letters or other writings, while two other events, which would seem to us of trivial import, loom large in his correspondence and his life,—the slightly irregular election of a patriarch, and the rehabilitation of an unfrocked priest. The former of these matters soon subsides into the background, but the second becomes the cause of a schism, and calls forth passionate appeals to distant authorities and efforts towards the formation of a party and a policy. Yet if we look at these three events together, those which seem so insignificant to us and of such deadly importance to Theodore, have their place in the great stream of affairs. They indicate, and even in a small measure help to determine, the course of circumstances by which Eastern and Western Christendom were partly sundered, partly held together in tangled and flexible cords. The questions as to rival authorities, civil and ecclesiastical, which seemed settled, but were really opened up afresh at the foundation of the Holy Roman Empire, were posed and answered by the Studite monks in their opposition to Patriarch and to Emperor.

The story of the coronation of Charles has been of late so often and so ably told that we need not dwell on it at length, especially as we are only concerned with it as it affected the Eastern Empire and Church.[1] The main events, however, may be briefly recapitulated.

Before matters came to a crisis, it had been thought, by some Western scholars with imperial traditions, that the title Augustus, with the world-wide Empire connoted thereby, would be more befitting to the great champion of Christianity and order, who ruled over so many Western lands, than it was to the comparatively feeble and unsuccessful Emperor at Byzantium. True, the title was not absolutely essential to the establishment of a great kingdom, or even to the union of many kingdoms under one sceptre. Alaric the Visigoth, Theodoric the Ostrogoth, Clovis the Frank, had ruled over many tribes and over widely spread dominions, and so far from aspiring to the imperial title, had been content to receive a sanction for their power in some conferred title—such as *consul* or *patrician*—which might seem slight in comparison to the natural name of *rex*. We read, indeed, that Adolf the Visigoth had at one time aspired to the imperial title, but preferring substance to shadow, had changed his ideal and made it his

---

[1] See discussion of historical authorities in Bryce's "Holy Roman Empire," Hodgkin's "Italy and her Invaders," vol. iii. ch. v., and Gasquet's *L'Empire byzantin et la Monarchie franque*.

motive not to destroy but to invigorate. Again, the most ambitious of Clovis' grandchildren, Theudibert, is said to have dreamed of an expedition to Constantinople and an assumption of the imperial dignity; but he came to an untimely end. At various times, while an emperor yet resided in Italy, one or another pretender had been set up by the power of barbarian swords. But no great Teutonic leader had ever adopted the imperial style. On the abdication of Romulus Augustulus in 476, the insignia of his office had been restored to Constantinople. The great king Theodoric had stamped on his coins the effigy of the Emperors at Constantinople. The recovery of Italy and of Africa by Justinian had brought the reality more into harmony with the theory, and the conquest of the Exarchate of Ravenna, first by Lombards and then by Franks, had left intact the claims to universal sovereignty vested in the heirs of Augustus. The political scheme was not a convenient one. The greatest secular authority could only be recognised as such by means of a prudent fiction. Yet that fiction might have lived longer but for the cruel deed of Irene and her unbridled ambition, and if it had not come to an end just how and when it did, the political ideas and to a large extent the political events of the Middle Ages would have been different. As it was, the loftiest of titles was bestowed by ecclesiastical hands on the *de facto* governor of the western world, and both those who conferred and those who received the honour handed down their claims to many generations after them.

We have spoken of the *foundation* of the Holy Roman Empire without of course meaning to imply that anything was now supposed to be created by the action of Leo and of Charles. But the fact that the Pope took the first step, and that the new Emperor, whatever his wishes may have been, was never acknowledged as either colleague or superior by the Eastern power, while his own powers were interpreted as universal, made the event of Christmas Day 800 the beginning of a new epoch.

Leo. III. had become Pope in December 795, and had at once written to Charles a letter promising obedience and fidelity in terms that are at least as subservient as any that might have been addressed by a Byzantine ecclesiastic to his Emperor. Leo was unpopular in Rome, and in 799 he became the victim of a conspiracy organised by Paschalis and Campanus, nephews of the late Pope Hadrian. He was seized while conducting a religious procession, and cruelly mutilated. The accounts are somewhat confusing. We can hardly accept the statement that his eyes were pulled out twice, or that his tongue was amputated, and that he only recovered power of speech by angelic intervention. He must have suffered considerably, but not so much that his disfigurement would hinder any public functions in future. After a brief imprisonment, he escaped to Spoleto. Thence, according to some chroniclers, he wrote to Constantinople for help. But these accounts are late and doubtful. If such an application was made, it received no attention. Leo crossed the Alps and was kindly received by Charles at Paderborn. After Pope and King had spent some months together, Leo was escorted back to Rome in princely fashion, and ten commissioners appointed by Charles investigated the matters which had led to the outbreak. Charles himself did not arrive till December in the next year, 800. Leo purged himself by oath of the charges brought against him. He was exculpated, and the chief conspirators received the sentence of death, afterwards commuted for that of banishment. Then the ecclesiastics of Rome and the followers of Charles consulted together on the next step. Finally, on December 25, as Charles attended in state the service held in St. Peter's, the Pope placed a crown of gold on his head, and all present, Romans and Franks, saluted him as *Carolus Augustus magnus et pacificus Imperator.*

Many writers of subsequent times have tried to discover the motives of Leo and of Charles, but difficulties still remain. Leo desired, of course, as solemn a sanction as possible for the great champion of the Church, and he saw his opportunity in what he conveniently regarded as the abeyance, for the time, of any legitimate imperial authority. One of the Chroniclers[1] states—what probably many people believed—that Charles had not heard of the blinding of Constantine and the usurpation of Irene—which had occurred three years before—until his arrival in Rome. The usurpation furnished an excuse. Had the throne in Constantinople been held by an iconoclast, a similar excuse would have been afforded on the ground of heresy. Everybody must have seen that changing circumstances were being used to justify an irrevocable decision. The Empire had been heretical and had become orthodox. The throne was held by a woman and was shortly to be filled again by a man. But the people of Italy cared not for the Greeks, and the Pope felt no brotherhood with the Eastern Patriarch, no deference to the oriental ruler. It was to Charles, not to Con-

[1] Of Moissac. The Frankish Chroniclers of this period are mostly to be found in the *Monumenta Germaniæ Historiarum,* Ed. Pertz, vol. i.

stantine, that Haroun al Rashid had lately sent the banner of Jerusalem and the keys of the Holy Sepulchre. He was the one hope and defence of the Church. By taking upon himself to accomplish this momentous act of coronation, Leo may have seemed to be magnifying to its utmost the authority vested in the successors of St. Peter, and to have secured for the future the co-operation of the principal factors in the Church and the world.

But what did it all mean to Charles? Here we may quote the words of his best biographer, Eginhard:[1] "Karl therefore went to Rome, and stayed there the whole winter in order to reform and quiet the Church, which was in a most disturbed state. It was at this time that he received the title of Emperor and Augustus, to which at first he was so averse that he remarked that had he foreseen the intention of the Pope, he would not have entered the church on that day, great festival though it was. He bore very quietly the displeasure of the Roman Emperors, who were exceedingly indignant at his assumption of the imperial title, and overcame their sullenness by his great magnanimity, in which, without doubt, he greatly excelled them, sending them frequent embassies, and styling them his brothers in his letters to them."

This second paragraph would indeed have sounded strangely in a Byzantine ear. That a usurper should show magnanimity in styling the legitimate rulers his brothers might seem a curious inversion of relations. Yet this paragraph throws light on the former. If —as seems quite possible—Charles did not wish then and there to be crowned Emperor, the reason for his

[1] Eginhard's "Life of Karl the Great," translated by W. Glaisher, chap. 28.

reluctance was twofold: he did not wish to bear the semblance of receiving the diadem from the Papacy; and he did not wish to break with Byzantium. He may possibly have foreseen in the former course the germ of the long strife between mediæval popes and emperors, and in the latter the final separation of East and West.

The proof that Charles did not wish to take up a hostile attitude towards Constantinople is shown in at least three ways: (1) in his cheerful acceptance of Irene's own account of the disagreeable affair in which she had been implicated; (2) in his friendly reception of the Sicilian embassies who represented the imperial authority; and (3) in his negotiations with Irene, which, at least according to the principal Greek account, would have led to a matrimonial alliance but for the catastrophe which deprived her of power—and possibly of life. The same line of policy as shown in his dealings with her successors will concern us later on.

I. In the *Annales Laurissenses*, we read,[1] under the year 798, that when Charles had returned to Aix he received ambassadors sent from Constantinople by the Empress Irene (whose name is barbarized into *Herena*), whose son Constantine had been seized and blinded by his followers on account of the impropriety of his conduct.[2] This is undoubtedly the account which the ambassadors gave of what had happened. The object of the ambassadors, Michael and Theophilus by name, was to obtain the liberation of Sissinius, brother of the Patriarch Tarasius, who had been taken prisoner in battle. The boon was granted, a sure sign that Charles did not wish to pick a quarrel with Irene. He surely

---

[1] Ed. Pertz, *M.G.H.* p. 185.
[2] "Propter morum insolentiam a suis comprehensus et excæcatus est."

had ample excuse, since the dethroned Emperor had been promised to him as son-in-law. But, however soldiers and courtiers regarded the matter, it did not seem to Charles that the imperial authority was in temporary abeyance.

II. The year before, according to the chronicles, Charles had received a messenger from Nicetas, Præfect of Sicily, bearing letters from the Emperor. These letters may have been written by Constantine just before the great catastrophe, and it has been conjectured that he was looking to Charles for help against his mother. But of this we have no proof. Constantine was not one to conceive far-reaching plans, nor had he much opportunity for independent negotiation. And besides this, the blow seems to have come suddenly. Theoctistus was hospitably entertained and dismissed, but we know nothing of any results to his commission. Other negotiations with Sicily are of ambiguous import. In 799, there was an ambassador from Sicily at the Frankish Court, and in 801 or 802, we find a refugee[1] from Sicily who is at the same time an emissary of peace. Theophanes, the Greek chronicler, tells us that Charles, after his coronation, meditated an invasion of Sicily, but changed his mind, and decided on an alliance with Irene. Whether this was the case or not, Sicily, so often the battle-field of the nations, was not on this occasion to witness the decisive conflict. It remained as an appendage of the Empire till it fell under the yoke of the Saracens.

III. The matrimonial scheme of Charles and Leo forms a strange episode. The sceptical historian is inclined to doubt whether it was quite seriously under-

---

[1] *M.G.H.* pp. 187, 222, &c.

taken. The particulars of the embassy are derived not from the Franks, who are silent as to the project of marriage, but from Theophanes. According to him, the ambassadors (Jesse the Bishop and Helmgard a nobleman, as we learn from the chronicles) were accredited agents of Pope and Emperor, to unite East and West in the matrimonial union of Charles and Irene. They arrived in Constantinople in 802.

Charles had lost his last legal wife two years before. As we have already seen, he had not taken up a position of moral censor with regard to Irene, and the proposal on his part, if not quite according to modern decorum, need not prove that he was guilty of hypocrisy. The action of the Pope—if the Pope had used the crimes of Irene to justify the elevation of Charles and then sought to unite the two—would have been more reprehensible. But we have not the material for a moral judgment.

If the object had been a determination of mutual relations between the Empire of Irene and that of Charles, we cannot tell what the proposed relations would have been. It was no mere question of border territories, but of conflicting claims to universal dominion, and of the possession of the city that must, however fallen in material prosperity, still figure as the head and mistress of the world. The fear of what might happen if Irene formed an alliance, which could hardly have been one of equality, with the great monarch of the West, might well have aroused general trepidation in Constantinople, apart from the selfish aims of particular courtiers. But to understand the general state of affairs, we must go back to consider the fortunes of the Court and the Empire during the sole reign of Irene.

This period had been full of dangers and discords. We have already noticed the ravages of the Arabs, which had made Saccudio an unsafe place for the abode of the monks. Troubles from the Bulgarians were chronic. There was another rising (strange to say, not the last) of the miserable, mutilated uncles. And worst of all, as rendering the other difficulties harder to cope with, and presenting fresh problems of their own, were the bitter feuds among the chief ministers of Irene—Stauracius, Aetius, and Nicetas.

The last proud moment, perhaps, in the life of Irene, was the occasion on which, after the defeat of the uncles, she rode on a chariot through the streets of Constantinople, drawn by four milk-white steeds, which were led by four patricians, while she scattered largess to the applauding crowd. But very soon after this came the fall of Stauracius, on the accusation of Aetius and Nicetas, and within a short time his sudden death, which seems to have warded off one conspiracy and made room for another. At this juncture Irene had recourse to popular measures and remitted certain taxes due from the citizens of Constantinople, while she also lightened the duties (*commercia*) paid by the ports of Abydos and Hieron. It seems possible that her efforts to obtain the liberation of the brother of Tarasius, already related, may have been designed to render the party of the Patriarch—now entirely united with the Studites—more zealous in her support. But neither the people nor the Church was likely to avail her against the ambition of Aetius and Nicetas. Aetius, indeed (after obtaining for himself the government of Thrace and Macedon in addition to his previous offices) had designs of setting a brother of his own, Leo by name, on the imperial throne. Possibly he may have aimed at inducing or forcing Irene to adopt Leo as her son. But any plots of his would prove unavailing if the ambassadors of Charles had their way, since, whatever their actual instructions, they were evidently believed by the Byzantines to have come with projects of marriage between Charles and Irene, and of union between the two empires, or rather, since the idea of duality was inconsistent with that of Roman imperialism, to bind in one the parts which had lately been severed.

But there was a party in Constantinople opposed alike to Charles and to Aetius, at the head of which were Nicetas and his brother Sissinius.[1] These seem to have gained over some of the military leaders, and to have made an instrument of one of the secretaries— the Chief Logothete Nicephorus. The Empress was at that time residing at a palace called Eleutherium, in the suburbs of the city. There she spent her last night of freedom. For the leading conspirators spread a report that Irene, fearing the wiles of Aetius, had proclaimed Nicephorus her colleague in the Empire. The imperial residence, Chalce, was overpowered. Then a band was despatched to Eleutherium to secure the Empress and bring her back into Constantinople. Her foes were now visible on all sides, her friends singularly ineffective. Next day Nicephorus, who had already been crowned, attended by several patricians, waited on the Empress, with expressions of good-will towards her person, of regret at the undesired honour that had been thrust upon himself. In corroboration of these sentiments, he pointed to his black shoes—for had he aspired to the throne, they would have been

[1] The name is that of the Patriarch's brother. Does this point to any kinship or secret connection which prevented the Patriarch from intervening on behalf of Irene ?

purple. He promised her a life of comfort and dignity and requested her to reveal the place where her accumulated treasure was hidden. Irene complied, acknowledging Nicephorus as her sovereign, and asked to be allowed to live in the Palace of Eleutherium, which she had herself built. At the same time she is said to have made some devout reflections on the instability of human fortunes and the need of submission to the Divine will. Nicephorus naturally took possession of the treasure. He would not allow her, however, to retain Eleutherium, but confined her in the monastery which she had founded in the Island of Princeps. Subsequently she was removed to Lesbos, where she soon afterwards died.

Meanwhile what were Charles's ambassadors doing? Why did not he choose the moment of confusion to rescue the lady who was quite ready to become his bride, and to reseat her, with himself, on the throne—as it would henceforth be—of a united Christendom? And what was the Church doing? Was Tarasius, who had received so much good at the hand of Irene, were Theodore and Plato, who had by her been restored to liberty and honour, and who were only too ready to ignore her worst offences, utterly unmindful of her cruel fate?

The answer seems to be that neither of these parties was satisfied, but that both were compelled to hide their feelings and to await the course of events. The Frankish ambassadors were sent home. Charles was not even now determined to break with Byzantium, and, as we shall see, he renewed his efforts for an alliance, even after Irene had been deposed and superseded by Nicephorus. The ambassadors had probably told him that there was no element or party in Constantinople on which he could rely.

But was there not a party in the Church ready to support his policy and that of Pope Leo? Undoubtedly there were many who, according to Theophanes, "living in piety and reason, wondered at the Divine judgment, which had permitted that a woman who had struggled and suffered for the true faith should be ousted by a swineherd" (an epithet not to be taken literally). These were undoubtedly the feelings of Theodore, who had shortly before written a panegyrical letter to Irene on the occasion already mentioned of the remission of the tribute. But what was he to do? Nicephorus did not wish to break with the monks—at any rate for the present. The Patriarch had, as before, shown a want of backbone. We find him, soon after, crowning the son of Nicephorus as joint-Emperor, and he is mentioned as negotiating for an amnesty to be granted to some insurgents. The Studite monks were acting for the time in concert with the Patriarch, and were included in the new Emperor's apparent good-will. But they, at least, were not often found to be invertebrate. Why did not they rally round Irene?

The answer is not an easy one. We may suggest that *possibly* they did not entirely believe in Irene after all, except in so far as she represented orthodoxy, and the best chance would be given to orthodoxy if they remained in alliance with Nicephorus and held back any possible movements towards an iconoclast policy. But even if they had felt confidence in Irene, or in Irene and Constantine, how would they feel with regard to Irene and Charles, or as it surely would have come about in the end, to Charles and Irene? Those who know Theodore's standpoint with regard to Rome as taken up in the controversy which was to follow—

his recognition of the Pope as successor of St. Peter, and as the highest spiritual authority—may wonder whether he might not have concerted measures with Leo's delegates. But we must remember that at this time Tarasius was alive, and was, in a sense, Theodore's superior, also that the Western Church had never entirely accepted the Second Council of Nicæa. Possibly there may have been a rapid growth of Theodore's notions as to Papal supremacy owing to the visit of the Roman legates to Byzantium, and to the light in which they would probably represent the Pope, as the acknowledged superior of the secular power. But, however this may be, Studium weathered the storm, and Theodore's work as abbot seems to have been little affected by all the turmoil around.

The policy of Nicephorus, in matters political and ecclesiastical, is not easy to unravel. Perhaps we may safely set him down as an opportunist, who had not long anticipated his elevation, and had no very definite programme. His ancestors, according to tradition, had, from personal motives, abandoned first the Christian and then the Mohammedan faith. He was said, by the monastic party, to be orthodox in semblance only. Some[1] have regarded him as a tool of the iconoclasts, yet he does not seem to have taken any steps towards a distinctly iconoclastic policy, and, as we have seen, he was careful to remain on good terms with the Patriarch. The lenient treatment of the Manichees for which Theophanes reproaches him, may possibly mark some inclination in that direction, and doubtless other acts of his may be interpreted in the same light. But he was all through his brief reign in embarrassing

---

[1] Notably Gasquet.

circumstances. The frugality with which he tried to remedy the effects of Irene's lavishness was naturally construed as avarice, yet it did not suffice to maintain effectual resistance to the Saracens—over whom Haroun al Rashid was now reigning at the highest point of magnificence—nor even to overawe the Bulgarians. In one quarter, indeed, the Empire held its ground, though not till after some reverses, and that chiefly by the co-operation of local patriotism. The war between East and West, which paved the way for a partial recognition of the co-existence of two Empires, was carried on not —as originally seemed most probable—in Sicily, but in the neighbourhood of the Venetians. Nicephorus had sent his ambassadors to accompany the returning embassy from Charles, but no definite pact was obtained. Meantime, Venetia had been stirred by the rival claims, and a party had appealed to Charles. The story of the struggle for Venice, which was lost to the Empire in 806, recovered for Nicephorus by the patrician Nicetas in the same year, practically abandoned again after the invasion of Pippin in 810, but finally, by the arrangement of 811, left under the permanent lordship of the Emperors at Constantinople, only indirectly belongs to our subject. It is remarkable chiefly in the history of culture as marking the future situation, and the beginning of what we may call the ducal independence of the city of Venice.[1] It is memorable in the history of East and West, because in the correspondence and negotiations to which the whole affair gave rise, we have statements made by those in authority which recognise the fact of a politi-

---

[1] Duke Agnellus, or Angelo Participazio, was elected under the presidency of the Byzantine Spatharius, Arsafius, and ruled for sixteen years.

cally divided Christendom, and allow us hereafter to speak of an Eastern and a Western Empire. In a notable letter of Charles, written early in 811,[1] he expresses his disappointment that the efforts made in the first year of Nicephorus "to make peace with us, and to join and unite these two [what? would he say Empires?] in the love of Christ" had not been crowned with success. But now he hopes for better things. The delimitation of frontier was made, although the ultimate recognition of two distinct spheres of government was not made with Nicephorus, but was left to his successor.

Meantime, Nicephorus had a sufficient task on his hand to replenish his coffers, and to conciliate parties at home. It is possibly to both of these motives that we may attribute an action of his, to which little attention was directed at the time: he brought the miserable Constantine VI. out of his place of retirement and received him as his guest in the palace.[2] His object, according to the unfavourable historian who relates the incident, was not to show pity, but to discover hidden treasure, and here Constantine, with his usual simplicity, served his purpose, for he revealed to him that much wealth lay hidden in a place called the Sigma, hidden under marble slabs. After the information had been given, Constantine was of no more account. Now it seems an unusual step to employ a blind man in seeking for treasure, though, of course, Constantine may have known of old all the ins and outs of the palace. But it seems more probable, if we take this story in connection with the subsequent conduct of Nicephorus, that he had ulterior views. The name

---

[1] Partly translated in Hodgkin, vol. viii. p. 246 *seq.*
[2] Theophanes Continuator. Bonn edition, p. 31.

of Constantine's grandfather was still potent among the soldiers. Again, Constantine also seems to have had a child, or children, by Theodote, who had been pronounced illegitimate, but whom Nicephorus might possibly befriend and find useful.¹ However, if there was any such prospect in view, it was not realised. Constantine died early in the reign of Nicephorus, and his body was given for burial to his first wife Mary, while his child was pronounced illegitimate.² This decision seems to have been made at some council held by the orders of the Emperors Nicephorus and Stauracius, Theodore himself being present, and the whole affair suggests an attempt at a new departure made by Nicephorus, and a temporary reversal of policy forced upon him by the party of the Patriarch and the monks. The legitimate child of Constantine, Euphrosyne, lived and took the veil. But, like others of her race, she underwent various experiences. We meet her again in Byzantine history as the wife of Michael II.

In the year 806, the Patriarch Tarasius died, and it was extremely important to all parties who should become his successor. It is difficult to understand how the historians of the monastic party eulogise his character, since he seems all through to have acted a weak part. But we must remember that he had a difficult and complicated rôle to play, and after all, it may have been due to his influence that the change of dynasty was accomplished without bloodshed, and that any renewal of iconoclastic persecution was postponed till after his death.

---

[1] Possibly the child pronounced illegitimate may have been Leo, who died in infancy.
[2] See very important letter of Theodore, i. 31. *Cf.* note at end of this chapter.

The object of the Emperor seems to have been to find a man who would further him in his desires of asserting a more independent ecclesiastical policy than had been possible for him while Tarasius was backed by Theodore. At the same time, wishing to stand well with Studium, he desired that his candidate should be approved by the monastic leaders, and actually asked the advice of Plato[1] on the appointment to be made. It seems most probable that he demanded the opinions of both Plato and Theodore, as practically colleagues in the government of Studium, since we have a reply which they drew up jointly, though in all probability it was the work of the younger man.[2] This document is remarkable as an Eastern manifesto of the relations of Church and State. Its language reminds us more of Rome than of Byzantium, and suggests that the Studites had seen something of Pope Leo's ambassadors during their sojourn in Constantinople.

They begin by congratulating Nicephorus on having been divinely appointed to rule over "the Christians" ($\beta\alpha\sigma\iota\lambda\epsilon\acute{u}\epsilon\iota\nu$ $\tau\hat{\omega}\nu$ $\chi\rho\iota\sigma\tau\iota\alpha\nu\hat{\omega}\nu$. Is this a tacit denial of Charles's concurrent claims?) in order that the secular government might be delivered from its evil condition and that the leadership of the Church ($\dot{\eta}$ $\kappa\alpha\tau\grave{\alpha}$ $\tau\grave{\eta}\nu$ Ἐκκλησίαν ἡγεμονία), if it were in any way failing, might be restored. With regard to the world, he had accomplished his mission. It was now his turn to see to

---

[1] Th. St. *Or.* xi. 34.

[2] *Lib.* i. *Ep.* 16. It is not quite easy, though by no means impossible, to reconcile this letter with Theodore's statements in the Panegyric on Plato. In the former no candidate is named. In the latter, Plato is said to have given a vote. Perhaps the demand for a vote was subsequent to the letter. It is rather strange that the transaction should be absent from the "Lives" of Theodore.

the interests of the Church by approving a lawful and free election to the vacant see. The writers have no candidate of their own, though they doubt not that suitable men are to be found. The qualification on which they lay stress is that the person to be chosen should have regularly ascended the successive grades of the hierarchical ladder, in order that, having been tempted in all things like the lesser clergy, he should be able to succour those that are tempted. The choice should be made by a select council of leading men both of the higher clergy and of the hermits and monks. The choice of these councillors was apparently to be made by the Emperor, but it was practically laid down that the whole body of the clergy was to be consulted. Even the Stylites were to descend from their pillars,[1] the recluses to come forth from their retirement, to take part in a measure which concerned the common good. With their advice the Emperor was to choose the fittest person. So would he (or *they*, for Stauracius seems to be included in the address[2]) be blessed and thrice-blessed, and the Empire likewise. Finally comes the clear statement of their conception of Church and State, with a pointed practical application: "Since God has bestowed on Christians two gifts, the priesthood and the empire [ἱερωσύνην καὶ βασιλείαν], by means of which terrestrial things are ordered and governed even as things celestial, whichever of the two fails, the whole must needs be imperilled. Wherefore, if you wish to acquire the greatest goods for your Empire, and through your

---

[1] They are to come *down*. Thus it is evident that the Stylites, who formed, apparently, a distinct order, dwelt habitually *on* their columns, not within them.

[2] The expression is curious: καὶ μακάριος εἶ, μᾶλλον δὲ καὶ τρισμακάριοι.

Empire for all Christians, let the Church receive as her president one who equals, as far as possible, the imperial excellence. So shall the Heavens rejoice and the Earth be glad." Adulatory language, even when the meaning is anything but adulatory, tends to become ambiguous. Did the abbots mean to say: let somebody be chosen who is as good, if possible, as yourselves; or, let a head of the Church be chosen equal in dignity to the head of the State? We seem to find in the East also a conception of the Holy Roman Empire and a Holy Roman Church whose respective heads should possess co-ordinate authority over things secular and things spiritual.

It need hardly be said that Nicephorus had no mind for a free election,[1] still less for the appointment of one who should be a colleague equal to himself. He had already found his man, a member of the official circle, who bore his own name, Nicephorus. Apart from his being a layman, there was no objection to this Nicephorus, who seems to have been orthodox personally and by parentage, and of general respectability. Plato, however, refused to accept his candidature, but made a nomination which the clergy were ready to accept, but which the Emperor rejected. It has been supposed that the person whom he nominated was Theodore himself. The words in which Theodore tells of the transaction may seem to favour that view: "He sent his vote—to whom it was given I forbear to say, but he sent it as in the presence of God."[2] Still, if his nominee had been some other person—such, for instance, as Joseph, Theodore's brother, afterwards

---

[1] Yet he seems to have observed the forms of one, since according to Theophanes, Nicephorus was chosen by the vote of clergy and people.

[2] *Or.* xi. 34.

Bishop of Thessalonica—it might still have been undesirable to mention his name. The approval which the nomination received among the clergy is difficult to explain. Probably the conclave was small and secret. In any case, Plato seems to have exerted himself considerably, as he secretly left the monastery to use his influence with a monastic friend about Court. On his return, he and Theodore were both seized by the order of the Emperor and kept in custody for twenty-four days—that is, until preliminary matters were settled and the ordination and consecration of the new Patriarch were accomplished. When this was over, they returned in no placid mood, yet they both thought it their duty to yield to the inevitable. This was not a matter sufficient to cause a schism. In fact the appointment of laymen to important episcopal sees had probably been of late rather the rule than the exception. But they had asserted their principle. The time was at hand when the imperial policy would bring the hidden discontent to light and would force to a decisive issue the rival claims of the imperial and the ecclesiastical power.

NOTE ON THE DEATH OF CONSTANTINE VI.

The death of Constantine VI. must have occurred some time between the accession of Nicephorus and the final breach between the Emperor and the Studites. The story quoted above from the Continuator of Theophanes gives the earlier limit. The latter is supplied by the letter of Theodore to the Community of Saccudio, which Baronius places in 808, but which refers to events that had occurred some time earlier. The important words are these:—

ἀλλ' αὖθις [ὁ Κύριος] εὐδόκησεν ἀποδοκιμασθῆναι τὴν ἐπιχαρμονὴν τῶν μοιχοζευκτῶν καὶ μοιχιφίλων Ναζιραίων, διὰ τῆς τῶν εὐσεβῶν ἡμῶν βασιλέων δικαιοκρισίας· ἀποδωσάντων, μετὰ τὸν θάνατον τὸν μοιχὸν τῇ νομίμῳ αὐτοῦ γαμετῇ· ἀποκαλεσάντων δὲ τὴν μαχλῶσαν, μοιχαλίδα· καὶ τὸ μοιχογέννητον τέκνον, ἐασάντων ἄκληρον, ὡς ἀθέμιτον καὶ ἀνομώτατον· ὡς ἐν ἐπηκόῳ μοι τὸ τίμιον αὐτῶν στόμα λελάληκε κατὰ τοὺς Ῥωμαϊκοὺς νόμους.

This letter seems to show that there had been a meeting to decide on the matter under Nicephorus and Stauracius. The superscription is rather puzzling, as it is to the Brothers *in* Saccudio, a point to which we shall recur.

The opinion that Constantine died almost immediately after the blinding must be attributed to the expression of Theophanes: ἐτυφλοῦσιν αὐτὸν δεινῶς καὶ ἀνιάτως πρὸς τὸ ἀποθανεῖν αὐτόν, which does not, of course, imply that death followed immediately. The view that he lingered on till about 820 A.D. is derived from a passage in the *Continuator* of Theophanes (ii. 10), who says, of the conspirator Thomas, who raised a rebellion against Michael II., that he feigned himself to be Constantine, son of Irene, who τηνικαῦτα δὲ καὶ τὸν βίον μετηλλαχὼς ἦν.

The τηνικαῦτα is repeated by Cedren (Ed. Bonn. p. 75). On the other hand, and confirming the opinion we shall derive from Theodore, is the statement of Genesius (Migne, *Patr. Gr.* 109. 35): καὶ ἐξ ἀνθρώπων ἠφάνισται μετὰ βραχὺ τῆς ἐκπτώσεως, καὶ ὁ τοῦδε νεκρὸς ἐν τίνι κατετέθη σορῷ τότε τῶν ἐν τῇ βασιλευούσῃ σεμνείων.

The ex-empress Maria does not seem to have felt very proud of her melancholy present.

[Since writing this note, I have found that Dr. G. A. Schneider quotes the above cited letter of Theodore (i. 31) to prove the date of Constantine's death.—*Theodore von Studium*, p. 25, note 1.]

CHAPTER VII

CONTROVERSY CONCERNING THE REHABILITATION OF THE STEWARD JOSEPH — THEODORE'S SECOND EXILE — DEATH OF NICEPHORUS AND ACCESSION OF MICHAEL I. — RESTORATION OF THEODORE — DEATH OF ABBOT PLATO

IF Nicephorus had been somewhat more wary in his ecclesiastical policy, he might, throughout his reign, have had the Church on his side. The reasons why he took measures which were certain to alienate the monastic influence are not clear. We can assign three possible causes: he may possibly have desired a trial of strength, in order to assert his authority. This view is adopted by many historians, but does not seem altogether probable. Or he may have been actuated by a political motive, and have wished to secure the fidelity of those who looked back with regret to the days of the strong Isaurian Emperors. It is noteworthy that more than fifty years later, two successive pretenders arose, claiming to be the dethroned (and unblinded?) Constantine. That name was still a potent one to conjure with. Or there may have been lurking in his mind a possible return to the policy of iconoclasm. Charity might suggest a fourth hypothesis: that Nicephorus only desired to unite all parties and make them promise to let bygones be bygones. But if this was his object, he appears in the light of an exacting and persecuting advocate of toleration,—a character after all not unknown to history. He was tolerant to heretics of certain types, and thereby vexed his orthodox subjects. The sovereign of a distracted realm must often feel drawn to seek for unity by means of toleration, but when such means are taken as are contrary to law and privilege, all the liberty-loving instincts of the people will join hands with their fanatical passions to oppose the suggestion. In the Eastern Empire there was not much liberty in the state nor in the bishops and clergy, but there was still a spirit of freedom and a sense of spiritual equality surviving among the monks. Religious innovations called forth a constitutional opposition such as was impossible in secular matters. In attempting to use imperial authority to allay strife as to points of doctrine, two strong Emperors, Zeno and Justinian, had signally failed. Nor was Nicephorus likely to succeed in asserting his authority on a question of ecclesiastical discipline.

In narrating the course of the controversy between the Emperor Nicephorus and the Patriarch on the one hand, and the monks on the other, we may say at the outset that the exact order of events is not to be determined with absolute precision, since our data are somewhat scattered. It is easy, however, to discern the main current of affairs and the part played by each of the principal actors in the drama.[1]

[1] Our sources are, of course, Theophanes (though he seems to regard Theodore and Plato as out of communion with the Patriarch all along, on account of his uncanonical appointment); a good many letters of Theodore, seemingly written with a present object; others narrative and retrospective; his life of Plato, and the two lives of Theodore himself. For all this part I have found Karl Thomas in general a very serviceable guide. Marin seems to regard the whole dispute as a continuation of that regarding the election to the patriarchate, but I think that Theodore's letters to the Patriarch are here quite decisive.

It seems to have been soon after the appointment of the Patriarch Nicephorus that the Emperor began to devise means for restoring to the priesthood the man who had been the scapegoat in the last controversy—the steward Joseph. This might be done, he considered, by the Patriarch, in virtue of a special dispensation or act of grace (οἰκονόμια). Nicephorus the Patriarch showed no objection, and held a small council, chiefly of bishops, to decide on the matter. Theodore was in custody, but was brought out of the place of confinement where he lay owing to the former troubles, to be present on the occasion.[1] The following day, fearing that the meaning he had expressed had not been made clear, he wrote a letter to the Patriarch.[2] In this letter his attitude is mainly apologetic. He does not repeat the arguments which he had stated the day before, but explains his personal position. He is anxious not to appear fractious or inflexible. He is willing even to admit of dispensations in special cases where there is just cause for such. His acceptance of the apologies made by Tarasius and his acknowledgment of the office of the present Patriarch show his disposition in that respect. Though his language is full of deference, and though he appeals to Nicephorus, as a good shepherd, to exclude one diseased sheep from the fold, lest the whole flock should be infected, yet there is a threatening tone in his language: "We testify to your Holiness in the presence of Christ and in the hearing of the holy angels, that you are causing a great schism in our church. If, being men, we bow to authority, yet it is by the authority of the sacred and divine canons,

---

[1] This has been gathered from *Lib.* i. *Ep.* 25.
[2] *Lib.* i. *Ep.* 30.

knowingly, or against our will, that we are ruled and are obliged to live."

By action, even more than by words, Theodore showed that he did not wish to push matters to extremities. For two whole years,[1] apparently, it was possible for Theodore to refrain from communicating with the Patriarch and yet to avoid an open breach. As he repeatedly declared, it was not really with the Patriarch that the offence lay, nor yet with the Emperor, but with the steward Joseph. As things were, however, to communicate with the Patriarch would have been, in his own eyes and those of the world, to communicate with Joseph, and to offend against canonical law.

The crisis was brought about, apparently, on the return of the Emperor from an expedition against the Saracens, in 808, when the Master of the Public Post conducted an inquiry into Theodore's conduct in thus holding aloof. At the same time he made similar complaints against Theodore's brother Joseph, who had just been made Bishop of Thessalonica. When Joseph replied that he had nothing to say against either the Pious Emperors or the Patriarch, only against the wicked steward, the Logothete replied somewhat brusquely: "The Pious Emperors do not want you, either in Thessalonica or anywhere else." This amounted to a declaration that Joseph had been deprived of his see by the imperial authority. He had already had to send an apology for having accepted it,[2] and had been forbidden to come to Court. His plea was that the

---

[1] 806-808. *Ep.* 25. Theodore in his letters mentions a long delay before his sentiments were declared. See especially *Ep.* 31.

[2] *Lib.* i. *Ep.* 23. To Simeon the Monk, who evidently stood high in the Emperor's favour and employment.

people of Thessalonica had sent a special deputation begging him to take it, and that the Emperors had given their consent. It would have been wrong to shirk the task, though he would personally have preferred waiting till the question of the steward was settled. This excuse, however, did not satisfy the Emperor. Joseph had to suffer for the cause, and throughout the conflict stood by his brother, who, in addressing him, expresses, along with much brotherly affection, all the deference due from an abbot to a bishop.

With regard to the main issue, the Studites had plenty to say to the Master of the Post, and to other interrogators. The ground on which Theodore stood was the fact that the steward Joseph, having been guilty of an uncanonical act, could not be released from the ban under which he lay, and restored to the priesthood, by means of the secular authority. As regards the point immediately in question, the matter seemed a small and personal one. But it rested on two great principles: that the rules of ordinary morality are as binding on sovereign princes as they are on private individuals: and that ecclesiastical censures can only be removed by the free action of the ecclesiastical power.

With regard to the illegality of Joseph's act, Theodore quoted a canon which forbade a priest to take part in a wedding feast in the case of a second marriage. How much more must he refrain from so doing when the marriage is actually of a bigamist? He cited the beautiful words of the Eastern marriage service, to show the profanity of applying them in a wedding of this kind: "Stretch forth Thy hand, O Lord, from Thy holy habitation, and join this

Thy servant to this Thy handmaid. Bind them together in unity of mind. Make those whom Thou art pleased to join to be of one flesh. Let this marriage be honoured. Keep their bed undefiled. Be pleased to let their dwelling together be without offence, in purity of heart."

The excuse that Joseph had acted at the bidding of the Patriarch was no excuse. If the ceremony were a lawful one, why did not Tarasius perform it himself? The unlawfulness had been recognised in Joseph's double degradation. True, there was a time for restoration. But Joseph ought to have applied within a year of his degradation, and to have sought absolution for his sin. In resuming priestly functions, without long previous penance, and doing so publicly and without shame, he had brought scandal upon the Church.

Of course the reply might be made, and was made,[1] that dispensations from general rules must be allowed in special cases. St. Chrysostom and St. Basil had thus remitted punishments. But the cases, it was urged, were not in any way parallel. Again, the second marriage of Valentinian I.[2] was by no means a desirable precedent. The plea put forward by the opponents: that the peace of the Church demanded a compromise, was turned back against them by Theodore. For if only those in authority would now do what was just and fitting, peace and harmony would be at once restored. The root of the matter was contained in the principle that the wishes or commands expressed by the sovereign rulers had nothing whatever to do with moral right or canonical

---

[1] See especially Theodore's letter to Theoctistus, *Lib.* i. 24.
[2] See Gibbon's "Decline and Fall," ch. xxx.

legality. If Constantine VI. had broken any of the commandments, he was not to be excused any more than a private person. If Nicephorus wanted to go against the decisions of the Church in order to vindicate Constantine and those who had sanctioned his conduct, the wishes of Nicephorus could count for nothing. "The laws of God are supreme over all men." If not by words, by deeds, Joseph and his abettors had declared that John the Precursor had erred in reproving Herod, and had not been worthy of the martyr's crown.

These arguments occur in varying order and connection in Theodore's letters, with a good deal of repetition, even in writings addressed to the same person. Of course we have not the arguments on the other side, except as stated merely for purpose of confutation. But there can be no doubt that in this case Theodore was the champion of moral law and of spiritual equality.

Meanwhile he was in correspondence with friends about Court. He wrote two letters (perhaps three) to Simeon the Monk, who seems to have been related to the imperial family, and one to Simeon[1] the Abbot; also one to the high official Theoctistus. But none of them seem to have effected anything for him in high quarters, any more than they succeeded in changing his own views. The priest Simeon he pronounced to be double-tongued. Of the Patriarch he seems to have soon lost all hope. "What is the use of saying any-

[1] The reader will have observed the difficulty occasioned to the student of Byzantine history by the paucity of proper names. Thus we have these two Simeons; we have Nicephorus the Emperor and Nicephorus the Patriarch; Joseph, Bishop of Thessalonica, and Joseph the Steward; among women there are not only several Marias, but various ladies bearing the names Irene, Euphrosyne, &c.

thing to the Patriarch, who sends no answers, and will not listen to any representations, but manages everything for the Emperor?"[1] However, he sent, probably after the return of the Emperor, a last desperate appeal to the Patriarch Nicephorus. He complained bitterly that he had heard from a colleague and pupil John, who had gone to pay his respects to Nicephorus, that the latter had stigmatised Theodore and his party as guilty of schism. He insisted on his orthodoxy, and on his recognition of the Patriarchate of Nicephorus, whom he commemorates in the daily services. He had refrained himself for two years, considering that an abbot has not so great a right to make protests as a bishop. He suggests as the only admissible compromise that he may be left in quiet. He would only implore the Patriarch to avert a schism.

But the Emperor and the Patriarch had made up their minds to resort to force. Studium was seized by a band of soldiers, and Plato, Theodore, and Bishop Joseph were again taken into custody. It is not surprising that they should have stood firm, but it is more remarkable that the brothers in Studium, deprived of the stimulating presence of their fathers, should have shown equal tenacity. The Emperor sent for them to the Palace of Eleutherium, and demanded that they should return to communion with the Patriarch. Those who would comply were to go to the right, those who refused, to the left.[2] When every single man passed to the left, the Emperor ordered that they should be distributed in various monasteries, the whole community being broken up. Either before or after this event, a council of the clergy was called,

---

[1] *Lib.* i. *Ep.* 26, to Simeon the Abbot.   [2] *Vita B*, 27.

at which, in spite of the Studites, resolutions[1] were carried in the sense desired by Emperor and Patriarch.

Under these circumstances Theodore once more found himself a prisoner and an exile, and yet again separated from his brave old uncle, on whom, owing to his age and infirmity, the blow came with greater force. Plato was, according to Theodore, treated with shameful brutality, and kept in close imprisonment. Theodore himself was moved from place to place, and probably detained for the greater part of the time in Prince's Island. What became of the monastic buildings we do not know. They were probably for a time left empty. But the imprisonment was not in all cases so severe as to prevent any sort of communication with the outside world. Thus Theodore was able to write to some members of his flock as well as to influential people at a distance, and his "sons" or "brothers" must have been able to receive his letters. Notably there is one from which we have had to quote which was addressed to the Brothers in Saccudio, and which shows that this monastery, the mother of the revived Studium, had been reoccupied, and was in close alliance with the community to which its leading men had migrated.

Theodore had two main objects in view: to keep his party together, especially by showing how the right lay on his side; and beyond this, if possible, to bring some pressure to bear that might lead to a reversal of policy at Byzantium.

We have already seen by what arguments he maintained his cause, and also how eager he was to meet the accusation of causing a schism in the Church. He

---

[1] We have not their exact wording, since the account which Theodore gives is, if correct in general purport, quite rhetorical in style.

contended again and again that not he but his opponents were schismatics and heretics, and invented an ugly name for this new heresy—the Mœchianic, or Adulterous. He consequently had to meet a further charge: that of indifference to matters of faith, since it was the accepted view that heresy consisted in wrong belief, not in perverted principles of action. There was a certain non-catholic sect—they are mentioned in the great work on heresies written by John of Damascus—called Gnosimachi, or opponents of subtle religious inquiry, who held that Christianity consisted not in knowledge but in action. In an interesting though not very lucid passage,[1] Theodore refers to these heretics, and also to those who make much of *gnosis*, and seems to regard both alike as bound to recognise heresy in his opponents. No number of names, whether of the learned or the unlearned, can prevail against the voice of truth and of the established law.

But it was in gaining or seeking to gain support from a distance that Theodore struck out a bolder line. It is of great importance here to observe his relations to Rome, and his correspondence with Pope Leo, whom he hoped to make his ally.

The relations between Constantinople and Rome in matters ecclesiastical were, throughout the reign of Nicephorus, unfriendly if not hostile. According to Theophanes, Nicephorus the Patriarch was not allowed to hold any communications with the Papacy till after the Emperor's death.[2] Cause and effect may here have

[1] *Lib.* i. *Ep.* 48.
[2] Theophanes, 770 B. In the 100th volume of Migne's *Patrologia* we have a lengthy epistle from the Patriarch Nicephorus to Pope Leo, in which he apologises for delay, and asserts his own orthodoxy and deference to the Pope. This was probably not written till 811 A.D.

been working mutually. The strained relations between the Empire of the East and the Papacy, necessitated by the hand-in-hand alliance of Leo and Charles, along with the hostile attitude of the two sovereigns to one another, especially in Venetia, may have led Theodore to hope for sympathy in Rome. At the same time, a suspicion that the Pope was in correspondence with the recalcitrant monks may have made the Emperor all the more desirous to have nothing to do with the Church of Rome.

We have already suggested that Theodore's notions of ecclesiastical politics had probably been affected by converse with deputies from Rome. Certainly, in his letters to Leo, he shows no trace of any recognition of the "œcumenical patriarchate" of Constantinople, the assertion of which had led long before Gregory the Great to read a lecture on humility to the aspiring metropolitan of Byzantium.[1] Theodore believed, as we shall see in the later controversy, in the patriarchal system,—according to which the assent of the five great bishops (of Rome, Constantinople, Antioch, Alexandria, and Jerusalem) was necessary to make valid the decrees of councils professing to be œcumenical. But he shows at this juncture and after that the authority of Rome ought, in his opinion, to preponderate over all others. For the Pope is the successor of St. Peter, who had received from Christ the gift of the keys and the injunction "Feed my sheep."

Theodore did not approach the Pope without efforts to gain other supporters in Rome. In a letter to a certain Abbot Basil, resident in Rome, he powerfully

---

[1] For the early relations of the sees of Rome and Constantinople, as treated from a Roman Catholic standpoint, see Introduction to Hergenröther's *Photius*.

urges his cause.¹ The chief intermediary, however, seems to have been a Studite named Epiphanius. The first letter from Theodore to Leo has been lost. The second² is addressed to him in even more than Byzantine terms of adulation. At the same time Theodore has no hesitation in exhorting the Pope to fulfil his high vocation, following in the steps of Christ, who saved His disciples in the storm, and who deigned to communicate in writing with King Abgarus;³ also in those of the earlier Leo, who had stifled the heresy of Eutychius. The ruling authorities in the East had arrogated to themselves, for heretical purposes, the power of calling a synod, a power which, apart from the sanction of Rome, they did not lawfully possess, even if their purpose had been orthodox. Let the Pope call a council of legitimate authority, to annul all their wicked acts, or let him at least send an authoritative letter. Theodore writes in his own name only, because his uncle, Plato, and his brother, Bishop Joseph, though sympathising with all his sentiments, are in separate custody and so cannot subscribe to the letter.

It is hardly necessary to say that Leo did not act as Theodore desired. Apart from the fact that he must have desired, as soon as possible, the establishment of peaceful relations between the two Courts, he must have seen that this was not a seasonable occasion for intervention. In fact, to any one really conversant with the circumstances, there would have seemed something grotesque in the notion that the Pope should come forward as universal censor in matters

---

¹ *Lib.* i. *Ep.* 35.   ² *Lib.* i. *Ep.* 33.
³ The story of Abgarus naturally comes up again *à propos* of *icons*, and shows that Theodore had already familiarised himself with the literature of the icon-defenders.

THE SECOND EXILE 127

matrimonial, seeing that his doughty champion, the pious and orthodox — and really heroic — Emperor Charles, had divorced at least one wife, and had had five recognised concubines, besides three other regular successive consorts. However, Leo sent a letter to Theodore, which gave him some satisfaction, and called forth a response, in which the name of Plato was associated with his own.[1] But while he professed himself greatly gratified by the Pope's consolations, and the assurance of his prayers, he insists again on the necessity of a lawful council. He goes a little more into the facts of the case, and insists very strongly on the evil of admitting "respect of persons" in matters of morality. He has to defend himself against the charge of heresy, which, as Epiphanius has related, has been preferred against him in Rome, and anathematises the heretical leaders whose opinions he was supposed to favour.

That these letters should have been allowed to go to Rome (though in the case of the second, we have no actual certainty) seems to show that Theodore's confinement in the islands by no means isolated him from the world. He managed, at the same time, to pour forth letters of exhortation and confirmation to his followers and friends. He compiled, from the writings of Eulogius of Alexandria, a treatise on the vexed question of dispensations. He devised a system of cypher[2] by means of which he might the more freely communicate with his correspondents. He laid down principles as to communion with persons infected with heresy;[3] examined, following St. Basil, the nature of heresy, schism, and segregation;[4] explained again and

[1] *Ep.* 34.
[2] *Ep.* 39, 40.
[3] *Ep.* 41.
[4] *Ep.* 40.

again the nature of the grounds of his disagreement with the authorities. Nor does his labour seem to have been entirely in vain. The Patriarch, certainly, did not find it possible, during the Emperor's lifetime, to retrace his steps, but he became very ready for peace as soon as any accommodation was possible. And among the people generally, the cause of the monks seems to have gained ground.

The end of the whole matter came about by the unsuccessful expedition of the Emperor against the Bulgarians and their terrible king, Crumn, which brought about the death in battle of Nicephorus (July 811) and the severe wounding of his son, Stauracius. Even if Stauracius had been whole, he would probably not have succeeded his father, for Nicephorus was unpopular, and the minister Theoctistus (to whom Theodore had written an appeal, and who was probably a friend to the monastic cause), had a rival candidate. This was Michael, Guardian of the Palace, who had married a daughter of Nicephorus, and who stood high in reputation for piety and orthodoxy. The result was that Stauracius was forced to retire into a monastery, where he soon after died. His wife, Theophane, whom he had illegally married, also withdrew from the world. Michael I. was crowned by Nicephorus, and promised to defend the faith and restore peace to the Church; and the exiled monks were permitted to return.

Whether or no the story is true that Theodore had foretold the destruction of Nicephorus, if he went forth to fight with Crumn, there is no doubt that he and all his party looked upon the death of Nicephorus and that of Stauracius as an intervention of Divine justice on behalf of the good cause. What is more to their credit, they readily embraced the proposals of the Patriarch and the new Emperor, and when once the single point at issue was satisfactorily decided, the schism came to an end. Joseph the priest was once more degraded. The aged Plato, with all the other sufferers, entered into peace with Nicephorus and the Church, and returned to their deserted monastery.

But Plato only came home to die. He was nearly seventy-nine years old, and his afflictions must have diminished his remaining strength. Nevertheless, he bitterly regretted that necessity compelled him to abandon his ascetic practices, and to use the comforts which his spiritual children were so ready to provide for him. After his death, in March 812, Theodore composed, for the Studite brothers, the stirring account of his life from which we have often had to quote. Plato's sister, Theoctista, had probably died before the last troubles began. The memory of the two, and the constant friendship of his brother Joseph, remained as a strength to Theodore in the strenuous and troubled days to come. He had much to endure, but was spared at least one of the most grievous pains by which loving and devout souls are often assailed,— the conflict between the claims of family affection and those of religious and public duty.

CHAPTER VIII

REIGN AND OVERTHROW OF MICHAEL RHANGABE— RENEWAL OF THE ICONOCLASTIC PERSECUTION BY LEO V.

THE accession of Michael Rhangabe must have seemed to the monks and their friends bright with hope for the future. True, there were enemies threatening abroad and subterranean mutters of discontent at home. Haroun al Rashid had died a year or two before, and the disputes among his sons rendered the Saracens, for a time, less formidable to the Empire. But the Bulgarians were as strong as ever. Crumn was drinking from a cup made of the skull of the Emperor Nicephorus, and his people were elated with their victory and ready to follow it up by devastating raids. In Constantinople itself there were some who looked back with regret to the great Isaurians, and who cared little for Michael and his house. But to Theodore and his friends, outward fortunes were of little account in comparison with inner rectitude, or rather, the most adverse experiences, if the heart and mind were sound, seemed at the worst a severe and wholesome discipline. And the new government was, they believed, sound at heart. The new Emperor had solemnly promised to the Patriarch to keep the faith, and to avoid the shedding of Christian blood, with all persecution of monks and clergy. Furthermore, Michael showed himself ready to listen to the advice of the Patriarch and of the monastic leaders. In everything he seemed willing to reverse the policy of his predecessor. Where Nicephorus had been sparing, he was lavish. While Nicephorus had allowed the laws against heretics to remain a dead letter, but had persecuted those among the orthodox who resisted his authority, Michael was willing to put down heresy and to work in all things in close alliance with the Church. Whereas Nicephorus had practically kept his Patriarch from communications with Rome, the advent of Michael was the signal for the reopening of correspondence between Patriarchate and Papacy. Theodore himself, mistrusted, threatened, finally imprisoned by Nicephorus, now appears in the character of an active adviser of the new Emperor.

Michael must be regarded as a *Pfaffen-kaiser*. The part was not a dignified one, and he did not show any particular ability for playing it well. He was not a strong man. He had an ambitious wife and a family for whom he was ambitious. His task required more character than he could show. It was the more difficult in that the body of the clergy, by whom he was generally swayed, was not all of one mind in everything. The party which followed the Patriarch was more pliant and less averse to all manner of compromise than was that of the Studites. Yet it was to the Studites that he chiefly deferred. We may probably see the hand of Theodore in the two creditable and honourable actions of the reign,—the establishment of an *entente cordiale* with the Frankish Empire, and the refusal to abandon Christian refugees to the Bulgarians. The second of these measures is undoubtedly due to Theodore, and it seems natural to suppose that he was consulted in the first, the results of which were entirely in accord with his principles.

We have already seen[1] that at the end of the reign of Nicephorus, negotiations were on foot between the Eastern and the Western Courts for settling the frontier question in Venetia and Dalmatia, and for establishing some kind of *modus vivendi* between the two Emperors. The embassy of Nicephorus had been accredited to Charles's son Pippin, whom his father had appointed to rule over Italy with the title of *King*. But Pippin had died in 810, and the ambassador, Arsafius, had proceeded to Aix, and held a conference with Charles. The result had appeared in the interesting letter already quoted, about the union of the two Empires (as we must almost certainly understand the words) in the love of Christ. With Arsafius, when he returned, were a bishop and two nobles, charged to restore to the "Constantinopolitan Emperor," as the chronicler still calls him, all claims over Venetia and the sea-coast towns in Dalmatia. Possibly this did not imply that Venice was to be free from any money payment to the rulers of Italy, but that such payment was not to involve subjection.[2]

Unfortunately, we have no details of the reception of Charles's ambassadors in Constantinople or of the persons with whom they held consultation. Yet that embassy must have been eminently successful. Like Arsafius, they had to negotiate with another sovereign than him to whom they had been dispatched, as Michael was now on the throne, and his son Theophylactus, crowned, or shortly to be crowned, as his

---

[1] Above, p. 108.
[2] This is the interpretation of Otto Harnack. The evidence for the payment is scattered and the question is not unanimously decided.

colleague, was specially included in the arrangements.¹ The issue of it all was that three ambassadors : Arsafius again, Michael, and Theognotus, were sent to Aix to grant to Charles the greatly coveted title which probably seemed to him of as much importance as any Adriatic cities. The conditions of the treaty were presented to Charles, with his clergy and nobles, and solemnly accepted by them in the church at Aix. On the conclusion of the treaty, the Greeks formally saluted Charles as βασιλεύς or *Imperator*. The proceedings fitly terminated with a hymn of praise,² which seems to find a continuation in Charles's letter to Michael:³ "In the name of the Father, &c., Charles, Emperor and Augustus, King of the Franks and Lombards, to his beloved and honourable brother Michael, the glorious Emperor and Augustus. . . . We bless our Lord Jesus Christ, who has vouchsafed so greatly to prosper us as in these days to establish the long sought and ever desired peace between the Eastern and the Western Empire, and to unite in our times the members of the Holy Catholic Church, which reaches over all the world, under His guidance and protection."

It is a very notable thing that the ambassadors proceeded directly to Rome, where they received the solemn written sanction of Pope Leo to the treaty that had been made.

Charles had thus obtained the reciprocation of the

¹ From the words of Theophanes, περὶ εἰρήνης καὶ συναλλαγῆς εἰς Θεοφύλακτον τὸν υἱὸν αὐτοῦ, the Latin translator, and some historians following him, have spun the imaginary web of a proposal of marriage with some Frankish princess.

² Dr. Hodgkin thinks that the giving of the title was in the course of the thanksgiving (Lauds). Others take *lauds* in the non-ecclesiastical sense. It is certain from the Monk of St. Gall that these ambassadors or their followers were skilled in Greek church music, and thereby greatly delighted Charles.

³ *Ep. Car.* 40 (Jaffe).

title of *brother*, and an acknowledgment of the duality of the Empire and the unity of the Church. Some of the words used in his letters require careful attention. In those days the designation of fraternity between monarchs was not a mere piece of diplomatic politeness. The profession of uniting in the love of Christ was not only pious commonplace. It has been pointed out by an eminent French historian,[1] that the whole tenor of the document and the expressions it employs correspond closely to those of the treaties by which the dominions of Charles were afterwards divided among his descendants. The brotherhood there was physical, but the idea was the same. The unity was that of the Catholic Church. The two Empires were not the Roman Empire as divided for administrative purposes under Diocletian, or under the sons of Constantine. The administrative separation was acknowledged as complete, but the spiritual union was to keep all Christendom together, and the spiritual head was acknowledged in the Pope at Rome.

If Nicephorus the Patriarch had been a strong man, he would probably have made some protest. But Nicephorus was a strange combination of saint and courtier, nothing at all of statesman or diplomat. And Theodore, as we have seen, had adopted, in all its consequences, the doctrine of the Keys. To him, the whole proceeding must have seemed the recognition of the great seats of authority in the Church and in the World. Small blame to him and to his partisans if they could not discern that the separation of the churches must needs follow on the gradual cleavage in character and customs, and that the closing of one

[1] Gasquet, *L'Empire byzantin et la Monarchie franque*, v. 2.

MICHAEL RHANGABE

ecclesiastical controversy only made way for more. For the time, at least, East and West were alike orthodox, and both bowed to the authority of Rome. Similarly, Charles could not foresee that after a few years, ῥῆξ would again be the most dignified word with which the Eastern Emperors would condescend to address his successors. When he lay on his death-bed, only two years later, he fondly believed that he was leaving a united Christendom, which he had saved by his wars, and bound in unity by the arts of peace.

Meantime, Michael had to make head against the Bulgarians. In his expedition he was at first accompanied by his wife Procopia. Her presence seems to have annoyed the soldiers. Probably they thought it implied that the Emperor did not mean business. Their disaffection was quelled, but the Bulgarians had taken advantage of the temporary confusion to press forward and make themselves masters of some strong places in Thrace.

Whether in order to gain time, or in consequence of temporary reverses, the Bulgarian king, Crumn, sent at this time an embassy to the Byzantine Court, to make conditions of peace. These conditions, as to frontier limits and commercial intercourse, were the same as those arranged between King Cormisos and Theodosius III., the last Emperor before Leo the Isaurian. The Emperor was not very warlike, the people were broken-spirited, and the Patriarch was strongly in favour of peace. The one hitch that occurred in the affair was the stipulation that on both sides refugees, captives, and deserters should be given up. It was on this point that Theodore, who was summoned to take part in the imperial council, had strong views, which did not coincide with those of the

Patriarch. The refugees, whom the Byzantines would have been bound to give up, were Christians, likely to suffer evil things at the hands of Crumn if they were left to his tender mercies. The captives taken by the Bulgarians had probably already been ransomed,[1] or else sold into slavery, and so were not easily recoverable. The advantage of obtaining the persons of the Christian deserters, who were teaching the Bulgarians the use of Greek fire and military machines, seems not to have come into the account. Theodore supported his position by a text of Scripture that he was fond of quoting in other connections: "Him that cometh unto me I will in no wise cast out." He applied it in the government of his monastery, never refusing candidates for admission. Here, of course, he used it to denounce any proposition involving the betrayal of those who had sought the imperial protection. His councils, taken up by the Magister Theoctistus, prevailed in spite of the Patriarch and his party, who urged that the few must sometimes be sacrificed for the good of the many. Unhappily, the bold decision was not followed up by bold deeds, and Theodore's opponents were able to accuse him of singular imprudence in causing the rejection of a much-desired peace. Whether, if an ignominious treaty had been signed, the relief would have been permanent, we need not stop to inquire.

We may observe that in another affair, Emperor and Patriarch were heartily at one in carrying out Theodore's maxim. The raids of the Saracens were at this time laying waste the habitations of many monastic communities in the Holy Land. There was a general flight to Cyprus, whence many of the desti-

---

[1] This is the view of Finlay, who, though not as a rule too favourable to Theodore, approves his conduct on this occasion.

tute monks passed on to Constantinople. They were received with a liberality and hospitality which, if disproportionate to the measure of relief which a prudent financier would have approved, were at least creditable to the good intentions of Michael and his councillors.

Meantime the Bulgarians were advancing. Mesembria fell into their hands in November 812, and with it, a good deal of the machinery for producing "Greek fire." Next spring the Byzantine army took the field, and for a very brief time seemed successful, owing, apparently, to an epidemic that attacked the forces of Crumn. In the campaign which followed, there seems to have been a want of determination in the Emperor and of unanimity in the generals, though the accusations afterwards brought against Leo the Armenian, of foul play, do not seem well substantiated. The Emperor and Empress had first visited the tomb of Tarasius, now reverenced as a saint, and surrounded it with silver plates. It might indeed seem as if the vacillating spirit of the deceased Patriarch were presiding over the plan—or no plan—of the campaign. Some of the people, guided by a truer instinct, flocked around the grave of Constantine Caballinus and invoked the aid of one who would never, had he lived on, have allowed his country to fall into such sad plight. They saw him, they said, mounted on his steed, ready to charge the Bulgarians. The orthodox party might call them Paulicians, or Athingians, or other bad names, for calling on one who had long dwelt in Tartarus, in the company of demons. But the facts were not altered. The heretics had certainly proved the best men of war. The battle—if battle it may be called—was fought near Adrianople, where, more than four and a half centuries before, the Emperor Valens had lost his life and his army in fighting the Goths. The imperial army fled so readily that Crumn suspected a feint. The Emperor returned to Constantinople, and proposed to abdicate, but his wife was naturally in opposition to this step. It seems rather strange that his rival should have been one of the unsuccessful generals, Leo, the governor of the Anatolian Theme. But the army knew him to be a man of military capacity, who might do something if only he were independent of so weak a figure-head as Michael. Nicephorus the Patriarch was not unwilling to support him, so long as he guaranteed the security of Michael and his family. This he was ready to do. He entered the city by the Golden Gate —close to Studium.[1] Michael and his family took refuge in a church. They were spared on condition that they entered the monastic life. Michael lived on for many years, and one of his sons afterwards became Patriarch of Constantinople, and also author of some biographical works, which are useful for contemporary events, though in themselves of doubtful merit.

Leo was crowned by Nicephorus, and seems at first to have shown a degree of orthodoxy which was satisfactory to the clerics, and of energy which aroused the hopes of the soldiers. He appears, however, to have declined to give a written confession of faith.[2] The worst thing known of his early days is a dastardly plot to assassinate Crumn at a conference. This miscarried, and the suburbs of Constantinople suffered terribly from the ravages of the barbarian host. How-

---

[1] Whence, apparently, the procession was formed.

[2] So Ignatius says: *Vita Nicephori*. But the passage is obscure, as he makes the Emperor already bound over to heretics and demons. Theophanes seems to have felt quite satisfied with things at the beginning, though he had to suffer when the persecution broke out.

The Golden Gate (in Theodosian Wall of Constantinople) near to Studium.

ever, next year, owing partly to the death of Crumn, partly to the vigorous preparations of Leo, the barbarians were decidedly beaten, not far from Mesembria. It was now the turn of the Bulgarians to suffer from a raid of Romans. A peace or truce for thirty years was subsequently signed between Leo and Mortogon, successor to Crumn, and for some time the Bulgarians seem to have given little trouble to the Empire.

In other directions, also, the change of sovereigns seems to have worked for good. By the testimony of his opponents, Leo was an energetic administrator and a lover of justice. Yet his barbarian ancestry—he was said to be half Assyrian and half Armenian—made him obnoxious to some of the upper circles. The forces of superstition—the ravings of soothsayers and the dreams of visionaries—could by his enemies be turned against him. It is possible that he felt the need of making himself strong in the respect of the armies. The memory of the crowd invoking the ghost of Constantine Caballinus may have suggested a reversal of the ecclesiastical policy of the last reign. Many who felt contempt for the feeble administration of Michael or suspicion of an ultimate swamping of secular interests and policy in the endeavour to reach a monastic ideal, were quite ready to suggest reasons for a return to the policy of Leo the Isaurian and a new campaign against the icons.

It may, however, be gathered from what we know of the character of Leo, hateful as it seemed to those whom he caused to suffer for their faith, that there was less of brutal violence, more of a desire to appeal to reason and to effect a compromise, than there had been under Leo III. or certainly under Constantine V. Leo was, of course, high-handed and autocratic, but he preferred, if possible, persuasion to force. One at least of his strongest supporters, possibly a prime originator of his policy, was a man of learning and intellectual ability, John the Grammarian. There may have been cruelty—though the sufferings of martyrs, detailed for the edification of the faithful, can seldom be observed in a clear light—but there is no ribald mockery. Leo would probably in any case have been likened to a roaring lion—the temptation of his name was too strong—but compared with other emperors, he does not seem to have been remarkably violent in meeting open resistance to his authority. Moreover, he seems to have been a religious man, taking pleasure in the sacred music which was at that time one of the glories of the Byzantine Church, and ready to accept the rôle presented to him of a new Hezekiah. Yet perhaps all the more because he was in some respects a better man than the Isaurians, the persecution which he directed was more disastrous to the Church.

Leo first attempted to get the Patriarch on his side. It is surprising that Nicephorus, so pliant on previous occasions, should suddenly have shown himself capable of resistance even to the loss of position and of liberty. Perhaps his conscience was more sensitive on matters of cult than on such as had to do with discipline, or, more probably, the stern and uncompromising character of Theodore had acquired an ascendency over his more yielding nature. In any case he used all his influence against the innovations, and held all-night services among the faithful. The Emperor had no scruple in taking matters into his own hands, and issued an edict apparently similar in tenor to that of Leo III. Meantime he had set to work some of the ablest men about him to search out and record all the Patristic and Biblical statements by which his cause might be supported.

Of these adherents of Leo, three in succession became Patriarchs of Constantinople. The first, Theodotus Cassiteras, was a layman, who, from the course of events may naturally be suspected of designs on the throne of Nicephorus. He seems to have worked on the superstitious fears of the Emperor. It is a curious fact that there was a certain party among the monks in or near Constantinople ready to denounce the icons and their worshippers and to promise long life and prosperity to the sovereign who might put them down. The threats of a "possessed" woman and of a priest named Sabbatius, and the machinations of Theodotus to bring them home to the Emperor, are detailed at length in some of the chroniclers, but need not concern us here.[1]

Antonius, Bishop of Sylæum, is said to have been a man of law, who fled from the world in consequence of an accusation made against him, and became first monk, then priest, finally bishop. He was regarded with contempt as a *mythologus* (story-teller?) but seems to have been a man of parts. The Patriarch Nicephorus, on discovering his tendencies to iconoclasm —probably before the Emperor had openly declared his policy—held a synod by which Antonius was con-

---

[1] With the accession of Leo, we lose the guidance of Theophanes, which is hardly made up by his Continuators, two unknown authors, together with Symeon Magister, George the Monk (Hamartolus), Genesius, and others. There is some account of the beginning of the persecution in the "Epistle to Theophilus" bound up with the works of John of Damascus. The Life of the Patriarch Nicephorus, by Ignatius, is, of course, strictly contemporary, but it is vague and prolix. The two Lives of Theodore are, of course, useful, and far more so are his letters, for the beginning of the persecution. Hergenröther is of great help as to the persons who figure at this crisis. The stories agree in the main, though the exact order of events is not always certain.

demned as a heretic. He agreed, however, to read a full recantation, though very soon afterwards he explained to Leo that this act had been merely formal and that his sentiments were the same as before. This tergiversation, when known, brought upon him a second condemnation.

But by far the most interesting of the iconoclastic advisers of Leo was John the Grammarian,[1] a man about whom we should like to know more, as he certainly shows versatility of character and talent, with originality and boldness not common among his companions. In fact, he was probably the only great iconoclast to whom Theodore wrote in terms of respect.[2] He was regarded by his contemporaries as an adept in the magical arts, especially in that of foretelling events by means of a metal basin, whence the name by which he is often called of *Lecanomantis*. It is not impossible that he may have had some acquaintance, derived from Arabic sources, with the physical sciences, and if this is so, it is by no means improbable that, not being over-scrupulous in his dealings with the people, he may have encouraged the general opinion that he possessed occult powers. He was said to be remarkably proficient in literature and in rhetoric. He had been abbot of the monastery of St. Sergius, in Constantinople, and was now one of the Court clergy. He must have been fairly young at this time. In the next reign we find him made preceptor to the young prince, and afterwards sent as ambassador to Bagdad and greatly

---

[1] His father, Pancratius, was, according to Symeon Magister, σκιαστης, a term variously rendered as "embroiderer" or "umbrella-bearer." There are a good many references to him in *Theophanes Continuator*, in the "Lives" of Theodore, &c.

[2] *Lib.* ii. *Ep.* 168, 194, 212; if the superscriptions are correct, *Ep.* 194 would have brought John into connection with Abbot Plato.

LEO V.—RENEWAL OF PERSECUTION 143

impressing the Caliph and his Court with his liberality and his powers. On his return, he induced the Emperor to imitate the Moorish style of architecture in some of his palatial buildings. He is said to have had a house underground, in which he carried on his mysterious operations. It is quite possible that at this earlier date he may have had intercourse with Mahometans, and have accepted their principles, at least so far as to reckon a pure monotheism inconsistent with pictorial representations of any being reverenced as divine. We have a graphic description of a scene in church, after the beginning of the iconoclastic measures. It fell to the part of John to read aloud the passage in Isaiah: "To whom then will ye liken God, or what likeness will ye compare unto Him?" Turning to the Emperor, John said: "Do you understand, Emperor, the Divine message? Let no man make you repent of the work begun, but remove far away every likeness that is thought sacred, and cleave to the true worship of those who adore not such things." This man, at least, was not a mere tool in the hands of the secular power. His learning and energy were turned to account by Leo, who chiefly entrusted to him the task already mentioned of searching out authoritative statements against image-worship,—an occupation on which John was employed from July to December 814.

Meantime, the Emperor held private colloquies with the Patriarch which, as might be expected, led to no result. He then summoned a meeting of the clergy at his palace. There Nicephorus had a strong following, even among the bishops, of whom Euthymius of Sardis was a decided champion, though Theodore seems to have taken the lead.

The accounts of this conference are not of course to be taken as verbatim reports, but though one cannot be at all sure what Nicephorus said—whether he tried to elude the demands of the Emperor with a logical quibble, or made a long-winded speech about miraculous icons, there seems to be no doubt as to the ground taken up by Theodore. He simply refused to acknowledge the right of the secular power to interfere in the affairs of the Church. This refusal is more intelligible than a general assertion that the points at issue were not capable of logical argument. Theodore himself, as we shall see, was by no means hesitating in the conflict of reason, and believed as much as other Greeks in the power of argument; but it was one thing to write out logical treatises for the benefit of waverers, or even to meet a theological foe on a fair field, and quite another to consent, in the presence of an autocrat, to the reopening of a question which a lawfully constituted council had settled not many years before. Yet this bold championship of ecclesiastical autonomy was naturally more irritating to the Emperor than any opposition on purely theological ground could possibly have been. He showed signs of great irritation, and declared that he had half a mind not to let Theodore return to his monastery. But he was still reluctant to use force and unwilling to bestow too cheaply the crown of martyrdom. Theodore retired to his faithful "fathers and brothers" the hero of the day. He was forbidden to speak on the controverted subjects, but refused to obey. Nicephorus, though miserably ill, in consequence, no doubt, of the nervous strain, was first dealt with. He was forcibly removed, imprisoned, and declared to have forfeited his see. On Easter Day, 815, Theodotus

LEO V.—RENEWAL OF PERSECUTION

Cassiteras, till then a layman, was set on the patriarchal throne.

The Sunday before, Theodore had taken a step which was too defiant of the imperial authority to be overlooked. On Palm Sunday, he ordered a solemn procession around his monastery, in which the prohibited icons were conspicuously borne aloft. Nevertheless, he seems to have received a summons to the synod called by the new Patriarch to give ecclesiastical sanction to the iconoclastic decrees. Needless to say, he declined the invitation and refused to recognise the intruder. He must have known that the time of banishment was nigh at hand, and he devoted all his energies to confirming the resolution of his monks and to arranging matters for their government during his absence. He chose a kind of committee of seventy-two, to exercise oversight over the rest. He was before long removed by the orders of Leo, and forced to retire to a place called Metopa, near to the Lake of Apollonia, in Northern Phrygia.

Three spirited letters of Theodore remain to us of this critical period. The first,[1] a general encyclical to the monks, was written to protest against the order presented to them for signature, that they should cease to hold meetings and conferences for mutual exhortation and support. In it he shows the power so necessary to a great party leader of making each member, however inferior his grade, realise his personal responsibility in maintaining a great cause: "At this moment, when Christ is being persecuted in His image, it is not the duty of those only who are eminent in rank and knowledge to contend, in conversation and

[1] *Lib.* ii. *Ep.* 2, order of Sirmondi. That of Baronius is slightly different.

instruction, on behalf of true doctrine. But those who occupy the rank of pupils are bound to be valiant for the truth, and to use all freedom of speech." To sign the document would be to betray the truth and to deny all spiritual authority, to give up the apostolic position that "We ought to obey God rather than men." He cites examples of clerical resistance to imperial authority, and appeals to the blessing pronounced on those who confess Christ before men, the curse on those who hold back. How is he himself to act up to his maxim: "Him that cometh unto me I will in no wise cast out," if he promises to reject those who come to him for counsel? He exhorts them to save their own souls and to support him by their prayers.

The letter to Nicephorus[1] resembles many of the catechetical orations in setting forth the glory and the joy of suffering for the truth and enduring the reproach of Christ. Besides the eternal reward of his constancy, the Patriarch has, if he looks around, the satisfaction of seeing his sheep, if physically separated, joined together in unity of spirit by his example and his prayers. Theodore's regard for the person and the authority of Nicephorus is shown again in the letter[2] which he drew up for signature by all those who rejected the summons to the synod called by Theodotus. Such synod, without the authority of a lawful bishop, was incompetent to settle any matter of doctrine and discipline, and the remonstrants have the sanction, not only of the Second Council of Nicæa, but of the great See concerning which the promise had been made: "On this Rock will I build my church."

[1] *Lib.* ii. 18. [2] *Lib.* ii. 1.

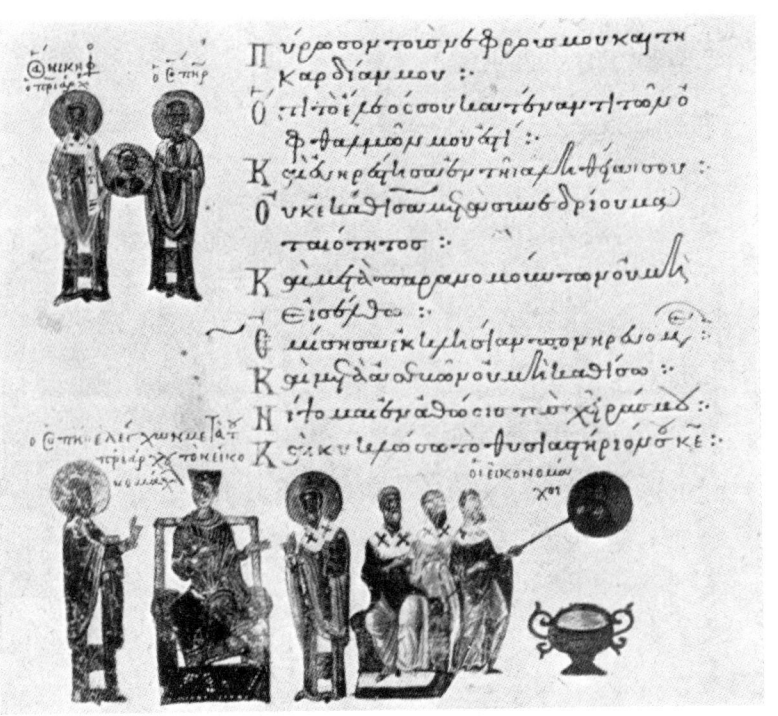

PART OF A PAGE FROM A STUDITE PSALTER OF THE ELEVENTH CENTURY
IN THE BRITISH MUSEUM.
ABOVE, NICEPHORUS AND THEODORE, WITH AN ICON BETWEEN THEM.
BELOW, THE SAME ARGUING BEFORE THE EMPEROR.
THE WORDS ARE PSALM XXVI. *vv.* 2--6. (XXV. IN SEPTUAGINT).

This letter contains also a dogmatic statement of the principles held by the objectors. The whole theological, aspect of the question, however, is so fundamental for the understanding of the controversy and of Theodore's part in it, as to need a special investigation, such as we are to make in the next chapter. The boldness and zeal of Theodore at this crisis show that he believed in his cause and that he was able to confirm the faith of others. The question what that cause actually was now claims our careful attention.

CHAPTER IX

THEODORE'S CONTROVERSIAL WORK AGAINST THE ICONOCLASTS

FROM what we have hitherto seen of Theodore's life and character, we should expect to find all his controversial writings marked by unity of purpose and fixity of principle. Nor are we to be disappointed. Nay, more: it is in these writings more than anywhere else that we find a clear expression of those dominant ideas which were at once his goal and his aspiration throughout his career. For Theodore was not, like many learned men whom an adverse fortune has placed in an uncongenial atmosphere of religious controversy, a theologian by accident. In whatever age of the world's history he had lived, he would have devoted his energies to the examination of theological principles and the elucidation of religious doctrine. The controversy of his day was one with which he became as closely identified as was Athanasius with the opposition to Arius. And, although Theodore himself would certainly have deprecated any suggestion of placing him on an equality with so famous a champion of the Catholic faith, yet possibly he may for us have an almost equal interest. For the conflicts of Theodore's time are more easily translated into terms of modern thought, and brought to act on our sympathies and antipathies, than are those of the fourth century.

For when we look back on the theological controversies of bygone times, we are inclined roughly to distinguish between three kinds. There are some which are to us not only unintelligible, but quite incapable of being stated so as to convey any kind of meaning. We can only look for their origin in a confused state of mind which has no notion of the inadequacy of definitions and arguments to the matters to be defined and argued about, and for their continuance in some half-forgotten prejudice, personal or national, which has become attached to a catch-word or has given significance to a peculiar rite. There are others in which we seem to see some of the thoughts and feelings of our own day represented in forms which we would fain identify and translate, but which we need to approach with caution lest insufficient historical training and imagination should land us in total misconception. And again there are others in which it is comparatively easy for us to realise the warmth of feeling they aroused and the deep speculations to which they led. Such are all controversies which have to do with cult and with habitual religious worship and aspiration. Among these last is the controversy with which we have here to do, though when we examine it closely we see that it comprised many elements likely to be overlooked by a hasty or unhistorical mind, and that many associations have come to belong to it which are not found at its origin.

A side question, involved, so to speak, accidentally, yet very deeply, in the controversy is, as we have seen, that of the nature of spiritual authority. Whatever the supreme voice in matters of cult and of doctrine might be, it was not, to Theodore and his companions, that of the secular government. We have already seen the stout opposition they made to the imperial government in upholding the prerogative of ecclesiastical law, whether in matters of ethics or of ritual. The authority of Councils was generally received, but the question as to *which* councils were to be regarded as authoritative was not always an easy one. The presence of the five Patriarchs was still made an essential condition, but, as we have seen in the case of the Second Council of Nicæa, the principle of representation had to be considerably stretched in order to find representatives of dignitaries whose sees were under Mohammedan sway. Theodore himself may have been quite prepared to cut the knot in the fashion now followed in the West, and to look to Old Rome as the centre of spiritual dominion. But we can hardly think that he would have quietly accepted the decisions of a Pope who received his instructions, with paternal injunctions and exhortations, from a Frankish Emperor of the West. Still less would the rank and file of Byzantine clerics and monks have adopted such an attitude. A united, self-governing Church, comprehending all Christian peoples, was still the object of pious hopes, a desideratum which historical events were constantly proving to be impossible. Written authorities: Scriptures, Canons, Patristic writings, were acknowledged on both sides. But here many fields were open for differences of interpretation and discrimination. And in this place, we may recognise one good thing in what may seem the least intelligent part of the controversy, that the need of examining authority was favourable to at least a rudimentary criticism. The question whether or no any prohibitions laid down by divine authority are universally binding or admit of limitations and exceptions, is one that must be agitated before those who accept Holy Scripture as authoritative can attain either to a rational exegesis or to a theory of progressive revelation. The meaning and authority of canons necessitated a study of Church history and of the principles of conciliar action. The right estimation of patristic saws implied—or ought to have implied—not only familiarity with a large body of literature, but some skill in discriminating genuine from spurious writings. In this direction, Byzantine scholarship had not advanced very far. To take an example: the Treatise of Barlaam and Josaphat is frequently quoted as St. Basil's. But the very recognition that some textual discrimination was needful was surely good for the cause of learning.

When, however, we come to the kernel of the controversy, the question whether or no it is lawful for Christians to represent pictorially the figure of their Lord, and to show reverence to such representation, we soon feel that we are on burning ground. For whereas, in many theological disputes in which an appeal has been made to the people, the popular interest seems forced and adventitious, we see here that men and women are contending for that around which their deepest and tenderest feelings are turned, the evidence to their souls of a divine power and presence. And to thinkers, whether lay or cleric, the question involved rival conceptions as to the central doctrine of Christianity and the deepest practical problem of all religion. It determined the meaning to be attached to the doctrine of the Incarnation, and to the real or symbolic apprehension of spiritual truth. No theological acumen is needed to see that the doctrinal basis of iconoclasm was utterly destructive of any belief in a human Christ, and that if extended to its furthest logical limits it would break down the bridges by which impotent man has thought to obtain communication with Infinite Power and Love.

It must not, of course, be expected that the disputants on either side fully acknowledged, in all possible bearings, the principles for which they strove. But perhaps in this controversy, more than in most, the profoundest of the points at issue were actually brought to the fore, and it is to the credit of Theodore that he excelled the other disputants on his side both in his realisation of the nature of the struggle and the lucidity with which he marked out the ground.

We may, then, take these two great religious principles, the human nature of Christ and the necessity of symbolism in religious worship, as constituting the positive side of the teaching which Theodore opposed to the practice of the iconoclasts. True, neither of these principles, put in dogmatic form, would have been denied by his opponents. They accepted the Nicene Creed and they reverenced the Eucharistic elements and even some of the material objects displayed in Catholic ritual,—such as the Cross and the Book of the Gospels. If it had not been so, all argument with them would have been futile. But they did not, as a rule, accept either doctrine as corner-stone of their whole system of life and thought. With Theodore it was otherwise. In every act of his strenuous life, he regarded himself as sharing in the efforts and the sufferings of a human Master, who, if incapable of pictorial representation, was a mere phantom, no suffering Saviour. And in every act of worship, he felt that in paying reverence to the symbols of the divine, whether to the imitative representation of a divine person, or to any other material suggestion of a divine presence, the object

WORK AGAINST ICONOCLASTS

of his devotion was the same, and the reality of his worship was beyond doubt. Hence we find that not only in his directly controversial writings, but in his catechetical exhortations to his monks and even in his private correspondence, he frequently breaks out into expressions coming from the regions in which his mind was always occupied; as when he says to a friend who has written for instruction in Christian duties: "The true Christian is nothing but a copy or impression of Christ,"[1] or announces to the brethren the deep philosophic principle that "The Archetype appears in the Image."[2]

Yet lest we should fall into the common error of giving too modern an air to an old-world controversy, we may notice a few points in which this one is linked with earlier disputes, and in which it most notably differs from those which might seem to resemble it at the present day. The old notion of the inherent impurity of the flesh, the contamination which spirit must suffer by subjection to material limitations, had been handed down by Pagan Neo-Platonists to various semi-Christian oriental sects, and in the several branches of Manichæan doctrine had exercised a powerful influence upon those who had already adopted the ascetic ideal of life. The anti-iconoclasts rightly saw something akin to Manichæism in the notion that a picture of Christ in human form was an insult to His divine nature. John of Damascus, who was not a student of Plato, refuted the charge by declaring that matter itself was a good creature of God.[3] Theodore does not take this ground, but he shows that the

---
[1] *Lib.* ii. *Ep.* 122.
[2] *Lib.* ii. *Ep.* 38, quoted from Dionysius the Areopagite.
[3] John Damasc. *Anti Icon.* i. 15.

opinions of his opponents would involve the Manichæan heresy that the body of Christ was a mere phantasm.[1] He, as well as his fellow-disputants, regard the points at issue in connection with those as to the Person of Christ which had filled the preceding centuries with bitterness. The modern mind cannot feel much indignation against the doctrine of the Monophysites or the Monothelites. In fact, from the ordinary lay standpoint, it may seem that to *divide* the nature or the will of any conceivable being would be utterly destructive of any unity of person, and would remove the being so divided from the whole region of actuality. We can hardly say whether or no this were the feeling of the fierce Egyptian monks, who, raging against the orthodox with the words: "Let those who would divide Christ be themselves divided," cut down their opponents with the sword. But on the orthodox side there is another point to be remembered. At that day, belief in the divinity of Christ was so entirely dominant, that but for the hypothesis of the Two Natures and even the Two Wills, there would have been no room for any human qualities at all. We can trace this tendency in another direction. Some of the Iconoclasts, especially the Emperor Constantine Caballinus, wished to reject the term, "Mother of God," as applied to the Virgin Mary. What, he asked, was the dignity of a box that had once held gold? Would it not be more fitting to speak of Mary as Mother of Christ? This was rejected as arrant Nestorianism. Nestorianism, however, was not the assertion of the humanity of Christ, but rather the reduction to a minimum of all the con-

---

[1] *Lib.* ii. *Ep.* 72, 81. Antirrheticus, iii. 15.

comitants of human nature as affecting His life on earth. Birth from the Virgin Mary, — a doctrine which in later times has seemed to over-emphasise a supermundane origin and threatened to destroy the possibility of normal human life — was probably, to those who opposed Nestorius, certainly to those who opposed Caballinus, the one guarantee of Christ's human existence, beginning, as all such existence must, in generation from a woman. So strange and even opposite are the meanings of theological symbols or articles at different periods.[1]

Then again—though, when he is dealing with questions of worship, Theodore seems to be on ground where we can safely follow him—we must not expect to find in his works the comparisons which a psychologist would make between the thoughts and feelings aroused by the sight of a picture and by the mental contemplation of the reality. The distinction between psychology and metaphysics was not observed in the Greek writings of those days. True, there were arising in the West a few lonely thinkers who realised that the feelings and thoughts suggested by an object must actually belong to the subject, that the soul of the thinker must be some measure of the world of thought and feeling in which he moves and dwells. But in general, men who wished to ask what they worshipped and why, naturally looked above or around rather than within. To us the saying of St. Basil, more quoted than any other in this controversy, "The honour paid to the image goes up to the prototype," might seem capable of intelligible explanation. For we might interpret it to mean that the feeling of reverence

---

[1] See the Author's little book: "Studies in John the Scot."

first evoked by a pictorial representation and then associated with that representation by conscious cultivation and expression, is exactly similar to the feeling which would be excited if the original were contemplated by itself; or—in case this condition were an impossible one—that what one really venerated in the image was the suggestion of that of which it was a copy, and that therefore the reverential feeling was similar to that aroused by other copies of the same object. But the Greek theologians of this time were not as psychological as we are, besides the fact that the words translated *worship* and *honour* were only too prone to become associated with physical prostration or genuflexion. Therefore they use metaphysical modes of thought, and dwell on the intimate relation between copy and prototype. Here again, the modern thinker is surprised to see no stress laid on the degree of adequacy with which the copy has been artistically rendered. It might seem to us that the iconoclasts might easily have said : " Are these poor, stiff figures worthy to be regarded as in any sense a representation, or even a useful reminder, of beings whose countenances must have beamed with a divine glory and beauty ? " And it would have been easy to answer, on the other side : " Perhaps the icons are hopelessly inadequate. But art has generally been, and might always be, the handmaid of religion. And if we forbid the representation in art of all that we deeply reverence, art will fall—as it has fallen among the Mohammedans—to the level of a sumptuous decoration of material life." But these arguments would not have appealed to a generation that, while it possessed the art treasures of the past and retained some skill in such art as was structural and decorative,

WORK AGAINST ICONOCLASTS

had lost the secret of copying nature, and with it all capacity for criticising art pure and simple. To the people of the ninth century the picture or icon, *qua* icon, was like the original, and it was in virtue of this likeness that it was to be venerated or rejected. The skill or want of skill possessed by the artist was merely a question of degree.

Nor was the common-sense or educational view of the icons much appreciated by Theodore, though, as we have seen, it was much regarded by the Latin fathers, and had found expressson at the Council of Frankfort. The notion that the walls of a church might be made a picture Bible, for the instruction of the illiterate, had commended itself to the practical mind of Pope Gregory the Great, who, more than a century and a half before this time, had issued a reprimand to Serenus, Bishop of Marseilles, for removing from his churches those pictures or statues which were practically the books of the unlearned. The use is not denied by the Greek disputants, but they generally prefer to take higher ground.

Nevertheless, they do not take the highest ground possible. Among the Fathers whom they quote are some—notably the pseudo-Dionysius Areopagitica—to whom the whole material universe, as it appears to mortal sense, is but a reflection, or an image, of the spiritual and divine. If man is to be prohibited from worshipping by means of symbols, he will never be able to worship at all, for no human mind can rise to the contemplation of Deity absolute. The Incarnation of the Logos and the Sacraments of the Church are alike in being a necessity for the limited nature of finite creatures. If icons are regarded in the same way as the sacraments—as pledges of an incomprehensible reality—the reverence paid to them is not only justifiable, but constitutes in itself an element in our worship of the Divine. But the wings of mysticism had been more or less clipped by the ecclesiastical shears, though the Areopagite himself was accounted a saint. The reverence paid to the eucharistic elements was regarded by Theodore as *sui generis*. He prefers to compare the *icons* to venerated crosses and books.

One point in the controversy shadows forth the conflict of a later, but still mediæval period. The stress laid on the identity of *name* in the thing represented and its original (as, when we see a picture of a palm, we say "this is a palm") anticipates the views of the Nominalists. But fundamentally, the position of the icon-defenders is nearer that of Realists.

The purely theoretical bearings of the question are somewhat obscured by the fact that on both sides the leaders had to keep a party together. Thus the arguments and appeals used are always liable to shift as they are addressed to thinking people or to the prejudiced and ignorant. The iconoclasts could always cite the Second Commandment and could express disgust at the weak superstitions of the time, and they probably found a good deal of support in the undoubted fact that the most determined iconoclasts had lived successful lives and died peaceful deaths, whereas many of the iconodules had brought disaster on the Empire and misery on their own heads. The champions of the images had their philosophic and theological grounds, and could defend them with ability and zeal, but they were not above the use of silly stories about miraculous pictures, and—whether consciously or not—

they encouraged acts which seem at least to indicate the grossest superstition. Thus Theodore writes a letter to a certain John the Spatharius, who had taken an icon of St. Demetrius as sponsor for his child. This deed, says Theodore[1] shows a faith like that of the centurion in the gospel, but reversed. The centurion believed in the power of the Word to act instead of physical presence, the Spatharius believed in the power of the physical presence of the image to act instead of the archetype. He need not doubt that his gift has been accepted and that the holy martyr has taken charge of the babe.

It is quite possible that Theodore, like many other intellectual persons, may have under-estimated the dead weight of materialism which loads the spirit of the average man. Some of the combatants on the other side, by no means oblivious of the material condition of the problems involved, would, if they allowed the images to remain, have placed them beyond the reach of physical contact, and thus prevented kisses, though not genuflexions. We do not, strange to say, meet as yet with the fantastic theory which ultimately gained ground in the Eastern Church, that images in the round were to be prohibited, pictures in the flat to be respected. These distinctions do not enter into the general theory of the subject, and some of them were refinements of a later age.

Another point that bewilders the modern reader is the inclusion of images of saints in the prohibition to represent divinity in material form. To Theodore and his friends this prohibition seems a sacrilegious

---

[1] *Lib.* i. *Ep.* 17.

attempt to deprive Christ of His followers. This objection may seem to us rather futile. We might have expected him to say that anything which stimulates our gratitude and admiration for the great men of the past must needs, if the characters admired are noble and worthy, raise our souls to the contemplation of the Divine Excellence, since, as was often repeated, man was made in the image of God. The iconoclasts' view of the Virgin, to whom no more statues were to be erected, was regarded as disparaging the human birth of Christ, not—according to a quite possible interpretation—as raising her to the rank of divinity.

Thus looking at the general nature of the questions involved in this controversy, we may say that the arguments urged by the anti-iconoclasts were psychological, metaphysical, and dogmatic. On the psychological side, neither they nor their opponents made the most of the case, because none of them considered that "the proper study of mankind is man." On the metaphysical, Theodore had a very strong case, which, though he used the names and some of the ideas of its greatest formulators, he hardly dared to set in its strongest light. On the theological side also he had a clear vantage-ground, and he used it with great argumentative skill.

The most formal treatises of Theodore on the subject of the icons which have come down to us are the three *Antirrhetici adversus Iconomachos*. Other writings, which he sent to friends and afterwards refers to, have been lost, unless in some cases they may be identified with some of his longer dogmatic epistles. It is not at all likely that anything has perished which would throw much light on the subject as it presented itself to his mind. In the catechetical discourses, wherever the subject comes up, as it was never far from his heart or lips, and in letters to wavering disciples or to inquiring correspondents, he not only insists on the same principles but uses the same quotations and illustrations, though they naturally seem to wear a slightly different appearance according to the type of mind to which they are addressed. A brief account of the Antirrhetici, supplemented by reference to some of his more private writings, will sufficiently show his general views and methods.

The first Antirrheticus is in the form of a dialogue between a heretic and an orthodox believer. The advantage of this style of treatment is that the ordinary stock objections to the writer's own views are brought forward, with all the scriptural and patristic citations commonly used in their support. There is, however, no exhibition of dramatic skill, not the faintest reminiscence of a Platonic dialogue. The persons speaking are not characters, but mouthpieces of divergent schools. And the colloquy in which they are supposed to be engaged does not exhibit any graces of courtesy or forbearance.

The first charge brought by Hæreticus is one of quasi-pagan idolatry. This is easily refuted by distinguishing between false gods and the true God incarnate. There was no question here of giving to the creature the honour due to the Creator, nor was there any attempt to represent the Divine in tangible form. When Heretic goes back to the Divine nature of Christ, Orthodox shows that His birth and sufferings marked Him as man, circumscribed in the flesh,— not mere man, or man in general, but a particular man, who ate and drank, hungered and thirsted, laboured

L

and rested.[1] Heretic now shifts ground and cites, the total prohibition of images by the Mosaic Law. Orthodox opposes the Cherubim and the Brazen Serpent, made by divine command. If the Jews were not allowed to liken Divinity to any creature, they were still permitted to use symbols. And the words of the prophets denouncing vain idols do not apply to the human Christ. Other points are brought up: the multiplying of objects reverenced, while the real object of worship is One; the sufficiency of the Eucharist as sole image of Christ; the duality of worship where the original and the image are worshipped together. These are answered by reference to customs of Church ritual,—at Christmas and Easter and on Palm Sunday—and by assertion of the principle that, in all cases, it is not the material object, but the Divine Being thereby signified, to Whom reverence is paid. The identity is of name, not of nature, the image on a coin being an apposite illustration. Heretic attempts a dilemma: If the Divinity of Christ is in His image, it is circumscribed; if not, the worship is unlawful. Orthodox answers that the Divinity is present, not in nature but by type. Heretic would, as a compromise, have the images exhibited, but not worshipped. Orthodox distinguishes the two kinds of worship or reverence—$\lambda \alpha \tau \rho \epsilon i \alpha$ and $\pi \rho o \sigma \kappa \upsilon \nu \eta \sigma \iota \varsigma$. The orthodox arguments are clenched by the assertion, that if the contrary is true, the Church has greatly erred,—an impossible conclusion. At the end, a list of iconoclastic state-

---

[1] I have not yet been able to discover whether the expression $\psi \iota \lambda \grave{o} \varsigma$ $\mathring{\alpha} \nu \theta \rho \omega \pi o \varsigma$ here, is the same as $\kappa \alpha \theta \acute{o} \lambda o \upsilon$ $\mathring{\alpha} \nu \theta \rho \omega \pi o \varsigma$ in Antirrheticus iii., or whether it is *mere man* in the sense of *ordinary* or *normal man*.

ments is set forth for condemnation, the first and the seventh being :—

I. "If any one shall not confess our Lord Jesus Christ, come in the flesh, to be circumscribed in flesh, whilst remaining in His Divine Nature uncircumscribed—he is a heretic."

VII. "If any one worshipping the image of Christ shall say that in it physically the Divinity is worshipped, not in so far as it is a shadow of the flesh united thereto, since the Divine is everywhere—he is a heretic."

The Second Antirrheticus goes over much the same ground, in the same way, but gives a larger number of citations and deals with intermediate positions. Here the heretic acknowledges at the outset that Christ was circumscribed in the flesh, but denies the propriety of reverencing His likeness. Orthodoxus tries to show that, since the Incarnation, Christ has been the Prototype of His own image, a doctrine which the heretic denies. The relation of image to prototype, and the one adoration paid to both, is illustrated by sayings from the Fathers, especially Basil and Dionysius, to the latter of whom are attributed the words: "The true in the semblance, the archetype in the image, each in each according to the difference in substance." With regard to the absence of teaching as to images in Scripture: "There are many things which are not written in so many words, but which are taught equally with the Scriptures by the Holy Fathers. The doctrine that the Son is of one substance with the Father is not in the inspired Scriptures, but was proclaimed afterwards by the Fathers; also the divinity of the Holy Ghost; and that the Mother of Our Lord is Theotokos—and many more."

There is a description from Sophronius of a great picture in a church representing Christ with the Virgin and saints, apostles and martyrs. A story is told (ascribed to Athanasius), of an image or picture of Christ, which, when pierced, shed blood and water. The analogy of the venerated cross is again brought in. When, in reference to the sacred things of the Jews, Heretic says that they were not worshipped, Orthodox tries to draw him on from point to point, to confess that what is holy should be venerated, then worshipped. The idolatry paid to the Brazen Serpent is said to be not a case in point, since the Serpent was not a true type of Christ. Heretic seems to have an apostolic saying on his side : "Though we have known Christ after the flesh, yet henceforth know we him no more." But since this interpretation of the text would only mean that the risen body of Christ had no physical properties, Orthodox is able to refute him easily from the Gospel story of the doubt of St. Thomas. He concludes by proving the spuriousness of the passage from Epiphanius quoted against him, and denouncing the heresy of Manichees and Valentinians, that God dwelt among men in appearance and imagination only.

The third Antirrheticus is more logically arranged than the two others, and is not in dialogue form, the objections from the iconoclastic side being stated impersonally.

It is divided under four heads :—

I. On the bodily representation of Christ ;

II. That Christ circumscribed has an artificial image, in which He is made manifest, as it in Him ;

III. That the worship paid to both is one and undivided; that to Christ and that to His image; and

IV. That since Christ is the prototype of His own image, He has one similitude (or relation? = ἐμφέρεια) with it, as one worship.

Under the first head, Theodore shows how the assumption of humanity by Christ involved the assumption of a body with all necessary human attributes. He could thus be seen, even more than heard, since sight is prior to hearing. The Manichæan doctrine of an incorporeal Christ, as well as the conception already noticed of a Christ who was "man in general," not a particular man, are mentioned to be condemned, and the possibility of depicting Christ without denying either His divinity or the incorporeal nature of the Godhead is made to depend on the dogma of the "two natures."

The Second Statement to be established: that Christ *has* an artificial image, takes the word εἰκών in the general sense of *bodily form*, not in that of *image* in particular. A form or similitude may be natural or artificial. The Divine similitude of Christ belongs to Him through His Divine Father. The human similitude, in virtue of which He can be presented to human sense, comes from His human Mother. Suffering humanity involves earthly properties and an "image."

The Third Proposition, as to the *one* worship of Christ and of His Image, follows from what has been already laid down. *Prototype* and *image* are correlative. There cannot possibly be rivalry between them. The worship of the image is worship of Christ because the image is what it is in virtue of likeness to Christ. Thus when we come to the Fourth Proposition, that Christ being the Prototype of His own Image, His relation (or resemblance = ἐμφέρεια) to it is single, and so also is His worship, we seem to have in it a restatement of the intimate relation between archetype and copy, which does not amount to identity of nature or substance, but which involves complete resemblance. If it is objected that " we walk by faith, not by sight," the answer is that we, nevertheless, do see—though "darkly, as in a mirror." If what the mind perceives is not also presented to the eye, the mental vision itself will not remain.

In the many letters which Theodore devotes to this subject, the same arguments and explanations occur. In some,[1] he cites the authority of Councils, especially that of the Quinisext or Trullan, which ordered that crucifixes should henceforth bear the figure of Christ, not, as formerly, that of the Lamb. To John the Grammarian,[2] he writes learnedly on substance and accident, worship and service. He often insists, to his pupils, that the worship of images is only relative (σχετική) and he writes a very severe letter[3] to one who had embarked on the controversy without a clear understanding of the terms used, and so had risked falling into many heresies. In another letter[4] he refutes, by a quotation from Basil, the opinion that images are a condescension to the illiterate. Perhaps Basil is quoted more than any other Father throughout the controversy, and his saying, "Honour goes up from the image to the Prototype," though originally applied in a quite different connection, is constantly brought in for explanation and comment.

---

[1] Especially ii. 72.
[2] As above hinted, I have some doubts whether the superscription is correct.
[3] *Lib.* ii. 152.   [4] *Lib.* ii. 171.

Possibly this summary account of the writings of Theodore against the iconoclasts may leave in the mind a feeling of weariness, and of protest against his logomachy and want of actuality. If, it may be said, great questions were at issue, their greatness is obscured by the haze of pseudo-science and logical subtlety. Theodore seems hardly to have grasped the great idea which the Greek Fathers had derived from Plato, that the whole universe is but a sensible manifestation of a reality beyond mortal apprehension.[1] He can scarcely be said to have woven his conceptions of the visible and the invisible into a sacramental theory of religion and of life. Yet if we examine his career and his influence on others, we can, perhaps, feel pretty sure which aspect of the subject was most constantly and practically realised by him and his followers.

There is a verse of sacred song, written by a Studite monk of the next generation, who had deeply imbibed the spirit of Theodore, often sung in our English churches[2]:—

"Oh happy if ye labour,
  As Jesus did for men;
Oh happy if ye hunger,
  As Jesus hungered then."

The lines are not of great literary merit. Nor do they contain any teaching which might not be accepted by John the Grammarian or, for matter of that, by

[1] See the last sentence of the *Timæus*: "This universe hath come into being living and visible, the image of its Maker, most fair and perfect, even this one and only-begotten world that is." (Mr. Archer-Hind's translation. If the other reading, νοητοῦ for ποιητοῦ be adopted, we have a yet closer approximation to Neo-Platonic ideas, both Pagan and Christian.)

[2] See Neale's "Hymns of the Eastern Church," p. 245.

Constantine Caballinus himself. But they strike a deep vein of Christian feeling, and after all, it seems hardly likely that they could have been written by any one who held that it was derogatory to the dignity of the Eternal Logos to delineate the form of Christ " circumscribed in the flesh."

CHAPTER X

THIRD EXILE OF THEODORE, 815-821

THE third period of banishment which Theodore had to endure may be regarded as historically more important than either of the other two. It was undergone for the sake of a great cause, not on account of a mere personal matter which even his lofty scrupulosity could hardly raise to a high rank of dignity. And, since the Patriarch and the monks were now united in opposition to the Court, it appears far more clearly than any of the former controversies in the light of a conflict between Church and State. In its relation to his personal character it is equally significant, as it brings to light his splendid powers of endurance, his indefatigable activity, and the paternal attitude, tender yet commanding, in which he stood towards the persons and the communities that looked to him for encouragement and guidance. Again, the work that was rudely interrupted by the imperial decree was much more complete and advanced than when last he had been obliged to leave it, and no greater proof of Theodore's powers as a leader of men is required than the fact that Studium weathered all these storms, and could afterwards look back on the period of persecution as the most glorious in the annals of the monastery.

There is abundant material for the history of these years in the multitude of letters written by Theodore from his places of imprisonment, taken in conjunction with the two Lives. The dates assigned to the letters cannot, however, be taken as certain, and the Lives, now, even more than formerly, show the fatal results, common in most biography, of preferring edification to truth. Certainly the character of the martyr does not gain thereby, and the whole question as to the nature of the persecution is rendered obscure.

As we have already seen, the persecution of Leo V. was very different from that of Constantine Caballinus, with which the biographers like to compare it. The plain facts that, through it all, Theodore was never for any length of time debarred from the use of pen and ink, or from the society of his friend and pupil Nicolas, and that he was generally able to receive communications, in letters and gifts, from various friends, is enough to show that the treatment he received was not peculiarly harsh. When we further reflect that on no occasion would Theodore promise to restrict himself in the use of any liberty of speech and writing allowed to him, and that his letters were generally of a highly inflammatory character, opposing, as strongly as possible, the policy of his sovereign, and even stigmatising his church as being in a state of schism, we wonder at the leniency of Leo's government. Unfortunately, however, it seems to have been on some occasions corruption rather than humanity that tempered the imperial severity. Theodore and his friends had no conscientious scruples against the use of bribes. In one letter, Theodore expressly thanks a lady for having bought kindness for him by her gifts to the gaolers.[1] And we may be inclined to attribute other instances of apparent clemency to the same cause. Doubtless the custodians

[1] *Lib.* ii. *Ep.* 94.

of the recalcitrant monks had orders which would have justified harsh measures. But some slight pecuniary inducement from the prisoner's friends—and Theodore, be it remembered, had friends in the higher and wealthier circles of Byzantine society—would secure his comparative immunity, until the discovery of some dangerous action on his part, or the machinations of a private enemy, might lead, for a time, to the use of a stricter rule. Of course the readiness to receive bribes may have operated along with more respectable motives. There can be no doubt that many people regarded Theodore as a saint and confessor, and that those who had custody of him were likely to be influenced by his popular reputation as well as by his dignified personality. Nor need we hesitate to accept Theodore's own statements as to his actual if intermittent sufferings, which, once at least, made him think that his last hour had come. But it is in action, rather than in suffering, in action that must needs bring the suffering which he has no desire to avoid, that Theodore appears at his best.

The place of Theodore's detention was twice changed. First of all, as we have seen, he was sent to Metopa, on the confines of Bithynia and Phrygia. The old division of the Empire into provinces had gradually been superseded by the system of *Themes*, which were more military in character, and each of which was ruled by an official bearing the title of *Strategus*.[1] The division is ascribed in the first place

[1] In the Lives of Theodore, the affected preference for variety in nomenclature is tiresome and puzzling. Thus in *Vita B*, 39, it is not easy to see whether by ὁ τῆς ἑῴας στρατοπεδάρχης is simply meant ὁ στρατηγὸς τῶν 'Ανατολικῶν. στρατοπεδάρχης seems to stand for a higher office than στρατηγός. But the Præfect of the East had been done away. In c. 42 we have ὁ τῆς ἀνατολῆς στρατοπεδάρχης.

to Heraclius, but it was further organised by Leo the Isaurian. Perhaps at this time there were already twenty-eight themes, sixteen in Asia and twelve in Europe. The Strategi were responsible for the prisoners sent into their respective themes, and apparently the variety of treatment which Theodore experienced was due to the variety of officials. Metopa was probably in the Opscian theme. Boneta, to which he was removed in order that his influence might be checked, was certainly in the Anatolic. Smyrna, his third and severest place of confinement, was in the Thracensian. The removal of Theodore from Metopa to Boneta was entrusted to a certain Nicetas, surnamed Alexius, with injunctions to keep him from oral or epistolary communication with outsiders. Theodore refused to become silent, and consequently Nicetas received orders to give his prisoner a hundred lashes. It may seem strange that the prisoner was regarded as the culpable party, not Nicetas himself. But Nicetas had, by honourable or dishonourable means, been won over to Theodore's side, and had recourse to a "pious fraud." He procured a thick sheep-skin, hung it over the prisoner's shoulders, chastised it in a manner not to hurt Theodore himself, and smeared the end of it with a little of his own blood in order to complete the delusion. Theodore thus escaped for a time. But shortly afterwards, a man of clerical status from the neighbouring theme, the Thracensian,[1] placed himself under Theodore's instruction, with the result that when he returned home, he caused his friends to separate themselves from their bishop, who was on the iconoclastic side. The bishop complained both to the

---

[1] Not, of course, to be confounded with Thrace.

Strategus and to the Emperor. Orders were sent down for another flogging, but again the design was frustrated,—it was said by the impression made on the gaoler by the dignified aspect of Theodore, who quietly took off his clothes, saying: "Child, do as you are bid." But unfortunately, a certain Anastasius, who seems to have had some commission from the Emperor, came to make inquiries into the execution of the orders given, and on discovering the state of affairs, gave fresh orders for a scourging,—which was this time actually inflicted—and for closer imprisonment. Theodore and Nicolas were, for a time at least, closely cooped up, and subjected to considerable privation.[1] Yet somehow, by fair means or foul, they managed to receive and to send out letters. A catechetical address from Theodore to his spiritual children was allowed to fall into the hands of the Emperor. The Strategus of the Anatolian Theme was ordered to inflict another scourging. The imprisonment had now lasted three years. Possibly the Emperor discerned that so long as he was in the Anatolian Theme, near to many of his old friends and colleagues, Theodore could not possibly be quite suppressed. He was accordingly moved into the Thracensian, to the city of Smyrna. According to his own testimony [2] his imprisonment was severer than formerly, yet the fact remains that he was able to say this in another catechetical letter. In all his sufferings Theodore showed a buoyancy of spirit and a joy in conscious martyrdom which, while it increases our

[1] According to the Lives their supply of food was cut so short that Theodore himself, leaving the prison supplies to Nicolas, kept himself alive on wafers (probably supplied by friends for celebration) until a superior officer (ἡγημονοκώτερός τις σατράπης) came and insisted on increase of rations.
[2] *Lib.* ii. *Ep.* 66.

admiration for the martyr, shows us also the difficult position of the persecutor, who was obliged either to allow his authority to be defied or to use great severity. Unfortunately for Leo, he failed on both sides. Theodore's influence continued to increase, while his painful captivity aroused the sympathy and emulation of all who heard of it. Smyrna continued to be his place of captivity until the death of Leo V.

It would hardly be desirable to attempt here a full account of the letters written by Theodore during his banishment, seeing that some hundreds[1] of them are still extant. We may briefly describe the general purport of his correspondence as it falls under three heads: (1) letters to his Studite monks, with those who belonged to Saccudio or in any other way came under the designation of "fathers and brothers"; (2) letters of exhortation to fix the purpose or confirm the faith of others, especially church dignitaries and heads of communities of women; and (3) letters written directly with the purpose of bringing pressure to bear on the Emperor and his officials, particularly those to Pope Pascal I. and to the other great Patriarchs.

I. Theodore had advised all the Studite monks to leave the monastery, and most of them seem to have followed his directions. But dispersion by no means involved abandonment of the monastic life. The weaker of them, however, felt sorely tempted to return to the world, and therefore the exhortations of their abbot were even more needed than in quiet times. But though we have many spirited letters "to the dispersed brethren," Theodore was not a father who

[1] There are 221 letters in Book ii., of which almost all belong to the Third Exile and the virtual exile that followed, and 296 in the Cozza-Luzi collection, of which a good many are of the same period.

SEVENTH CENTURY CAPITAL FROM THE CHURCH OF ST. JOHN, USED AS A TARGET FOR PISTOL SHOOTING BY THE TURKS.

regarded all his children in the mass, and a very large number are addressed to individuals. In some cases we have very stern denunciations of those who have been enticed away by an "Eve,"[1] in one instance, the delinquent is told to place his lady, if she consents, in a nunnery. Other letters are written to congratulate on firmness shown and to assist in arguments against heretics. All the arguments which Theodore had been using in his own writings and a good many of the passages from Scripture and the Fathers which he was in the habit of quoting, are collected for the use of his pupils. Evidently his favourite correspondent, one to whom a large number of letters were written, marked by signs of affection and confidence, and giving directions for all manner of occasions, was his "son" Naucratius, afterwards his successor at Studium, and probably already selected as such by Theodore. For a time,[2] at least, Naucratius was a prisoner, but he seems generally to have been at large and influential. It would seem that some of the Studite monks had been unable to flee, and had consequently been exposed to the vengeance of the authorities. The headship of the two monasteries, Studium and Saccudio, was given to a monk named Leontius, formerly a strong, or at least a demonstrative adherent of Theodore, now a renegade, though we find him returning to obedience later. Leontius seems to have been aided in asserting his authority by Bardas, a kinsman of the Emperor.[3] The treatment to which

---

[1] *Lib.* ii. *Ep.* 88, 102, &c.   [2] *Lib.* ii. 67.
[3] He is not, I think, mentioned in Theodore's letters, but the Lives give the story of a miraculous cure from a disease in consequence of the prayers of Theodore, who reproached him with the scourging of Thaddæus.

the faithful monks were exposed was so severe that one of them, Thaddæus, died of the effects. This monk seems to have been a special protégé of Theodore. He was a Scythian—*i.e.* probably a Slav— by birth, and had been emancipated from slavery and received into the monastery, where he distinguished himself by his zeal. But after all, it was a great thing for the cause to have a martyr, whose prayers might be invoked and whose example could be appealed to.[1] The means which Theodore used to keep his monks loyal comprised strict separation from all contaminated with the heresy, and mutual encouragement in persecution. As we have seen, he treated the Byzantine Church as a heretical branch. The buildings in which the iconoclastic clergy officiated were to be avoided, even for prayer. To receive the sacraments at the hand of an iconoclastic priest was a grievous offence. He gave instructions to Naucratius[2] with regard to the monks who had lapsed and then returned to obedience. They were to be rigorously excluded from the Communion till such time as a lawful and orthodox council should have been held, though should that event be long delayed, the time of penance might be shortened. Any prevarication or act of compromise done under compulsion could only be done away by prolonged penance. But these negative measures could, of course, have effected little, if there had not been a general readiness on the part of the faithful to minister to one another's spiritual and corporeal needs.

It is not easy to say where all the scattered monks were secreted to whom Theodore's encyclical letters were addressed. Some of them may have taken up

---

[1] *Lib.* ii. 5, 21, 37.   [2] Especially in *Lib.* ii. 11, 40.

THE THIRD EXILE

their abode in deserted monasteries or waste places, where the officials were too indifferent or too corrupt to interfere with them. Certain it is that many communities which looked to Theodore as to a spiritual father held firm and hoped for better times. His usual mode of exhortation may be illustrated in a general translation of one of his encyclicals, which shows both his weaker and his stronger points. It was written on the occasion already mentioned, of his punishment and closer seclusion after one of his addresses had been brought under the cognisance of the Emperor.[1]

"Rejoice, my longed-for brothers and fathers, for my tidings are of joy. Again have we, unworthy as we are, been held worthy to confess a good confession; again have we both been tormented for the sake of the Lord. For brother Nicolas also has striven most nobly and most faithfully. We, for all our lowliness, have seen the blood flowing from our bodies upon the ground, we have looked on our own scars and sweat, the effects of our stripes. Is not this joyful? is not this a thing for spiritual exultation? But what am I, wretched man that I am, to be numbered with you, worthy confessors of Christ, I the most unprofitable of all men? The cause whence all this came about was that a former Catechetical Oration of mine had come into the hands of the Emperor, who thereupon sent to the Commander [of the Theme, $\sigma\tau\rho\alpha\tau\eta\gamma o\hat{v}\nu\tau\alpha$] ordering that the leader of the band [$\kappa\acute{o}\rho\tau\eta s$ $\kappa\acute{o}\mu\eta\tau\alpha$] should come to us. And he having come, with officers and soldiers, in the middle of the night, they surrounded, with crowding and clamour, the little house in which we were, as if

[1] *Lib.* ii. 38.

they were tracking a wild beast, and having hastily broken down the enclosure with pickaxes, produced, scanned, and displayed the Oration. We confessed to having written it, as was the will of God. But he desired only one thing,—that we would yield to the will of the Emperor. We replied what truth demanded: 'Far be it from us! we do not set our God at nought!' And other answers we gave such as were fit. Thereupon he scourged us heavily. And the Brother (Nicolas) since his first imprisonment and indictment, has suffered as yet nothing very terrible. But I being low and weak, reduced by violent fevers and by severe labours, scarcely escaped with my life. But God in His mercy soon took pity on me, and the Brother gave what help he could. But still the marks remain and have not been completely cured. So things were, and I have told you of the suffering, knowing that you desire to learn so as to sympathise. But what came next? Fierce threatening and closer confinement. For our guards and their headmen have been charged with threats not to let us give forth any sound, still less to write any word. Shall we then tremble and be silent, having regard to the fear of men, not of God? Nay, verily. But so long as the Lord opens a door to us we shall not cease, so far as in us lies, to fulfil our task, fearing and dreading the judgment on our silence: 'If any man draw back, my soul shall have no pleasure in him. But we are not of them that draw back, but of them that believe to the saving of the soul.'

"Hence this letter of mine to all the dispersed brethren, grievously afflicted by persecution; and especially to you who are confessors of Christ. Let us endure, my brethren beloved, being ever more strengthened, not cast down, in our sufferings. We have bodies,[1] let us not spare them. We are tortured for Christ's sake; let us rejoice. He who has abounded in afflictions should be the more joyful, as one who has earned higher wages. If any man dreads the pain of the rod, let him think of the eternal torment, and shake off his fear. These are to those as a dream, as the missiles of babes. I entreat and adjure you, let us be made glad by our sufferings for Christ, severe as they may be according to the flesh. Let us look to that which cometh and remaineth, not to that which is now and is soon passing away. Let us desire that our blood may mingle with the blood of the martyrs, our portion with the lot of the confessors; that we may exult with them to all eternity. Who is prudent? Who is wise? Who is the good exchanger, giving blood to receive spirit, despising the flesh to obtain the kingdom of God? 'He that loveth his life shall lose it,' saith the Lord, 'and he that hateth his life in this world shall keep it unto life eternal.' Let us hearken to His words, let us follow Him. 'Wheresoever I am,' He saith, 'there shall also my servant be.' And where was He? On the Cross. And we are there, poor and lowly, as those that learn of Him. I exhort you to suffer this word of exhortation, for I have written but briefly. You know that we, sinful as we are, rejoice and keep up heart, if only you stand fast in the Lord. Greetings from Nicolas, my fellow-prisoner and fellow-labourer and fellow-soldier, and your most faithful brother. Greet one another with a holy kiss, as combatants your fellow-combatants, as persecuted your comrades in persecution, all as loving

---

[1] *Or* " they are flesh " (σάρκες εἰσί).

one another in faith. If any one does not acknowledge Our Lord Jesus Christ depicted in the body, let him be anathema from the Trinity. The grace of Our Lord Jesus Christ be with you. Amen."

This letter may seem to modern ears overstrung, self-conscious, abnormal. But the feeling it expresses is intensely real. We may dislike the tendency to dilate on personal sufferings. Yet if the blood of the martyrs is the seed of the Church, it were bad policy in the martyrs to check its operation. Even the curse at the end comes from a life-long conviction, and is not an ebullition of personal spite. Theodore wrote not for us, but for the men of his time, to whom he seemed to hold the rank of a spiritual father, who saw no weakness in his complaints, and were strengthened by his fortitude, who did not perceive his exaggerations, but were ready to receive his message.

II. It is not easy to separate the letters written with authority from those of a private and friendly character, since a good deal of importance was attached to all that Theodore said, and questions were continually being put to him on matters of doctrine and discipline. He seems, possibly through the posthumous influence of his mother, to have obtained great influence over a good many religious communities of women, and to have felt responsibility for their conduct and prosperity. "We are one church of cœnobites,"[1] he wrote to a nun, "I visit you by letter, my spiritual sister, and ask after your welfare in the Lord ;—whether you keep to the glorious confession of Christ ; whether you maintain securely the faith entrusted to you by the Holy Spirit; whether you are strong in the Lord and

---

[1] *Lib.* ii. 53 : μία Ἐκκλησία κοινοβιακή ἐσμεν.

not in terror of the impious." Both to individuals and to communities he wrote letters of encouragement and of warning. A community of thirty women who had held firm against persecution received his warm congratulations.[1] He shows discrimination in dealing with separate cases. Thus he sanctions,[2] for a short time only, the adoption of a secular habit by a nun who feared lest she might not be able to resist the demands of the iconoclasts. But she is not to retain that habit permanently. To a patrician lady, who seems to have been of monastic status,[3] he writes a kind letter on her return to the faith after having lapsed, and exhorts her, in her penitence, to have regard to her health. In general, however, he is no less strict in exhorting women than in his injunctions to men, and rejoices in their steadfastness as in that of his own monks.

There were a good many bishops on his side, notably his brother, Joseph of Thessalonica, Peter of Nicæa, Theophylactus of Nicomedia, and Theophilus of Ephesus. Joseph seems to have amused himself, as did Theodore himself,[4] in making metrical refutations of the iconoclasts' arguments, some of which had been lost in transit. To all ecclesiastical dignitaries, Theodore writes in terms of studied compliment, yet in a way that suggests anxiety to retain their adhesion. Several abbots received from him letters of encouragement and sympathy. We find also among his correspondents many laymen who held offices and titles,

---

[1] *Lib.* ii. 59.   [2] *Lib.* ii. 52.
[3] *Lib.* ii. 68, *i.e.* if we identify her with Irene, the mother of Euphrosyne, of whom more hereafter.
[4] Or is it possible that the verses attributed to Theodore were really written by Joseph? See *Lib.* ii. 31.

yet whom he evidently regards as well inclined to his cause. This fact would strengthen the supposition to which one is led in other ways, that, as a rule, the persecution was confined to the clergy and the monks and nuns. Indeed, Theodore congratulates a certain Gregoras [1] as being the only layman in authority who had made a good confession and therefore suffered persecution. There must have been a good many among the laity who received the sacraments secretly from orthodox priests, and who made some efforts to alleviate the sufferings of the confessors.

III. But from a more general point of view, the most interesting part of Theodore's correspondence is that by which he sought to obtain the help of the Roman See in putting down the heresies of the East. The cause was now one which had, *prima facie*, a better chance of receiving Papal attention than so purely personal a controversy as that concerning Steward Joseph. For the Papacy had definitely taken up the cause of the icons, though not quite as decisively as the Eastern monks might have desired, and a great Pope, anxious to restore ecclesiastical unity, might have felt strongly moved against the schismatic Emperor and Patriarch. But men and measures were, in the West, on a smaller scale than during the life of Charles, and those of Popes Hadrian and Leo. The Emperor Lewis the Pious might be ready enough to pray for the unity of the Church, but had neither power nor inclination to interest himself actively in the cause. Pope Paschal I. may have had wider views, but the management of affairs in Italy, and in the West generally, was sufficiently

---

[1] *Lib.* ii. 56.

engrossing, and his power in the Western Church was not altogether unquestioned.

It was, however, to Paschal that Theodore now appealed. The letter is shorter than that formerly addressed to Leo. With his own name, Theodore associates those of four other abbots. He addresses the Pope as "Master and Apostolic Father," and acknowledges him as possessor of the keys, and as corner-stone of the church. He narrates briefly the misfortunes that have occurred, the imprisonment of the Patriarch, the insult done to the sacred images, and through them to their Prototype; the exile of priests and monks; the great sufferings inflicted on the faithful; the general terror. "'And thou when thou art converted, strengthen thy brethren'; now is the time and place; help us according to the command received from God. Stretch forth thy hand as far as thou canst;—thou hast power from God in that thou art above them all. . . . Good shepherd, lay down thy life for the sheep. . . . Let it be heard under heaven that by thee the presumptuous ones have been synodically accursed." At the same time, Theodore wrote to friends in Rome, begging for their co-operation, especially to the Archimandrite Basil,[1] to whom he insisted on the essential unity of the Church. With the idea of a synod in his mind, Theodore wrote also to the other parties whose presence was necessary for a lawful council, the Patriarchs of Alexandria and Antioch, to whom he sent an identical letter, and to the Patriarch of Jerusalem.

The result was partially successful. In several letters written, apparently in the course of the follow-

[1] *Ep.* in Cozza-Luzi Collection, 192.

ing year, Theodore triumphantly asserted that Rome was on his side. In another letter to Paschal, he expresses delight and gratitude at the kind messages which the brothers whom he had sent to Rome had brought back with them. But in this second letter, there is no mention of a synod or council. Probably the Pope had suggested to the emissaries that some personal communication with the Emperor might be tried first. In any case, Paschal wrote to Leo, using the common arguments against iconoclasm.[1] It must have been the work of some Greek exiles, more bold and consistent in their sacramental doctrines than Theodore himself. The Neo-Platonic thought of the material as *image* of the spiritual, is handled as by a disciple of the Areopagite. It is not likely that, in any case, the representations from Rome would have changed the imperial policy. But a very different series of events was soon to restore the sufferers to liberty and hope.

From all that we can gather of the character of Leo V., by reading between the lines of partial and prejudiced chroniclers, he seems, in his government, to have been just and economical, and one likely to offend vested interests in his measures of administrative reform.[2] It is not easy to tell whether the fate that came upon him was provoked more by his good or by his evil deeds, but probably the machinations against him were devised by those who hated him as economiser, not as perse-

---

[1] The letter, in a somewhat mutilated state, has been published by Cardinal Pitra (*Jur. hist. et mon. Gr.* vol. ii. p. ix. *seq.*). See also Schneider, *Th. v. St.* p. 86.

[2] See an appreciation of his government in Finlay's "History of Greece," vol. ii. bk. i. ch. ii. But it is hard to acquit him of cruelty, or at least of ruthlessness, though he may only have followed the prevalent customs in espionage and torture.

cutor. The leader of the rebellion was Michael the Amorian, a soldier who had risen from the ranks, and who had come to possess the Emperor's confidence. His treachery was discovered by means of spies, and Michael was thrown into prison, a respite for his execution being allowed over Christmas Day. But Michael contrived to communicate with his fellow-conspirators through a priest whom the Emperor had, by special request, sent to receive his confession. A message from the prisoner was conveyed to the insurgents, to the effect that if they did not make an effort to release him, he would denounce them to the Emperor. The effort was made, by the cunning of a friend of Michael's, Theoctistus.[1] The Emperor was going to an early morning service in his chapel, to which a limited number of outsiders were admitted. Among these were some of the conspirators, in priests' robes, with daggers under their arms. Leo, who had a fine voice, himself took part in the singing. At a certain point in the psalms, the assassins, as previously arranged, rushed forward to despatch him. He resisted, using a cross as weapon; then, seeing his case hopeless, took refuge at the altar, and asked for mercy. "This is the time for killing, not for sacraments," was the reply of a rude giant among the conspirators. Leo fell dead. Michael was called forth from his dungeon, and set on the imperial throne. Leo's wife and sons were forced to adopt the monastic life.

The letters written by Theodore when he received the news of this most dastardly murder are by no

---

[1] Not, of course, to be confounded with the Theoctistus of whom we read under Michael I.

means pleasant reading. They recall the triumph of Athanasius at the sudden death of Arius, and are a fresh proof, if one were required, that persecution, if it braces the soul of the sufferer, does not always enlighten his judgment or refine his taste. Even the sacrilegious character of the deed does not seem to have shocked Theodore. The sacred building had lost its character when given up to schismatic and iconoclastic worship. But if he seems to represent the deed as non-criminal, it is simply because he regards it as an act of divine justice. He probably would have agreed that the conspirators were murderers, but from his particular point of view, they are instruments in the hand of Providence, as much as hail-storm and thunderbolts. After all, it was not his business to inquire into the rights and wrongs of an action for which neither he nor his friends were in the least responsible. He had but to receive the results of that action with all thankfulness, and to use his utmost efforts to make the most of the unexpected turn of affairs for the restoration of the exiles and the re-establishment of their cause.

CHAPTER XI

THE LAST FOUR YEARS

THE disappointments which proverbially lie in wait for restored exiles soon arrived to curb the jubilant delight of the monks at the supposed end of their sufferings and the restoration of the good cause. Michael, like most usurpers, would have preferred to reverse to some extent the policy of his predecessor without taking such decisive measures as to threaten a vigorous opposition and the downfall of his unsteady throne. He was no fanatic and not incapable of toleration. He seems to have been a fairly able general, and if it is true that he rejected the proffered aid of the Bulgarians against his Christian subjects,[1] he must have had some sense of the dignity of his position. He also, in his dealings with the great Western Power, appears somewhat of a diplomatist. But he does not show any greatness of character nor yet the statesmanlike ability needed to cope with the unusual difficulties which beset his reign: economic distress; political disaffection; formidable and hostile neighbours; and a bitterly distracted church.

One of his first acts—that which called forth the prematurely triumphant utterances of Theodore already referred to—was to issue an edict for the liberation of the persecuted monks and their friends. But it need hardly be said that to Theodore no liberation was to

[1] *Theoph. Continuator*, c. 17 (p. 65).

be accounted as such that did not carry with it full power to labour for the reassertion of the cause at stake. He welcomed the new Emperor not merely as a personal benefactor, but as a possible Josiah, to whom the task had been entrusted of restoring pure religion. This restoration would, to his mind, imply the return of the monks to their old possessions and their former ways of life; the dethronement of the schismatic Patriarch with the recall of Nicephorus; the replacing of the sacred icons where they had formerly received reverence; and the complete reconciliation of the Byzantine see with that of Rome.

The activity of Theodore was thus directed to his one object by various channels. He must write to his "spiritual children" everywhere, congratulating them on their improved position, but urging them to remit no efforts towards the achievement of their hopes. The Patriarch Nicephorus must be kept firm by definite though very respectful exhortations to do his duty. The arguments in favour of icon-worship must be repeated even *ad nauseam* to ecclesiastics, to statesmen, to the Emperor himself. And in all communications with the imperial power the principle must be kept in the forefront that no arrangement can possibly be satisfactory that does not acknowledge the Roman primacy, and the complete independence, in matters concerning religious doctrine and discipline, of the ecclesiastical authority, which can never be lawfully subordinated to that of the State.

Theodore could rely on the support of some powerful persons about Court, notably the Logothetes John, Pantoleon, and Demochares, and the Magister Stephen.[1] In his letters to these persons, Theodore

[1] Different from Stephen *a secretis* to whom Letter 75 is written.

THE LAST FOUR YEARS 189

expresses some disappointment with the slow pace at which things are progressing: "Tell me, most worthy friend, how is it that now the winter is over, we have not a perfect spring, but only a spell of moderate weather, with a suggestion of seasonable times? The fire has been quenched. Why has the smoke been left behind?" The disappointment may have been due to the answer sent by Michael to the representations of Nicephorus, who was probably acting under Theodore's direction in writing from his retirement to demand a reversal of policy and the restoration of the images.[1] To this request the Emperor returned the somewhat curt answer, that he did not intend to make any changes. If the ex-Patriarch wished for restoration to his office, he must comply with the Emperor's policy. Nicephorus held firm, strengthened by personal intercourse with Theodore, who visited him as soon as possible, and kept up frequent communications with him when they were both in the suburbs of Constantinople.

Theodore had also written very decidedly to the Emperor.[2] At first, apparently, he entertained, or at least manifested, no doubt as to the intentions of Michael. He congratulates him on the good work begun, and adjures him to complete it, by restoring the cult of the icons and the unity of the Church: "To believe in Christ is nothing else than to believe that the Son of God the Father, having become a complete man, was formed after our own image and likeness [ἐξεικονίζετει καθ' ὁμοίωσιν ἡμῶν] so as to be nought other than what we are [? ἵνα μὴ ἄλλο τι εἴη παρ' ἡμᾶς]

---

[1] *Continuator of Theophanes*, c. 8. Told at greater length in the Life of Nicephorus by Ignatius.
[2] *Lib.* ii. 74.

while He remained himself uncircumscribed with the Father and the Spirit in so far as He is very God." He goes on with the old comparison between the Emperor's head stamped on a coin and the picture of Christ. Recognition or denial of the copy implies recognition or denial of the original. Finally: "Our Church has of late torn herself away from the four Patriarchs, in vain lawlessness, but 'now is the accepted time,' O most Christian Governor, 'now is the day of salvation,' to reconcile us to Christ, by the mediation and with the approval of your pacific Empire;—to unite us with the head of the Churches of God, namely Rome, and through Rome with the three Patriarchs, that being like-minded we may with one mouth glorify God."

While the Emperor was considering the rôle suggested to him, the factions trying to assert their rival causes and interests, and the exiles flocking back to their homes, Theodore himself was travelling from Smyrna to Constantinople. He seems to have met with an enthusiastic welcome from the inhabitants of the religious houses at which he stayed on the way. He lingered for a time near Lake Metata and then at a place called Pteleæ. On the way two men of influence visited him or were visited by him, Leo the Consular, and Theoctistus who had been *Magister* and was now a monk. At Pteleæ he enjoyed a visit from his brother Joseph. He travelled on to Chalcedon, where he saw the ex-Patriarch Nicephorus, and then seems to have settled for a time at the monastery of Crescentius, close to Nicomedia. Here strange to say, we are in the dark as to the point on which we should naturally expect to have definite information: whether or no Theodore actually returned to Studium and resumed at once his

THE LAST FOUR YEARS

authority and his functions there. His modern biographers seem, perhaps too hastily, to have assumed that he did so. But neither the Lives nor the Letters are quite explicit on this subject. We are told that he returned to his beloved province (or Παροίκια), but this word may stand for those parts of Bithynia with which he had for many years been familiar, where his kinsfolk held property, and where there were many religious houses devoted to his cause. No doubt Theodore hoped to be reinstated before long at the head of his monastery, but such reinstatement was hardly implied in the bare remission of his exile, and it is almost impossible that he would have consented to return without a clear understanding that the old ritual was to be restored. Such an understanding, we can easily imagine, might have been taken by him for granted without formal leave, but in such case, we should probably have heard of some such occurrence as that of the Palm Sunday before his exile. From the data that remain to us we can only feel sure that the first weeks—perhaps months —were spent in strengthening his partisans, both lay and monastic, for the coming struggle. The space which would naturally be devoted to this important part of the narrative in the Lives is a lacuna, stuffed for padding with a very insipid and irrelevant series of miracles, including the drying up of a flood, the frightening away of a tiger, and the castigation, during sleep, of a Sardinian monk who had made light of Theodore's hymns. More pleasing, as certainly more probable, is the story of how he was consulted by an ascetic suffering under calumnious accusations, whom he advised to wear shoes in winter, and in his food and clothing to live a little more after the ways of ordinary people.

Michael seems, like many well-meaning autocrats

deficient in sympathetic imagination, to have thought that the whole iconoclastic controversy could be settled by a conference in which the leaders on both sides might be persuaded to accept a policy of compromise, with local toleration. We have among the Letters[1] one from an assembly of bishops and abbots, drawn up by Theodore in the name of the rest, in which they state that they are assembled by order of the Emperor, and request him to give them a personal hearing. The letter is very much to the same purport as the private one already quoted, but it insists yet more strongly on the supremacy of Rome, quoting the text, "Thou art Peter, and on this rock I will build my Church," and it rejects indignantly the proposal—probably made to the orthodox bishops and abbots in their assembly, that they should hold a conference with those of the opposite persuasion. Michael seems to have gone further in his proposed concessions than Leo had gone, in that he would have put the ultimate decision into the hands of persons acceptable to Theodore and his party.[2] But to Theodore, anything short of an œcumenical council seemed insufficient to determine the questions at issue. If the local conference were to have been merely preliminary, it seems not improbable that he would have agreed to it, but he doubtless saw that the Emperor would make it final, and would endeavour to settle fundamental points of doctrine by means of an irresponsible and manipulated debating society.

In the two Lives of Theodore there is a curious little divergence, since one[3] expressly mentions the

---

[1] *Lib.* ii. 86.
[2] This is to be gathered from *Lib.* ii. *Ep.* 229.
[3] *A*, 118.

THE LAST FOUR YEARS

Patriarch Nicephorus as taking part in the doings of the assembly demanded by the monks, and the other[1] as definitely excludes him. This must have been a crucial time for Nicephorus, since the iconoclastic Patriarch, Theodotus, died in this same year, and there can be little doubt that the Emperor would have been glad to help towards the extinction of the schism by reappointing Nicephorus, under conditions which might be agreed upon. It was in all probability Theodore who prevented any such conditions from being made. This supposition would account for the close union between the two leaders, and their mutual deference, which seemed to the biographers to afford a most edifying spectacle. Michael appointed to the vacant Patriarchate a leader of the opposite party whom we have already mentioned, Antonius of Syllæum.

Meantime, the desired audience was granted.[2] The bishops and abbots were introduced into the imperial presence by one of their friends at Court—probably one of Theodore's correspondents. They discoursed in defence of the icons, apparently without much lucidity, as the Emperor after a time turned from them to Theodore and asked him to state the case. Theodore repeated the arguments of the others, probably with greater clearness, and thus obtained a definite, if hardly satisfactory answer: "What you say is all very well, excellent in fact, but I have up till this time never worshipped an image, and I mean to leave the Church as I found it. I command that you have full licence to follow the teaching of what you call the orthodox faith. Outside the city, you may each of

---

[1] B, 60.   [2] *Vita A*, 118; *Vita B*, 60.

you do as he likes, without fearing or expecting that any interference will come to you from my government." So saying he dismissed the assembly.

The words "outside the city" were decisive. Local toleration with local persecution is seldom a satisfactory expedient, and in a state in which the capital is of such paramount importance as Constantinople was to the Empire, the concession seemed nugatory. To Theodore it meant that he must henceforth keep at a distance from Studium, and that the great monastery which owned his headship could not again become the headquarters of his party. He withdrew to Crescentius, near Nicomedia. Great as his disappointment must have been, matters were not quite hopeless. The persecution was stayed, and his influence was allowed free course both among his spiritual children and in the higher circles of the court and state.

It was probably in the religious houses of the coast and islands in the near neighbourhood of Constantinople that the influences were growing and spreading which led, though not in Theodore's lifetime, to the ultimate triumph of the icons. Among Theodore's correspondents were some women of high rank, including two ex-empresses, who were strong adherents of his cause. One of these was the Empress Maria, widow of Constantine VI., who had, with her daughter Euphrosyne, adopted the monastic life. Whether or no Euphrosyne had taken all the vows required for a religious profession may be doubted. In any case, she ranked as a nun, and was secluded in the Princes' Island. Michael was now a widower, and in spite of his attachment to his deceased wife, he listened to the suggestions of his courtiers and their wives

THE LAST FOUR YEARS

that he should marry again. It is another sign of the popularity, among a considerable section of the people, of the great Isaurian dynasty, that Michael decided to brave the censures of the Church in order to unite to himself a lady of that house. The marriage of Michael and Euphrosyne was odious to the monastic party on three grounds. They objected to second marriages in general; Euphrosyne was a nun; and any connection with the sacrilegious Isaurian family seemed unholy. Theodore denounced the marriage in a catechetical oration.[1] He also wrote to the Empress Maria,[2] of whose cause he had in former days been the champion, and who had lately sent him some token of friendship or regard. Her imperial son-in-law seems to have invited her to Court, and the world expected her to accept the invitation. But Theodore maintained that a higher authority than that of the world ordered her to remain where she was, and against the promptings of natural affection he quoted the bitter texts: "Who is my mother and who are my brethren?" and "He that hateth not his . . . daughter for my sake is not worthy of me." It is not clear whether Theodore meant that Maria's monastic vows compelled her to remain in her place of seclusion, or whether he simply intended to warn her against incurring the temptations of a misbelieving Court. Apparently Maria did not go, as another letter seems to congratulate her on having resisted the temptation.[3] But Euphrosyne, if we judge from subsequent events, was more inclined to the belief of her mother than to

---

[1] No. 74. This may have been delivered (1) orally to the monks who had come to live under him at Crescentius or elsewhere; (2) by letter, as was the case with many of his *Catecheses;* or (3) orally at Studium, during the insurrection of Thomas (see below).
[2] ii. 181. [3] Cozza-Luzi collection, 148.

that of her father's family. At least the monastic houses with which she was associated seem to have been orthodox. We have a letter written by Theodore to the canonesses of Princes' Island[1] in which he congratulates them on their purity of life and faith, though he warns against temptations. And the monastery of Gastriæ, said to be that of (or founded by) Euphrosyne herself,[2] and to which she retired in later life, was situated close to Studium itself. It was also very near the abode of a lady who worked a good deal in the cause of the images, Theoctista, mother-in-law of the Emperor Theophilus. Her name, being also that of Theodore's mother, might suggest kinship, and this suggestion is made more probable by the statement of a chronicler[3] that the place for the monastery had been bought from the patrician Nicetas, who is addressed as a kinsman in one of Theodore's letters.[4] Furthermore, we have another imperial lady closely connected with Princes' Island and with the island of Prota, also a stronghold of the orthodox, who was a correspondent of Theodore. The wife of the Emperor Leo, Theodosia, is said by the chroniclers to have urged on her husband the postponement of Michael's execution till after Christmas Day, an act which indirectly led to Leo's murder. There is, of course, no reason to suppose from this fact that she was in any way cognisant of the conspiracy, and the contrary would seem to be proved by her enforced retirement afterwards, when she was sent to Princeps, her sons to Prota.[5] According to a story current among the orthodox, one of these sons, named Constantine, but

---

[1] (ἡγομένη) *Lib.* ii. 125. Is the *dux* mentioned Maria herself?
[2] See George Hamartolus, p. 790.   [3] *Theoph. Contin.* p. 70.
[4] *Lib.* i. 27.   [5] Symeon Magister, p. 619.

now renamed Basil, became afflicted with dumbness in consequence of the cruel mutilation perpetrated, in Byzantine fashion, on all the sons of Leo. Basil, however, thought of calling in the aid of Gregory Nazianzen (the reason why this father was selected is not told), and immediately recovered his speech, and became a devout venerator of the icons. The story would not be worth relating if it were not that we have a letter written by Theodore[1] to the Empress Theodosia and her son Basil. The first part of it consists of congratulations on their having come over to the side of the truth. The second is a little ambiguous. The Emperor had assigned to them the Island of Chalcita, whence the monks and brethren were to be ejected. Theodore had felt distressed at the tidings, but had lately been partially reassured, on hearing that whatever was being done, was entirely by order of the Emperor. He requests the ex-Empress, however, and her son, to lessen as much as possible the sufferings of the exiles.

From these various facts we learn that Theodore had many adherents, both men and women, in the regions adjacent to the city. Before long, however, circumstances led to an unexpected recall into the city itself, and probably, for a time at least, to a temporary re-establishment of Theodore in his authority at Studium.

These circumstances were the disturbances connected with a serious revolt, which soon grew to alarming dimensions, and spread distress and insecurity throughout the Eastern provinces. The leader, Thomas, is an ambiguous figure.[2] By some he was identified—

[1] *Lib.* ii. 204.
[2] Even the Continuator of Theophanes is puzzled about him, and gives two accounts of his origin.

and this is the view commonly accepted—with the general of the same name who shared in the revolt of Bardanes and was afterwards promoted by Leo the Armenian. According to others, he was a Slav of obscure birth who had for a time served under the Saracens. He succeeded in gaining a party among the desperate and discontented, and is said to have actually posed as the unhappy Emperor Constantine VI., asserted to have survived his misfortunes. This pretension is inconsistent with the identity of Thomas the rebel and Thomas the general of Leo. One would have thought that such a claim could have been shattered at one blow by a refusal on the part of Euphrosyne (whether or no she were as yet Empress) to acknowledge him as her father.[1] Yet there have been no less strange and —one might suppose—easily refuted claims made by other historical pretenders. Thomas secured the co-operation of a certain Gregory Pterotes, brother-in-law and friend of Leo V. By an arrangement with the Saracens, he was enabled to travel to Antioch and go through the rite of coronation at the hands of the Patriarch Jacob or Job. He gathered a large fleet which assembled at Lesbos, overran great part of Asia Minor, and proceeded to lay siege to Constantinople.

Michael now showed a considerable amount of energy. He collected ships and munitions of war, put the city into a state of adequate defence, and with his son Theophilus, whom probably at this time he associated with himself as co-Emperor, maintained a vigorous and ultimately successful resistance to the besiegers.

---

[1] It may be observed, however, that the marriage with Euphrosyne may possibly have been a counter move on the part of Michael to the pretensions of Thomas.

The rebel army suffered from an inroad of the Bulgarians—though the Emperor had declined their help. The rebel fleet was scattered, and two attempts to storm the city alike failed. Thomas raised the siege, and was in turn besieged[1] by the imperial forces. He was shortly after betrayed to the Emperor and was, along with his son, put to death with disgrace and torture.

It was during or just before the siege of Constantinople that Theodore and his monks were summoned into the city. The measure was one of caution on the part of the Emperor, who feared lest they might favour the insurgents. Thomas seems to have been trying to win over some of the party by professed devotion to the icons, but it does not seem probable that either he or the monks looked to each other for assistance. The orthodox chroniclers write of Thomas with detestation. It is certainly unlikely that any pretender who meant to oppose iconoclasm would try either to perpetuate the traditions of the Isaurian dynasty or to attach to himself the friends of the murdered Leo. The only trace of action on their part, during this crisis, seems to have been the successful negotiations, carried on by a Studite monk, for separating Gregory Pterotes from the cause which he had adopted. Our want of information as to how Theodore passed the months of the siege, and as to the local warfare before and after, is probably not to be supplied. It would seem most probable that he was again in residence at Studium, delivering his fiery catechetical orations to his "fathers and brethren," and maintaining the strictness of their rule, with the observance of iconodulic ritual.

[1] Either in Adrianople or in Arcadiapolis.

It was probably at the end of the revolt that the Emperor made another effort towards a peaceful argumentative conference. A letter has already been quoted, addressed to the Emperors Michael and Theophilus,[1] in which, after a very respectful salutation, Theodore again refuses to discuss publicly with heretics, gives a confession of faith, goes through a good many of the arguments used against iconoclasm, and insists on the authority of Œcumenical Councils. A letter to the same purport with regard to Conciliar authority was written by him to the Sacellarius Leo, in which he referred to the offers made three years ago,—a fact which seems to prove that Michael had kept the same object in view during this time, but had been prevented by the rebellion from carrying it out. It seems that the Emperor had determined not to allow the cult of icons, or to listen to suggestions for the restoration of Nicephorus, till a definite arrangement had been made. Theodore retired first to the monastery of Crescentius, where he must have had fairly complete liberty, since he was able to see his friends and to write letters to his adherents. The country was still in a very unquiet state,[2] and he was soon compelled by an Arab inroad to leave Crescentius for the promontory of Acrita, where there was a religious house dedicated to St. Tryphon. It must have been about this time that he had the great sorrow of losing his brother, the Bishop of Thessalonica, who was afterwards buried at Studium.

The Emperor Michael did not prove equal to the task of settling the disturbances which had been partly

---

[1] *Lib.* ii. 199, placed by Baronius in 823 A.D.

[2] *Lib.* ii. *Ep.* 127, may perhaps be taken in connection with *Vita A*, 119, though they do not entirely coincide.

THE LAST FOUR YEARS

cause, partly effect, of the rebellion of Thomas. There were complaints on many hands of oppression and incapacity on the part of his government, and having little culture or tact, he failed to maintain a position of personal dignity in the eyes of his officers and of the public generally. The two great disasters that came upon the Empire soon after the suppression of Thomas are such as we cannot lay entirely to his charge, though they are part of the general failure of the Empire to defend the Provinces. These are the losses of Crete and of Sicily. Crete was overrun by a band of Saracens from Spain, whose leader burned his ships and forced his followers to make wives of the captive women and to settle as permanent colonists. The efforts made to recover the island ended in failure. The ancient Greek cities had to submit to Moslem rule, which remained in the island for nearly a hundred and forty years. The other loss to the Empire was still more serious, and it was permanent. A Syracusan citizen, said to have married a nun and to have raised an insurrection in order to escape the amputation of his nose, invited Arabs from Africa, who, after a considerable period, possessed themselves of the whole island. The fighting was not all over during the lifetime either of Theodore or of Michael. One cannot help thinking that the religious controversies, with the exile of the monks and their supporters, helped to bring about the catastrophe. The refugees, who must have existed in considerable numbers in these parts, were not likely to welcome the Arabs, but their influence cannot have tended to the loyal support of the imperial government.

But Michael showed himself sincerely desirous of internal peace, and he determined to look for it in the direction so often indicated by Theodore. He resolved, however, not to apply straight to the Pope,[1] but to approach the Papal See by means of the Emperor Lewis the Pious, with whom the relations of the Byzantine Court had continued, on the whole, friendly.

The attitude towards the Papal power of Theodore, Michael, and Lewis respectively, is characteristic and instructive. To Theodore, as we have seen, always ready to recognise "the archetype in the image," the Pope is both legally and practically the wielder of supreme power. Distressed Christians may appeal to him for aid as the disciples called to Christ when the storm threatened their boat. To Michael he probably seemed an inconveniently powerful prelate, whose action was embarrassing in many ways, but who might be presumed to stand to the Emperor Lewis in much the same relation as the Patriarch of Constantinople to the Eastern Emperor. Probably neither party realised how the complicated relations of the Papal and the Frankish Court made any effectual intervention almost impossible.

The name by which Lewis is commonly called—the Pious—suggests his habitual deference to the authority of the Church. But this by no means implies great respect for the Pope. Councils had been held in his dominions for the reform of monastic institutions and for the redress of ecclesiastical grievances, but these measures had not been undertaken at Papal instigation. The act of Lewis which showed

---

[1] All the transactions are given at considerable length in Baronius, *Annales Ecclesiæ*, xiv., and in Mansi, *Concilia*, xiv. He also wrote to the Pope (see his letter to Lewis), but apparently only to complain of the encouragement given to fugitives.

the most entire submission to the spiritual authority, the penance he underwent at Attigny for sins which modern historians commonly regard as no sins at all, whatever it was, was not a "going to Canossa." Pope Paschal, at the moment when Theodore was entreating the Emperor of the East to reduce the Church under the papal authority, was labouring under the charge of having caused the murder of two dependents of the Emperor of the West, and was only cleared after a commission of inquiry and a solemn act of expurgation. His successor, Eugenius, was appointed under the direct influence of the Emperor's son Lothaire, but was not inclined to adopt a very decided policy.

Michael's letter was a singular production. It abounded with commonplaces about the blessings of peace and unity. It repudiated any responsibility for the murder of his predecessor, and gave some account of the recent troubles with Thomas, which were urged in excuse of the Emperor's dilatoriness in opening negotiations with Lewis. It passed on to make complaints of the Iconodules, who refused, it said, any conference and compromise, and were guilty of all manner of superstitious practices, such as mixing the scrapings of the images in the sacred wine, taking statues as sponsors for children (a practice, as we have seen, not disapproved by Theodore), replacing the cross by an icon, and so forth. He expresses his own orthodoxy and moderation, carefully stating that he acknowledges the *six* œcumenical councils—thus excluding the second of Nicæa, and declares that he and those who have come to his conference have ordered the images not to be broken but placed beyond the reach of the worshippers' hands and lips. He requests Lewis to use his influence with the Pope against the calumnies of the fugitives.

The following events took a peculiar course. The ambassadors proceeded to Rome along with some messengers from Lewis.[1] The result was that permission was granted to the French clergy to meet in Council—or Conference—and draw up a collection of the opinions of the Fathers on the subject of Images and Image-worship.

The Council, or, as it is more precisely called, the *Collatio*, which was summoned in consequence of this permission, sat in Paris in 825, and drew up several very lengthy documents. The main part of their work was, of course, the collection of Patristic authorities. We meet in it many of the stock quotations, but it is incomplete and bears some marks of haste. The general result is a decision in favour of the mean—a reassertion, so far as doctrine is concerned, of the decrees of Frankfort. A moderate reverence is to be paid to images, the use of which is primarily educational and commemorative. The opinion quoted which seems most entirely to represent the view of the Frankish Church, is one already cited—that of Gregory the Great in his admonition to Serenus, Bishop of Marseilles :[2] "It is one thing to adore a picture, another to learn, through representation in a picture, what is worthy to be adored. For what the faithful who read receive from books is given to the simple in pictures; since by them

---

[1] It seems possible that the only communication which Michael held with the Pope was through the letters from him conveyed by this joint embassy.

[2] St. Greg., *Lib*. xi. *Ep*. 13.

the ignorant are instructed in their duty and in them the illiterate can read."

The Council drew up a letter for Lewis to send to the Pope and even one for the Pope to send to Michael. Neither of these epistles ever arrived at its destination. But two French Bishops, Jeremy of Sens and Jonas of Orleans, were sent to Rome, with a long paper of instructions bidding them deal very diplomatically with the Pope, and endeavour to persuade him to join with the Emperor in sending a peace-making embassy to Michael. It certainly would have been inadvisable to state plainly before even the most imperially minded Pope the condemnation that the *Collatio* at Paris had pronounced against Pope Hadrian for disapproving the articles of Frankfort. Whether the fault lay with Jonas and Jeremy or with circumstances we cannot say. But the Pope did not send any legates, nor did any sent by the Emperor effect the kind of understanding desired. All dreams of a spiritual force proceeding from the West to calm the storms raging in the East, proved a mirage. Different indeed were the hopes of Theodore from those of the Fathers assembled at Paris, but both were alike illusory.

There is but one passage in Theodore's correspondence which seems to refer to this attempt at conciliation. In writing to the monk Nicetas[1] he acknowledges a book which has been sent to him setting forth the doctrine that pictorial representations are an indulgence to the imperfect. This view, substantially that of the Synod of Paris, is extremely

[1] *Lib.* ii. 171.

repugnant to him. He objects to the division of the Church into the perfect and the imperfect (did he suspect Manichæism here?), and quotes as a *reductio ad absurdum* the instruction which the great Basil professed to receive from pictures. Whether he knew anything more about Western opinion we cannot tell. It is not impossible that some of his friends who had taken up their abode in Italy may have used their efforts to keep Eugenius from accepting the part which had been assigned to him by the French clergy and their Emperor.

The Frankish Church continued for some time to regard pictures and statues as educational aids. Some churchmen went the length of actual iconoclasm, especially the notorious heretic, Claudius of Turin. But there was no persecution. It seemed for the time as if diversity of view were more possible in the West than in the East.

Meantime, where conscious effort failed, an apparently unimportant circumstance connected with the negotiations helped ultimately and indirectly to bring the East nearer to the West. Among the gifts brought from Constantinople to the court of Lewis was a copy of the works of that prince of mystics, the pseudo-Dionysius the Areopagite. Lewis ordered that a translation should be made of them. The attempt failed, but the task was afterwards taken up by more competent hands.[1] There seems an irony of fate in the circumstance that the very same action which brought about a declaration of the most common-sense, unimaginative, one might almost say pseudo-rationalistic view of religious symbols, also brought

[1] See the Author's "Studies in John the Scot."

into Western Europe one of the most abundant sources of high-soaring mysticism. For from Dionysius arose the fountain that helped to fructify the whole spiritual field of mediæval thought, that nourished the philosophy of Scotus and even of Aquinas, the art of Botticelli, and the poetical imagery of Dante.

CHAPTER XII

THEODORE'S PRIVATE CORRESPONDENCE—HIS DEATH

THE events narrated in the last chapter bring us near to the close of Theodore's varied and strenuous life. But before we come to the final scenes, we may take a glance at a part of that life which is not confined within any limited period—at his epistolary intercourse of a more private nature than the letters already cited in connection with doctrinal controversies and official action. Not that in his case the public and private can always be kept quite distinct. Some of his most important declarations as to matters of principle were made to his near kinsfolk or intimate friends—to his uncle Plato, his brother Joseph, his spiritual "sons" Naucratius, Ignatius, and the others. And in his most private letters, his desires and his warnings often fall into the forms with which we have become familiar in his definitely theological works, just because these forms were a part of his perpetual mental environment. Thus the relation of Image to Prototype is never far from his thought. Nevertheless, we can roughly separate his dogmatic or authoritative from his friendly and personal letters, and these in many cases tend to give us a different impression of the man from that which we should derive from his professional utterances alone. There is more elasticity and urbanity about them, more recognition of the necessary conditions of civilised life, above all more "saving common sense."

The reader is at first struck by the vast number of letters that Theodore must have written, seeing that the many hundreds which have come down to us cannot be regarded as constituting the whole or even the greater part of his correspondence. A very large number are in answer to letters sent to him, most often of inquiry as to his opinion on difficult questions of discipline or of private conduct. A good many are addressed to bodies of men and women taken collectively. Several are expressions of thanks to men, or still oftener to women, for kindness shown during times of adversity. There is, as one would expect, a considerable variety in style, according to the object of the letter and its recipient in each case. Unfortunately, the stilted ceremonialism of Byzantine life had intruded even into private relations, so that one must not expect to find here the grace and simplicity which have made the epistolary literature of the best periods such an abundant and trustworthy source for contemporary social history. The third person generally prevails, the writer being "my humility," "my unworthiness," or something of the kind, and the person addressed "your magnificence," "your piety," and the like. Still, the man's real meaning generally succeeds in breaking through the crust. Occasionally the feeling of the writer is decidedly at variance with the respectful style of the epistle, as where an answer has to be sent to some tiresome person who has been asking unreasonable questions.[1] Far more often, however, the tone of politeness and of kindliness is maintained throughout.

Among the letters of the more ordinary and

[1] This is the way in which I would explain *Lib.* ii. 220, and 205. The former is to Machara, wife of a Spatharius, who seems to have wearied him with empty compliments.

o

complimentary kind are a large number written to persons of high station to condole with them on the death of some near relative. There is one to Stauracius[1] the Spatharius, probably (though not certainly) the prime minister and bad adviser of Irene, to comfort him on the loss of an infant son, his eldest-born. To Leo, the Guardian of Orphans, he writes to express sympathy on the death of a child, three years old, the third child the father had lost.[2] This letter is written in what seems a simple and natural way, and would lead us to suppose that Theodore had a soft place in his heart for children, and that he was not very emphatic on the doctrine of original sin: "For you this is sad, exceedingly sad; but by no means so for those that have been taken, since, unspotted and undefiled by sins, owing to their youth, they have departed from things here to the blessed and painless life, where in the bosom of Abraham they sing praises in chorus with holy infants, and make melody with the children who follow Christ."[3] He urges him to keep the mean, showing natural grief, but maintaining self-control, and he hopes that his wife the Chartularia[4] may bear him another and less short-lived son. The tendency to optimism as to the future of those who die young is shown more markedly in the case of a man who had died in vigorous youth, not in innocent childhood. In writing to the Turmachissa of Greece[5] (wife of the commander of turma?) to comfort her on the loss of a son killed in a battle, he says: "He had put on Christ in baptism, embraced the orthodox faith, and had not yet become

---

[1] *Lib.* i. 18.   [2] *Lib.* i. 29.

[3] The word is χριστοφόρων. Is he thinking of boys carrying the icons of Christ in a procession?

[4] Was Leo *chartularius* as well as *orphonotrophus*?

[5] *Lib.* ii. 145.

filled with the pleasures of the world, so much as to touch them with his finger-tips, owing to his youth. Wherefore we may believe that where, in his human life, he may have erred and gone astray, he will obtain forgiveness through his unexpected and unjust death." In another letter[1] he condoles with a nobleman whose young son had, after receiving a good education, died in chastity and orthodoxy. In his experience among his "spiritual sons" of frequent lapses and belied hopes, he may well have felt that whom the gods love die young. His letters of condolence often insist, in a commonsense way, on the duty of the bereaved to temper their affliction by devoted attention to those whom the deceased has left behind; at the same time he held that spiritually the living can help the dead. The high value that he sets on conjugal and domestic life[2] would be striking if we were not familiar with his dual standard of life, for those in the world and those out of it. The ordinary life of human society, even Court life, afforded scope, in his eyes, for the attainment of a high stage of Christian virtue, but those who had renounced the world were bound to aim higher, seeing that they were free from many temptations, and had received a divine call.

This view is strongly expressed in two letters to devout laymen, and in one to a lady who wished to leave the world but had not obtained her husband's consent. To Marianus the Spatharius he writes, after designating the chief vices to be shunned and virtues to be sought: "These and suchlike things pertain to the true Christian. Do not consider, my Lord, that what I have said only applies to the monk, and

---

[1] *Lib.* ii. 54; *cf.* ii. 145.
[2] See especially ii. 176, 186 and 188.

does not pertain equally to the laity at large (even though these things are most strictly enjoined on monks); with the exception of celibacy and poverty, in respect of which things those in the world are not condemned. But even with regard to these, there are times for abstinence and rules for self-denial."[1] And to Theodore the Hospitalarius:[2] "The true Christian is nothing else but a copy and impression of Christ, and ought to stand to Him as the branches to the vine and the members to the head." After speaking of reciprocal duties of masters and slaves, husbands and wives, parents and children, he continues: "Here we have slavery and marriage; in the world to-come both will cease, and all will be one, as are the angels." To Albeneca, the wife of the Protospatharius:[3] "It is a great thing, Lady, that you desire, and one hard to accomplish; . . . since you cannot easily be severed, after God has joined you together." She should tell her husband of her wish, and set forth the superiority of the monastic life. If he will consent, well and good. If not, she should remain with him, not vexing him with complaints, but winning him by her devout life. This lady seems to have had grown-up children, so that there was not any question of deserting a young family, but her high position made retirement difficult. Theodore told her that she must seek salvation in her married life, and hope that the way would be smoothed for her to something higher.

A vigorous exhortation to duty in lay and official life is to be found in a letter he wrote to a certain Demetrius the Consul,[4] on his appointment to an important command involving chances of war. But there

[1] *Lib.* ii. 117. [2] *Lib.* ii. 122.
[3] *Lib.* ii. 51. [4] *Lib.* ii. 148.

is a touch of stern asceticism in his admonitions, since, along with his injunctions to do justice, relieve the oppressed, and refuse gifts, comes the prohibition of laughter: "For they that laugh now shall mourn and weep hereafter."

Both men and women were accustomed to ask Theodore's advice on questions of casuistry, as well as on spiritual life and discipline. Thus he is called upon[1] by one of his "sons" to decide the old and knotty question whether it is ever justifiable to tell a lie. His answer is in the negative, but with a proviso that reminds us of the adage on "treason never successful"; if you tell a lie to save a brother or sister from destruction, and add, *sotto voce*, words which may give a true meaning, you have not lied. But this expedient is not to be used in order merely to avoid inconvenience to oneself. The reasoning is hardly cogent, as in arguing points of ethics Theodore has regard to authorities rather than to principles, but the result seems to be consistent with common-sense. In another letter[2] he protests against the diversion to the use of men of a religious house originally designed for women. In another[3] he condemns the intention of a father who had dedicated his elder daughter to the religious life, but on obtaining an eligible offer of marriage for her, was thinking of accepting it and devoting a younger daughter in her place. It is plain that such lax transference of vows would destroy altogether their binding character. It is gratifying to find a letter protesting against the cruelty of boycotting the family of a

---

[1] *Lib.* ii. 39.

[2] *Lib.* ii. 192. This is one of the letters to the Patrician Irene, and the monastery had been presided over by her daughter, and devoted to her memory.

[3] *Lib.* ii. 172.

suicide[1] and another addressed to an ecclesiastical dignitary, against capital or any corporal punishment of heretics.[2] Theodore's arguments would here seem to lead to a larger toleration than probably he would have wished to accord. He quotes the striking passage from a letter of pseudo-Dionysius in which the monk who is impatient for the destruction of the wicked is reproved by Christ, ready to undergo all His sufferings again for the sake of sinners. Theodore declares himself willing to lose his head rather than consent to the physical chastisement of heretics.

Among the letters of spiritual advice is one to a nun named Anna, on the subject of prayer.[3] This lady, to whom several letters are addressed, had ministered to Theodore's wants with motherly care. In answer to her inquiries, he bids her not to grieve that physical infirmity prevents her from fasting and labour, for a sufficient humility can make up for deficiency of abstinence. He bids her contemplate the goodness of God to her till she is moved to compunction: "whence comes illumination of the heart, delight in the spirit, a strong desire after God. When this takes possession of the heart, all that is evil flees away." In making confession, she is to call to mind all her sins, but not to dwell on them in a way that might be hurtful to the mind. The invocation to the Virgin, angels, and saints, comes last of the acts of prayer. "These things seem to me to comprehend what is of power in prayer. And though some may pray in certain words, and others in others, and even the same person may not always use the same words, yet the same power seems to me to be necessary for

---

[1] *Lib.* ii. 153.   [2] *Lib.* ii. 155. To Theophilus of Ephesus.
[3] *Lib.* i. 42.

all." There is nothing mechanical here, nor is there any mention of icons, or other material helps to devotion. In a letter to another lady,[1] who had asked how often she ought to communicate, he left the decision to her own discretion. He allowed no choice, however, as to the necessity of receiving the communion from an orthodox priest only.

Another lady, the wife of a Candidatus,[2] some high military official, was suffering from religious depression, from "a certain fear and trembling in the soul without any cause." Theodore counsels her to regard this infirmity as contemptible, and not able to work her real harm. She should strengthen herself against it by falling back on her profession and hopes as a Christian, remembering the words: "Thou shalt not be afraid of the arrow that flieth by day, nor of the terror that walketh by night," and, "if God be for us, who can be against us." She is to be of good cheer, pray and read, and never give way to lassitude.

There are a good many letters to heads, and collectively to members, of various religious communities. Among them are several addressed to an abbess named Euphrosyne (not, of course, to be confused with the Empress), for whom he seems to have felt something like paternal affection. Her mother, Irene,[3] was an Armenian by birth, whose husband had held a governorship, first in Armenia, then in Greece. After his death, she had adopted the monastic

[1] *Lib.* ii. 220.

[2] *Lib.* ii. 195. *Eudociæ Candidatissæ*—the same title as that given to Casia. (See note at end of this chapter.)

[3] *Lib.* ii. 113. I am inclined to think she was not the same as *Irene the Patrician* to whom several letters are addressed. The tone in which he speaks of her makes it improbable (though not impossible) that she had "lapsed" and repented. It was, however, probably to her as abbess that *Lib.* ii. 203 was written.

life, and became an eminent ruler of a monastery in Constantinople. Her daughter Euphrosyne was associated with her, and one of Theodore's letters was written jointly to them as his *sisters*.[1] He had not known them in their earlier life, but a strong friendship had been formed between him and them, and when Irene died, she asked Theodore to take her daughter under his especial care, a charge which he carried out with great zeal.[2]

The first letter that Theodore wrote to Euphrosyne after the death of her mother consisted mostly of a panegyric on the deceased, intended certainly for others besides the recipient. Soon after, in answer to a request from herself, he wrote again on the subject of her bereavement,[3] but chiefly with regard to the duties of abbess which had now devolved upon her. Among other pieces of advice, he exhorts her not to trouble herself too much with what is done in this or that other monastery. It is by our own law that we should test ourselves, not by the practice of our neighbours. He advises her to find a coadjutrix to relieve her of some of her responsibilities. He has written unreservedly to her and her mother, he says, as if they were really his mother and sister by physical kinship. They have one Father, one household, and one inheritance, and the love which binds them together has the sanction of Christ. In another letter,[4] he bids her try to know all her nuns individually, with their several tastes, capacities, and temptations, that she may be able to deal wisely with each one.

---

[1] *Lib.* ii. 104.
[2] Theodore also wrote two graceful epitaphs on Irene. See his *Iambi*, 117, 118.
[3] *Lib.* ii. 115. [4] *Lib.* ii. 118.

He seems to have found her inclined to regard the cares of office as a hindrance to the attainment of spiritual excellence, since he has, in another letter,[1] to insist that the care of the Sisters is a help, rather than a hindrance, to her progress. He dwells[2] in a way that modern taste might find morbid, on the high vocation of nuns as "brides of Christ," and our present standard would not allow a high place to the virtue of tearfulness.[3] But high-strung emotion seems to him the only safeguard against the tendency to become slack. Theodore seems to have derived real satisfaction from his intercourse with Euphrosyne, since he was able to congratulate her on the good order that prevailed in her monastery, which had become an "eye of Byzantium," with a high reputation for piety, hospitality, and general harmony. One definite point of discipline is referred by her to him.[4] A nun has tired of the rule and wishes to leave. Theodore is quite clear in his answer, for which he cites the authority of Basil. A nun may be allowed to depart if it is to take the oversight of another community, or the Abbess may allow, at times, a change likely to prove beneficial. But an impatient desire to throw off the yoke is never to be gratified. The term *Mother*, which Theodore often applies to Euphrosyne, precludes the idea of her being a young woman. But in addressing her, he takes the tone of a father or an elder brother. She is to be the living image (icon) of her Mother, whose name suggested peace, and in whose place he stands to exhort and encourage her in the ways of peace and holiness.

Another lady who received encouragement from

[1] *Lib.* ii. 134.
[2] *Lib.* ii. 150.
[3] *Lib.* ii. 177.
[4] *Lib.* ii. 196.

Theodore in the career on which she had entered was Casia, or Icasia, the poetess.[1] This lady, who became an eminent and prolific writer of religious and other poetry, is also the heroine of a strangely romantic story. Some chroniclers relate that the Empress Euphrosyne, seeking a bride for the Emperor Theophilus (her step-son) called together a number of maidens of good family, and bade the Emperor give a golden apple to the one he preferred. Theophilus was attracted by the vivacious appearance of Casia, and to test her, made the somewhat uncouth statement: "By woman came evil into the world." "And by woman," replied Casia, "came deliverance from evil." But her readiness in speech seemed to betoken a want of modesty, and the apple was given to another maiden, Theodora. Casia had lost her opportunity. She entered the monastic life, and attained a literary celebrity which she might not have obtained in the enervating atmosphere of a Court. So runs the story, but the letter from Theodore would seem to show that she had aspired to a religious life from her early youth. In any case it is interesting to find that she belonged to the circle of those opposed to the religious policy of the Emperors, and that, as her writings might lead us to suppose, she felt the powerful influence of Studium and its abbot. More than one letter is addressed to a person of her name, but the identity is doubtful.[1]

The letters on questions of Christian doctrine are mostly concerned with the controversy which filled his whole life as to images and prototypes, in relation to the dogma of the Two Natures. There is one on

---

[1] See note at end of this chapter.

a subject which belongs to the regions rather of mysticism than of dogmatism, but which the dogmatic spirit of the age brought within the area of authority: the hope of final restitution.[1] Theodore had been asked by his "son" Gregory to enlarge what he had said in some previous communication suggested by certain statements of the Bishop of Chalcedon. He follows Maximus and other Greek Fathers in acknowledging three kinds of future restoration: of each individual, according to his merits; of the whole physical creation, which is to be made incorruptible and immortal; and of the whole moral creation, whence sin is to be made to disappear, as the soul of man returns to the Infinite God. For sin has no real existence, since it is not a creature of God, and in the fulness of time it will perish, and he who has committed sin will be "saved as by fire." This statement would seem to give a far more optimistic view of the universe than is found in Theodore's works generally, but he seems to ward off dangerous consequences by his anxiety to assert that this is not the doctrine of the arch-heretic Origen, and to avoid pressing the words even of the authorities he accepts to their natural conclusions.

Some of Theodore's last efforts were devoted to the reclamation of a hermit named Theoctistus,[2] who seems to have taken up various heretical doctrines, but to have abandoned them in consequence of Theodore's persuasions. Both by letter and by personal intercourse, Theodore was active to the last. The last months of his life were spent among his followers and friends, who flocked to Acritas from all quarters. It

[1] *Lib.* ii. 160.   [2] *Lib.* ii. 116, 138, 166.

might seem that where he was, there was Studium, though the actual monastery was no longer his dwelling-place.

Theodore was now sixty-seven years old, but must have seemed much older, as his health had been broken by his anxieties and labours. More than once before, the end had seemed near, and after the last illness had taken hold of him, he had various rallies which enabled him to give his final injunctions to his monks. When physically incapable of addressing them, he wrote an address to be read to them. Until the very last, he allowed himself the minimum of relaxation from monastic discipline. He drew up (if he had not done so earlier) what is called his Testament.[1] He begins this document with an elaborate confession of faith and goes on to exhort his successor and the monks as to their mutual obligations and common objects. The chief points of the rule are recapitulated, especially as to poverty and seclusion. Finally he encourages them with the hope of the final reward of constancy, asks for their prayers, and promises to intercede for them after his departure. He had spoken much of the affairs of the community to Naucratius,[2] then acting as steward, afterwards, doubtless according to secret instructions left by Theodore, appointed his successor as abbot. When Naucratius asked about those monks who were under punishment or censure, he replied "God will be gracious to them all." He was not free from the terrors of the unseen, but he was full of thought for those he was leaving. He sent a respectful

[1] In Migne, p. 1814.
[2] Naucratius wrote an account of his death and funeral and sent it round as an Encyclical. It is published at the end of Theodore's works in Migne.

CRYPT AT THE SOUTH-WEST END OF THE CHURCH OF ST. JOHN.

HIS DEATH

message to the Patriarch, and greetings to various friends, and received each monk into his cell for a final benediction. He received the Eucharist, and was "anointed according to custom" on Sunday, November 11, 826, and about noon, feeling his strength fail, he bade them light candles and sing the hundred and nineteenth psalm, which seems to have been in use at funerals. As the words were being chanted: "I will never forget thy commandments, for with them hast thou quickened me," he passed away.

He was borne from the peninsula to the Island of Princeps in the midst of a storm,[1] and buried in the presence of a great concourse of people, many of whom had brought costly gifts of candles, wrappings, and spices. But even in death his bones were to have no lasting rest. Eighteen years later, when the cause for which he had so greatly suffered had become triumphant, his body was translated to Studium, to lie with that of his uncle, Plato, and of his brother, Joseph of Thessalonica, both of whom had fought with him and suffered with him, and might now seem, though late, to triumph with him, as they rested together in the home which had long been the centre of their labours and affections, but never—till the last—their permanent abode.

An adequate impression of Theodore's mind and of his achievements cannot be obtained without further study of his work, actual and posthumous, in various fields. But here we may pause for a moment to consider his personal character as it has shown itself to us in his labours, his exhortations, and his intercourse

---

[1] So *Vita A* and *Vita B*. Naucratius, in his Encyclical, only says that he was taken to the place where he had written books and served the Lord, and does not mention any boats.

with followers and friends. Perhaps the verdict of some readers will be: "A noble character, if only it had not been spoiled by religious controversy!" But Theodore himself would have had no satisfaction in such approbation, since he identified himself with the causes which he felt bound to maintain. And it seems probable that had there been no iconoclastic controversy raging in his time, he would still have been on the side of the opposition to current policy or doctrine. He was one of the men whose intense feeling of right and wrong has led them to attribute grave moral importance to matters which to most people seem practically indifferent. Thus he became not only the champion of great causes, but the leader of dissension where modern opinion would see no occasion for a breach of the peace. All will acknowledge that the question of the Emperor Constantine's divorce and remarriage was a moral one, and that the monks who opposed it did so in the interests of domestic purity against lawless despotism. But when we come to the schism caused by the rehabilitation of the wretched Joseph, who was, after all, but a cat's paw of Tarasius, the atmosphere seems to be charged with the venom of petty personalities. Similarly the opposition to Nicephorus when he was first appointed Patriarch seems hardly warrantable, even if based on legality, since the irregularity was not unusual, and Nicephorus afterwards seemed to Theodore a good man for the post. And in respect of the great conflict—that against iconoclasm—even those who may consider, after studying his arguments, that he had a good cause, may feel irritated at his obstinate rejection of every chance of compromise. Theodore was essentially of a combative nature, and one to whom every conflict was a duel between good and evil. Perhaps we may best express his essential character by the word *Puritan*. He had the austerity of manners, the contempt for worldly pleasures, the severity towards both himself and others, the absolute indifference to any consideration at possible variance with religious principles, which English people associate with the word *Puritanism*. It may seem paradoxical to apply the word to a man who devoted his life to the maintenance, in religious worship, of institutions which English Puritanism branded as idolatrous. But after all, Theodore was not a devotee of sacred art. He does not himself seem to have used the icons much as helps to devotion. He scouts the idea of their value to the weaker brethren. He only upholds them because certain doctrines to which he attached great value seemed to stand or to fall with them. Far from fostering the impulses of free imagination in religious symbolism, he discouraged the pictorial representation of the virtues, or any unauthorised flights of the religious fancy. In giving spiritual advice on prayer, he thinks of the soul and mind of the person, not of any surrounding objects.

Thus Theodore had both the noble and the less noble characteristics of the Puritan. He was courageous in meeting dangers and in reproving wickedness in high places. He was willing to undergo great personal hardships and risks for any cause even indirectly connected with the principal ones at stake. He was loyal to his friends, and had the solicitude of a father in Christ for the souls of those committed to his care. But he was a party man whom partial views had blinded to the better side of his adversaries and the weaknesses of some of his partisans. He either could not or would not see the pride, perfidy, and heartlessness of Irene. His rejoicings over the murder of Leo V., even if they find a parallel in some utterances of Athanasius, are none the less revolting. His political horizon was bounded by practical limitations which prevented his one far-reaching idea—the unity of Christendom—from ever being, through his efforts, brought nearer to realisation.

But with the faults which belong to his type of character, he had virtues peculiarly his own. He was from early years a leader of men. He had a wonderful power of attracting men and women and of inspiring them with his own enthusiasm. This power must have been in great part due to keen sympathies and a clear memory of the character and needs of each one of his friends. The advice which he gave to Euphrosyne, to maintain an intimate personal acquaintance with the members of her community he followed himself on a wider field. And when there was no call for the exhibition of any particular bias, he manifested a high degree of practical good sense.

Furthermore he was a scholar and a gentleman. We have seen that he had literary power, logical acumen, respect for learning, intellectual taste in his recreations. He was at home when writing or speaking to the most exalted persons in the state, and could vie with any courtier in writing complimentary addresses. And beyond all this, he was a man of strong personal affections. We have seen how his love for his mother, brother, uncle, and other relatives was strengthened rather than weakened by his religious zeal. Like most great men, he was capable of strong friendship, and unlike some, he was, while intensely suspicious of ordinary female attractions, strongly sensitive to the sympathy and approval of good women.

I have called him a great man, and in using this epithet I am in company with most students, of very various schools, who have concerned themselves with his life and writings. Yet in two respects, one mental and the other religious, he could not rise above his age, and was doomed to a painful restraint. His mind knew nothing of intellectual liberty, his religion was out of sympathy with nature and with healthy human life. Admirably bold in withstanding the authority of the Emperor, he bowed his head beneath the yoke of an authority which seemed to suppress his thoughts if ever they rose towards a freedom or an originality which might be suggestive of some condemned heresy. Intensely conscious of the reality of the spiritual world, he despised as vanity all things pertaining to that natural world which, in the eyes of the loftiest thinkers, derives from the spiritual its whole significance and beauty. He saw and felt the contrast between the real and the apparent, but, in his theory of the prototype and the image, he fell just short of reaching the standpoint from which he might have seen a divine harmony and glory shed on a world shrouded in confusion and gloom. Thus he ever walked under the yoke and in the shade. But he walked in confident hope of liberty and light in the world to come.

APPENDIX TO CHAPTER XII

THEODORE'S CORRESPONDENCE WITH CASIA

THE friendly relations of Theodore with the poetess Casia, which seem to be indicated in the letter mentioned in the text, are much what we might expect, considering the great respect in which Theodore was held by many pious Byzantine ladies, and also the resemblance of their tastes and styles in religious poetry. At the same time, the subject presents several difficulties. Almost all that can be told about Casia is put together in a most interesting article, by Dr. Krumbacher, published in the *Sitzungsberichte* of the Bavarian Academy for 1897, which contains copious selections from her poems. It is rather surprising that the author, though in his *Byzantinische Litteraturgeschichte* he does full justice to the character and talents of Theodore, and to the historical importance of his letters, seems to have passed over the letter to her in the Cozza-Luzi Collection, No. 270, which, if accepted as genuine, contributes some facts towards the further elucidation of her life and character. Dr. Krumbacher places the birth of Casia about the year 810, so that she would be about sixteen at the time of Theodore's death, and the letter would seem to come very naturally from an old and revered friend to a clever and literary young girl. The text is not throughout perfectly clear, but may be roughly translated as follows:—

"You have again favoured us, most honoured Madam, with writings so able and so learned as to fill us with admiration and with thankfulness to the Lord. Especially as all this wisdom is found in a quite youthful maiden! I cannot say that you have attained to the standard of the ancients, for we of the present time, both men and women, fall far short of our predecessors in knowledge and in skill. But among those of to-day, you shine pre-eminent. Your speech is beautiful beyond all temporal beauty, and what is yet more excellent, your life accords with your speech, and in neither is there any uncertainty of foot. If indeed you desire in the present persecution to suffer for Christ, you are not one who, after one chastisement, becomes impatient, and unable to support the burning passion of a good confession (in which may you ever be preserved). For you know assuredly that nothing is so fair or so joyful as to suffer for the truth and to abound in sufferings. Gold and silver, fame and luxury, all that seems to be desired of earthly goods, is in reality of no worth. It is but a flowing stream, a vision, a shadow. Your choice of the monastic life comes, you say, from the persecution. This is not strange to me, though it may seem strange. Why so? Each one judges of what is to come from what has gone before, and conversely. If there is smoke, there has been fire; if there has been confession of Christ, the desire for monastic perfection will shine forth. You are happy in respect of both. But do not look for consecration from me,—who am a sinner—but from that hand the imposition of which will sanctify you. I would send many greetings to her who has brought you forth again into the light of truth, the Mother of your day. I have received her presents and yours, and consecrate them as a gift to the Lord by thanksgiving, praying for you both. Of a truth I am burdensome to you, but you shall be relieved from your spiritual burden by Him who taketh away the sin of the world."

From this letter we should gather (1) that the person addressed was a talented writer; (2) that she was very young—these two points would make it highly probable that she was the poetess Casia; (3) that she had a pious mother; (4) that she or her family had suffered (not necessarily to any severe extent) for the cause of the icons, and had ministered to Theodore in his distress; and (5) that she had already decided to enter the monastic life. This last point—if the lady addressed is Casia the hymn-writer—would militate against the veracity of the story of Theophilus and the golden apple, since the chroniclers who wrote that story certainly suppose that Casia was at that time (three or four years after the death of Theodore) unbound and eligible for marriage.

The golden apple story is regarded by Dr. Krumbacher as undoubtedly historical. He considers that the other Byzantine apple story—of the means by which Theodosius discovered the infidelity of Eudocia, is too dissimilar to be a duplicate. Perhaps it may seem odd that a critical apple should figure in the lives of the two most celebrated of women poets of Constantinople. And there certainly seems to be something legendary in the complexion of the tale. It is not narrated by the best of the meagre chroniclers (the *Continuator* of Theophanes), and Symeon Magister is hazy about Euphrosyne, whom he represents as the own mother of Theophilus. If, however, no more information were forthcoming, it might hold its ground. The point to which I would here draw attention is that if Casia were a professed nun before the death of Theodore, the historical value of the story would disappear.

Now, besides the letter translated above, we have two purporting to be from Theodore to a lady called *Casia the Candidatess*.[1] One of them was certainly addressed to a nun, though in this case the term *Candidatess* is puzzling,—unless we consider that she was the widow of a military functionary, the Candidatus. This is not impossible, although Theodore has *heard* that she had followed a pious life from early youth. She has been kind to his spiritual son, Dorotheus, but while commending her bounty, Theodore warns her against enjoying male society. The apparent want of knowledge on his part of the circumstances of her youth makes it improbable that she is the same lady to whom the other letter was written.

There is yet another letter to a Casia—again called Candidatess, with a slight difference in spelling—in the Migne Collection of Theodore's letters. This letter is in a different tone, and is so personal as to be very obscure. The lady seems to have accused him of listening to calumnies against her, and he asserts his rectitude with some haughtiness. The letter contains allusions to her sister and to a Strategus and his wife with whom they were apparently intimate. There is nothing to show whether the letter is to a married or a single woman, but the general impression that it leaves is that it was written to a lady in society.

Thus it appears that there were—presuming the authenticity of all three letters, which does not seem to have been questioned—two, if not three persons named *Casia* or *Cassia* among Theodore's correspondents, and that only one of these was written to the poetess Casia; that this letter goes some little way to discredit the story of the Golden Apple; and that the acceptance of the second letter quoted as addressed to the poetess would demolish that story altogether.

Perhaps the most natural supposition would be that the famous

---

[1] Cozza-Luzi, 142, and Migne, *Lib.* ii. 205.

Casia had a relative—probably an aunt—of the same name and the same religious sympathies, who was also a correspondent of Theodore. The question arises: was *Casia* or *Cassia* a name frequently used at that time? Dr. Krumbacher, after enumerating the many different ways in which the hymn-writer's name was written, concludes that it was the same as that of the daughter of Job, Keziah. Two variants of quite distinct etymology would be *Icasia*, the female form of a classical Greek name, *Icasias*, and *Cassia*, a Roman gentile name. If the name of the poetess were of the third etymology, we should expect to find it recurring among her kinsfolk. But to whatever conclusion Byzantine scholars may come, we seem to have at least one interesting fact before us: that Theodore knew and appreciated the budding powers of the most original and prolific of Byzantine literary women, and that she desired, but was not permitted, to receive from him authorisation for adopting that monastic life to which she aspired in girlhood but—perhaps—only entered when disappointed of a seat on the imperial throne.

CHAPTER XIII

THEODORE'S PLACE IN CALLIGRAPHY AND HYMNOGRAPHY

THOSE who have realised the great variety of interests which claimed Theodore's attention, the restless energy of his mind and character, and the depth and extent of his influence, during life and after death, will not be surprised to find traces of his activity in other spheres than those peculiarly his own. If he had never been made prominent in his relations with Church and State, or earned fame as a theological protagonist and a monastic reformer, he would still have been a person whose services to the art of writing and the art of versifying merited the attention of the palæographer and the historian of literature.

We have already seen how Theodore, and Abbot Plato before him, gave much time and labour to the copying of manuscripts. In his funeral oration on Plato,[1] Theodore remarks both the zeal which his uncle had shown in collecting books, to the great enrichment of "the monasteries under us" (*i.e.* Studium, Saccudio, and others on the islands or the coast opposite) and his beautiful writing as copyist. "What hand ever drew out the letters[2] more artistically than his, or who ever showed more diligent care in writing?" Similarly Theodore's own hand was said by Naucratius to be elegant.[3] One of his biographers[4]

---
[1] *Or.* xi. 16.   [2] ἐσυρμαιογράφησεν.   [3] ὡραιογράφος.   [4] *Vita A*, 35.

CALLIGRAPHY AND HYMNOGRAPHY 231

says "of which books there remain to us still some beautiful copies, written with his own hand." In one of his letters, he expresses the pleasure and comfort he finds in the work of writing.[1] Further, in all the accounts we have of Studium, both in the Lives of Theodore and in the collections of Rules, we see how important a place was held by calligraphy in the work of the monks. The regulations and penalties by which they were bound were decidedly severe.[2] A man who broke his pen in a fit of temper had to prostrate himself thirty times. Copyists of Studium had to mind their stops, and to keep their manuscripts clean, on pain of a hundred and thirty prostrations.

It is noticeable that the Studite monk particularly commended by his biographer for swiftness and elegance in handwriting is that Nicolas[3] who was, as we have seen, the constant companion of Theodore in his longest and severest exile, and in all probability wrote many of his letters for him. As might be expected, the art was carried on in the monasteries which were founded from Studium, and looked to it as their head and fountain. Provision was made for calligraphy in the various rules of the Athos Monasteries which have come down to us. The witness of ancient records agrees with that of modern researchers who, in quite recent times, have reaped a rich harvest of manuscripts from the regions under Studite influence.

---

[1] Cozza-Luzi.
[2] *Pœnæ Monas.* 53–60.
[3] See his biography in Migne, 105. It is not a contemporary work, but the tradition here is probable. He was as swift in writing as Asahel (2. Sam. ii. 18) and ἄριστα συρμεογραφῶν. This last expression is almost the same used above about Plato. Some take it to refer to the long tails of the capital letters, but it may possibly indicate the cursive character of the hand.

But there is a more definite point, and one of great interest, in the services rendered by Theodore to the art of writing, and consequently to the dissemination of learning. Just at his time, and, we cannot help suggesting, greatly under his influence, a new form of writing was being elaborated, which in neatness, elegance, and practical usefulness, far exceeded that which had gone before. This was the *Minuscule* writing, which had gradually superseded the earlier uncial before the middle of the ninth century. It has been shown by various researchers that this character was not a new invention, but the adaptation to literary purposes of a style already in common use for informal writing.[1] Most unfortunately for our present purpose, there are very few manuscripts of the late eighth and early ninth centuries that can be definitely dated. But if we consider together the immense amount of writing of an epistolary kind done by Theodore himself; the great pains he devoted to the art of writing; the number of *books* copied by his hand or under his direction and placed in the libraries of the Studite monasteries; and above all, the exquisite specimens of minuscule writing which, in the two following centuries, were actually subscribed by monks from Studium or from Mount Athos, the probability that Theodore had great part in the elaboration of this hand amounts almost to a certainty. And our confidence is con-

[1] See Gardthausen: *Griechische Paleographie*; Batiffol: *L'Abbée de Rossano*; other authorities given by Marin: *De Studio*, chap. vii. The connection between the non-literary cursive and the early literary minuscule was clearly shown by Dr. Kenyon in his Sandars Lectures on Palæography given in Cambridge in 1901. See also Maunde Thompson in "Greek and Latin Palæography" in the International Scientific Series. A good specimen of Studite minuscule writing is given opposite p. 146, dating from the eleventh century.

firmed by our knowledge that Plato acquired his handwriting in an office of the Imperial Treasury, and our strong suspicion that the same was the case with Theodore, though even if he did not, it was under his uncle's influence and guidance that he first set to work as a copyist. Now it was in writings from the Imperial Treasury that the regular minuscule hand first appears. In Sir E. Maunde Thompson's "Palæography,"[1] there is an extract from an imperial letter dated 756 A.D., as to which that author remarks: "In this specimen of the writing of the Imperial Chancery, most carefully written, we have the prototype of the minuscule literary hand of the ninth century. Making allowance for the flourishes [Plato's "tails"?] permissible in a cursive hand of this style, the letters are almost identical."

Of the general character of the early minuscule writing, Sir E. Maunde Thompson writes[2]: "The writing of the period of the *codices vetustissimi*, of the ninth century and to the middle of the tenth century, as far as is shown by surviving examples, is very pure and exact. The letters are most symmetrically formed; they are compact and upright, and have even a tendency to lean back to the left. Breathings are rectangular, in keeping with the careful and deliberate formation of the letters. In a word, the style being practically a new one for literary purposes, the scribes wrote it in their best form and kept strictly to the approved pattern." Further on[3] he says, "the writing of this first division of the minuscule literary hand is subject to so little change in its course that it is extremely difficult to place the undated MSS. in their proper order of time."

[1] Page 144.   [2] *Op. cit.* p. 162.   [3] *Op. cit.* p. 165.

No doubt uncial writing was simultaneously practised at Studium, since that hand continued in use for some time in service books. But the minuscule was eminently better fitted for multiplying copies of treatises on topics of current interest, and for stocking the libraries of the ever multiplying monasteries in works of scriptural, patristic, and secular lore. It seems by no means impossible that in South Italy, whither a good many monks had fled before their persecutors, an impulse was given to calligraphy which came originally from Studium. But without venturing on any disputable ground, we may safely affirm that the work of the Studites, and pre-eminently of Theodore himself, in developing a new style of writing, both useful and beautiful, and employing it in the multiplication and dissemination of books, accomplished a great work, the fruits of which we have not even now entirely gathered.[1]

An analogy may be suggested—but not pressed into details—between the changes then taking place in the art of versification and that of handwriting. Theodore and his immediate friends and followers seem in both to occupy a transition stage, and—at least in the case of verse-writing—to show skill in the old and also in the new method.

We have already[2] mentioned the verses which Theodore wrote on the parts and the offices of his monastery. They are generally in iambic metre with a few elegiacs, and are on the whole decidedly graceful and pleasing. As may be seen from a few rough translations appended to this chapter, while written in a light vein, they show all the intensity of Theo-

---

[1] Krumbacher, in his great work on Byzantine Literature, frequently notices the importance of Studium in the history of learning.

[2] Page 71.

dore's nature, and his stern conceptions of life and duty. Thus his best wish for his dormitory is that it may not prove conducive to over-much sleep. Guests, however courteously received and entertained, are warned not to distract the monks with gossip about the outside world. Monks who walk abroad to see to the business of the monastery are enjoined to keep their eyes downcast and to return as soon as they can. Yet, as in the *Catecheses*, the ascetic tone is relieved by a strain of joyous activity, a sense of the dignity of the meanest labour, a certain hope of reward hereafter for all the toils of the present.

Along with these verses specially written for Studium, we have a number of epigrams of different kinds: addresses to various saints and to various churches; lines on the sacred images, especially on one votive piece of stuff with a picture on it; the epitaph already cited on Irene the Abbess and some others;[1] a sketch of the character of a recluse; a friendly address to the place of his captivity; a disciplinary charge to himself. Of Theodore as poet, Krumbacher says: "He not only fills a gap; it was especially due to him that the art of Epigram, which in the dark days from the middle of the seventh to the end of the eighth century, had fallen into desuetude, was recalled to life, and by skilful application to things of present interest, made worthy of continued existence."[2] The large number of manuscripts containing Theodore's epigrams shows their wide dissemination.

But it was not by any work of a classical form, intended only for educated society, that Theodore's

[1] No. 115 is on Anna, apparently his correspondent to whom he wrote letters 42 and 54, who had, with her children, adopted the monastic life by consent of her husband! By a curious error, it is addressed to *his* wife.
[2] *Byz. Lit.* p. 712.

poetical achievements became the possession of his church and people.

In the voluminous metrical liturgies of the Eastern Church there are a great number of sacred songs attributed to Theodore.[1] By the middle of the eighteenth century, Theodore's other works had been studied and admired by some learned Benedictine monks who felt puzzled and perhaps scandalised by these productions. They found it impossible to make them scan. A good deal of conscientious labour was wasted in their attempts. They had faith in Theodore's learning and they knew that he *could* write iambics and even hexameters. Why should he not have written classical odes? But these odes of his were not to be explained without a clue that the Benedictines did not possess.

This clue was not discovered till more than a century later, when Cardinal Pitra, during what he regarded as a captivity among barbarians,—a sojourn in North Russia—turning over the leaves of an ancient service book in his cell, and endeavouring to make out the significance of certain red marks, lit on the secret of the *hirmus* and *troparia*, which, when once recognised, found ample confirmation in the expressions, hitherto but partially understood, of Byzantine grammarians.[2]

---

[1] Of the two odes given in Migne's edition of Theodore's works, one, that on the restoration of the icons, can hardly be his. Cardinal Pitra has published a good many in his *Analecta Sacra Spicilegio Solesmensi*, tom i. Paris, 1876. A fine hymn on the Day of Judgment, taken from the Trisagion of the Greek Church, is fully translated in Neale's "Hymns of the Eastern Church."

[2] Cardinal Pitra described his discovery in *L'Hymnographie de l'Eglise Grecque*, 1867. The whole subject is expanded and discussed with much lucidity by Ed. Bouvy : *Études sur les origines du rythme tonique*. See also Stevenson in *Revue des questions historiques* for October 1876.

The fact is that the poetry of the Greek Church had, before Theodore's time, come to be measured, not by quantity, but by accent and by number of syllables. The manner in which the change came about is not a matter on which all are agreed, but the main cause is evident, that the differences between long and short sounds had ceased to be articulately conveyed in ordinary speech, whereas the tonic accent had become as clear and predominant as among us now. Why this should have happened is a further question which may be left to the student of phonetics and of their history. The fact itself is undoubted.

Here a natural question arises: how did it happen that as quantity declined and accent came to the fore, a new system was required rather than a modification of the old? Why did not accent simply step into the place of quantity in regulating the order of words in the ancient measures? We are familiar enough, in English, with hexameters based on accent, and when we read modern iambics, we hardly realise that originally iambics went by quantity. Why should not the Greeks have adopted a scheme of verse in which syllables of greater and less value succeeded one another according to ancient rules, but having that value determined by accent, not, as previously, by quantity?

The answer to this question is not easily to be found. It is to be observed, however, that to a certain extent, and in some kinds of poetry, the process above indicated was actually gone through. There was a long struggle between quantity and accent before they finally separated their respective fields. In Theodore's Iambi, to go no further for illustrations, we often find in place of a long syllable a short one with an accent. But in lyric poetry, or at least in that of the Church, the old metres were lost. Some investigators have here seen traces of the influence of Hebrew poetry on the early Church, but this influence is exceedingly problematic. Others have thought to find only a rhythmic prose, analogous to those Canticles from Holy Scripture which formed the earliest of church hymns. Others, again, have hoped against hope to find reminiscences of classical measures. The whole subject is bound up with that of church music, since it was the necessity of accommodating words to melody or melody to words that led to the new system.

Now the discovery of Cardinal Pitra was briefly this: that generally speaking, in Greek hymns after the sixth century, we can discover a model verse, not necessarily at the beginning of each hymn, with a certain number of lines varying in length and number, and following this a series of verses which correspond with the model pretty exactly in the number of syllables in each line and in the positions of the accents. The model verse is the *hirmus*, those that follow are the *troparia*. This we perceive from the explanation, previously misunderstood, of Theodosius of Alexandria: "If one wishes to make a canon he must first melodise his *hirmus*, and then bring up the *troparia*, equal in syllables and alike in accents to the *hirmus*, and according to one scheme.[1] Of course, not all Greek hymns are canons. The canon, in fact, was a collection of hymns or odes, properly

[1] Perhaps the words are still wanting in perfect clearness, but this is a *locus classicus*, quoted by most of the writers referred to, and by Krumbacher (*Byz. Lit.* p. 695): Οἷον ἐάν τις θέλῃ ποιῆσαι κανόνα, πρῶτον δεῖ μελίσαι τὸν εἱρμόν, εἶτα ἀπαγαγεῖν τὰ τροπάρια, ἰσοσυλλαβοῦντα καὶ ὁμοτονοῦντα τῷ εἱρμῷ, καὶ τὸν σκοπὸν ἀποσώζοντα. Of course the analogy of classical *strophe* and *antistrophe* will suggest itself, but the differences are obvious.

CALLIGRAPHY AND HYMNOGRAPHY 239

nine in number, corresponding to the nine Scripture canticles.[1] But to compose a canon you must make odes, and to make an ode you must choose a model from some accepted writer or make one for yourself. You may use considerable freedom in forming it, but when it is once formed, in all the succeeding verses you must closely follow your pattern.

If we could apply the terminology and the *general* process to English psalmody, we might take as an example one of the paraphrasists of the twenty-third psalm. He took as his model the verse or stanza :—

> "The Lord my shepherd is ;
> I shall be well supplied.
> Since he is mine and I am his
> What can I want beside ?"

In the succeeding verses he was bound to follow the first, since each was bound to consist of: (1) a line of six syllables and three accents ; (2) a line exactly similar ; (3) a line of eight syllables and four accents ; and (4) a line like (1) and (2). Apart from any consideration of rhyme (which, though not unknown, is not yet of any importance in Greek poetry), a choir would have to hear the whole four lines before knowing how the tune was to run. The four lines would then constitute the *hirmus* and the succeeding verses would be *troparia*. The analogy is very imperfect, since in English psalmody the *hirmi* or models are comparatively few, whereas in Greek they were

---

[1] *i.e.* the two Songs of Moses, that of Hannah, of Habakkuk, of Isaiah, of Jonah, the two Songs of the Three Children ; and those of Zacharias and of the Virgin, taken together as one. See Introduction to Dr. Neale's "Hymns of the Eastern Church." It seems strange that one so well versed in Eastern hymnology should have apparently failed to see the importance of the scheme of accentuation, and have spoken of the language as "measured prose."

many in number and various in form. One early hymn-writer, Romanus, who seems to have been a master of his craft, composed a large number, which were freely adopted by others. Thus we find an indication of the *hirmus* frequently recurring with metrical changes in the Greek liturgies, just as in English hymn-books there is sometimes given the name of the tune to which the hymn is to be sung. Romanus [1] doubtless exercised considerable influence over Theodore, though Theodore was quite equal to the task of making new *hirmi* for himself, and often did so.

The characteristics of the new form have varied greatly—like most other forms of verse—according to the powers of those who used it and the taste of those among whom it became popular. If dull and mechanical it may become empty and wearisome. If used to express great thoughts or powerful feelings, and manipulated by artists who know how to "build the lofty rhyme," it becomes both dignified and pathetic in the recurrence of its manifold series of similar yet varying sounds.

In some modern Greek monasteries, travellers have heard liturgic odes which have confirmed Pitra's theory as to the essential character of Greek hymnographic rhythm. M. Edmond Bouvy [2] cites a hymn to the Virgin sung in the monasteries of Mount Athos in which the relation of *troparia* to *hirmus* is made

---

[1] For Romanus see Pitra's *Analecta Sacra* already quoted, which gives many specimens of his poems. See also Krumbacher, p. 663 *et seq.* Though he seems to have been an epoch-making writer, his date is uncertain. He lived either under Anastasius I. (491–518) or Anastasius II. (713–716)—more likely under the former.

[2] He also remarks that visitors from the West commonly find Greek services interminable from the simple reason that they never stay to the end.

very clear, and he ironically observes that though a hymn in seventy verses all exactly alike is tedious even to a pious soul, it affords an excellent opportunity of ascertaining the laws of its metre. But generally the case is far less simple. No student may hope with Pitra's key to unlock all at once the elaborate doors of Byzantine metre. In the first place, though the principles of "isosyllabism" and "homotony" (if we may coin abstract terms from the expressions of Theodosius) hold good within limits, yet we cannot expect to find the accents always recurring with perfect regularity on corresponding syllables in every *troparion*. Then again the accents themselves are misleading, since we have to distinguish the tonic stress accent from that which was merely grammatical, and possibly by that time existed for the eye, not for the ear. Furthermore it may be necessary to have recourse to accents which are discerned by the ear and not marked for the eye, as in some polysyllabic words, which may have a secondary as well as the principal accent, the former only being written in.[1] And to maintain the rule as to syllabic equality, we have to allow a good deal for the elision, diæresis, or synæresis of vowel sounds. Then again, as we have said, the *hirmus* to which most of the *troparia* answer need not come at the very beginning of the ode. There may be a prelude or procemium, and in all elaborate Greek liturgies there are a number of verses intercalated which bear various names according to their position and purpose. The subject is one which requires special and close attention. All that is attempted here is to obtain some light on the kind

[1] I think it was the late William Morris who made "Canterbury-bell" scan $-\smile\smile\smile-$. An inferior versifier would have made it $-\smile-\smile-$.

of measure and harmony which we are to expect in the Church hymns written by Theodore and the other Studites. For—as we shall have to show later on—Theodore was not the only hymn-writer of his monastery. His brother Joseph[1] practised the art, and probably there were others similarly employed in that generation, as there certainly were in those that come after.

We have already said that one of the Church "canons,"—a series of nine odes—purporting to be by Theodore, which is printed with his other works, is almost certainly not by him. It commemorates the Restoration of the Icons, and contains expressions of exultation over John, Antony, and the other iconoclast bishops, which would, at any time in Theodore's life, have been highly premature. The other canon is on the Adoration of the Cross, but seems to have been composed for Easter. The poems collected by Cardinal Pitra[2] are generally in honour of various saints, but there is one of exceptional interest to be sung at the burial of a monk. The ode consists of thirteen stanzas which (except the first, which is a prelude, apparently borrowed) contain each eight lines besides the refrain at the end: Τὸ ἀλληλούια. Most of the lines are of eleven syllables and three accents, but the sixth is a long rolling one of fourteen syllables and five accents. The form seems well adapted to convey the ideas, always powerful with Theodore, which the occasion calls forth: the tragedy of the sudden change; the human cry after the departed friend; the longing desire for some communication from the unseen world; the triumph of the

---

[1] But Joseph, Bishop of Thessalonica, is *not* Joseph the Hymn-writer *par excellence*, a Studite monk who came from Sicily.

[2] In the volume i. of *Analecta Sacra* often cited.

CALLIGRAPHY AND HYMNOGRAPHY 243

self-renouncing life; the solemn warning, here put into the mouth of the dead monk himself, of the vain and transitory nature of all things mortal; the final hope, not unmixed with fear. We have the spirit of the *Catecheses* clad in poetical garb.

If we read Theodore's religious poems, paying attention to the accents and trying to forget quantities, we become aware of a kind of melody that, if the words were suited to adequate music, might have an impressive, if somewhat monotonous effect. One feels that such melody might well have charmed the ears and the soul of Charlemagne,[1] as he listened to the music brought to his Court from far away. And one may be inclined to regret that at least one fruit of the Greek mind in its later days has been lost to posterity, or has at any rate failed to obtain due recognition from those whose lives are devoted to Hellenic studies. For though it is a product of what is in some respects an age of decay, it is instinct with vigorous life. Critics may differ as to whether Theodore's classical epigrams or his Church hymns are better as literature. Probably he bestowed equal care on both, and he may not have realised the difference between them. But the former were probably intelligible to few—in fact, it probably needed a non-natural pronunciation to make them intelligible to anybody—and the latter became so absorbed in the voice of the Church as to sound familiar in the ears of many who knew not whence they had come.

The connection between controverted doctrine and popular hymnody seems to have been very close in early times. Arius had sought to make his views

---

[1] Page 133.

acceptable to the Alexandrian boatmen by embodying them in attractive song. We have seen[1] how an addition to the *Trisagion* had once aroused dangerous tumults in Constantinople. Similarly it seemed natural that in the Iconoclastic Controversy Theodore had to refute the poems (as the phrase went) of his opponents, and employed his leisure in making acrostic verses against them.[2] And when the cause of orthodoxy triumphed, the hymns of the Studites acquired ascendency. If a versifier were to be judged by his weakest performances, we might set Theodore down among the controversial poetasters of a feverish age. But if the power to utter words that touch the deepest veins of human nature and that express the never-ceasing laments and aspirations of man in dignified and melodious sound, belongs only to the real poet, then we may well give the name to Theodore, since his work, amid some hay and stubble, shows here and there pure gold.

[1] Page 69.   [2] Migne, xcix. p. 437 *seq.*

APPENDIX TO CHAPTER XIII

RENDERINGS INTO ENGLISH OF SOME OF THEODORE'S POEMS

(In translating Theodore's Iambics, I have merely attempted to give a general notion of the meaning and character of the pieces through the medium of English blank-verse, the accepted equivalent for this classical measure. In dealing with the Church hymns, I have endeavoured to follow as far as possible the metre of the original as to accents and number of syllables. The result is necessarily very inadequate, owing partly to the poverty of the English language in natural dactyls and anapæsts.)

I. IAMBICS

To the Doorkeeper

Be diligent, my child, and wait in fear
On this thy task. Here is God's entrance-gate.
Attend with caution, and with care reply.
Repeat and utter only what is fit.
Be silent on whate'er might evil work
To those within, without, our brethren here,
And strangers there. Open and shut with care.
Grant to the poor his boon. Or give good words.
Thus when thou goest hence, thy meed is sure.

To the Keeper of the Infirmary

Oh blessed task, to bear the sick man's load!
That work is thine, my child. Then labour well,
In diligence and zeal to run thy course.
When daylight dawns, stand thou by every couch,
To minister to each with fitting words,

And then to bring the timely gift of food,
To each what suits him best, as reason bids;
Each one belongs to thee. Neglect him not,
Thus shall thy service reap a rich reward,
Light unapproachable, the joy of Heaven.

To the Sewers of Leather

A noble art is his who works the shoes,
'Tis like the Apostle's. Seek to emulate
The zeal of Paul, who sewed the leather skins.
Welcome the daily task appointed you
As Christ's own workmen, thinking still of Him.
Cut well the leather, follow well your art,
Make old things new, and work the new aright,
Throw nought away, and waste not by misuse,
In negligence, if all is not the best;
Nor cut too close, but find the proper mean.
Thus doing all things fitly, ye shall win
The race, accomplishing the martyr's course.

The Dormitory

O Thou who givest sleep, and ease from toil
To those whom daylight calls to labour still,
Grant Thou to me, O Christ, Thou Word of God,
Sleep light and gentle, swift to come and go,
And pure from fancy visions profitless,
But filled with dreams of all things fair and good.
Then rouse me up, what time the clapper sounds,
Alert and sober, fit for sacred song.
Set well my feet to praise Thee while I go,
From evil spirits keep my spirit free,
And purify my tongue to harmony,
To sing and magnify Thy glorious might;
That rising early after perfect rest
I may behold the light of Thy commands.

II. CHURCH HYMNS

Hymn for the Burial of a Monk

Prooemium

(Scansion different—probably an older verse adopted by Theodore.)

Gone from things transitory, piously departed,
He rests in peace with the righteous ones,
O Christ, who art God,
E'en if as man he has sinned with us upon the earth,
Thou who art sinless, lay not to his charge
What he willingly did amiss
And what unwillingly;
So prays the Mother who bore Thee.
Thus may we join all our voices as we sing for him
Our Alleluia.

Troparion I[1]

Passing strange is the sight and the mystery
For he breathes not, my comrade of yesterday,
And the voice that was speaking it speaketh not,
And the eye that beheld, it beholdeth not.
Each of his members is silenced.
His decree hath God sent out against him as 'tis written,
And no more will he come to his place of old,
Where we mortals are singing and sounding the strain
Our Alleluia.

Troparion II

As a son of the day thou art gone afar,
But for us there are tears for the loss of thee,
As we think of the graces adorning thee,
All thy love, all thy zeal, all thy gentleness.
We keep thy glories in our memory.
On thy shoulders thy cross didst thou carry still in patience,
And didst follow the Lord on thy earthly way,
Wherefore come, and to God let us sound forth the strain,
Our Alleluia.

---

[1] The *hirmus* is, for this hymn, borrowed from Romanus.

Troparion III

Tell me now, worthy friend, what I ask of thee,
Tell me where thou dost dwell who art snatched away?
With what souls has thy lot been appointed thee?
Hast risen to the regions celestial?
Hast thou attained to the things thou hopedst for?
Hast thou found an abode in the shining light? O tell me
Where the choirs of the living make melody,
As the shout of their triumph goes up to the Lord,
Their Alleluia.

Troparion IV

For thy voice it was pleasant to hearken to,
Thy converse was gentle and courteous,
Thou wert brother beloved of the brotherhood,
Loving good, hating evil, and pitiful;
The truth thou spokest in sincerity,
With no craft in thy tongue to resist the Lord's commandment.
But on all men thy face looked in kindliness,
And for this he will love thee who sings to the Lord
His Alleluia.

Troparion V

Thou hast gone through thy conflict of holiness,
Thou hast finished thy course in obedience,
Though hast passed through the trenches, O valiant one,
Of all lustful desire thou art conqueror,
And to shame hast thou put the Evil One,
And in meekness thy neck hast thou bowed beneath thy shepherd,
And excelled in thy humble obedience,
And for this will he love thee who sings to the Lord
His Alleluia.

Troparion VI

Yet we seem in the spirit to look on thee,
And to see thee as still with us sojourning,

When together we joined in our harmony,
Working our God-given work in piety;
Work that delighted all our hearts to do;
And we fervently long for thee our sometime companion,
But our wishes are vain, for we find thee not,
With whom fain would we sing as we raise to the Lord
Our Alleluia.

Troparion VII

For a dream is our life and a vanity,
This thou knewest, for God had instructed thee,
Thou hast left thy parents at his word to thee,
And thy brethren and companions and family,
So great was thy desire for the Lord himself,
All the world and its glory didst thou esteem as nothing,
And instead thou hast life for eternity,
And for this he will love thee who sings to the Lord
His Alleluia.

Troparion VIII

Yet thou seemest to speak to us hearkening,
" O my brothers attend to the word I say
'Tis the hour, come and fight while the strife is on,
Now is the day, there is work to do
Now ere the stadium is closed to you,
O beloved, give diligence Belial to conquer,
That the glory from Christ may redound to you,
And a song shall ye sing to the praise of the Lord,
Your Alleluia.

Troparion IX

" O how pleasant the life ye have chosen you!
O how sweet 'tis to dwell in a brotherhood!
For the Saviour himself has commended it,
When he spake by King David in psalmody.
Rejoice then, brethren, in all joyfulness
In obeying your shepherd and each one loving other,
And your passions send far and spurn away,
That your song may resound with the praises of God
Your Alleluia.

Troparion X

" Yet a word would I say in farewell to you,
O my brothers, no longer you look on me,
And my voice never more shall be heard of you,
Till the Judge gives his sentence concerning me.
That day so terrible when we mortals
Shall present ourselves trembling before the throne Eternal,
Whence each soul shall receive all its recompense,
And the living shall sound forth the praises of God,
Their Alleluia.

Troparion XI

" Great the terror and fear all surrounding you,
Hasten then, wait not, zealously all of you,
In obedience ever directing you,
Let the law be your rule and accomplish it.
For Satan lurketh like a lion hid,
And he roars as he seeks for the prey of spirits living,
By hardness with meekness rise victorious,—
That ye all may sound forth to the praise of the Lord
Your Alleluia."

Troparion XII

We have heard all the things thou hast said to us:
Since to thee has the Ruler seemed pitiful,
For us all do thou evermore supplicate,
That receiving instruction we go our way,
And fight and labour in all discipline,
That our shepherd may bear his rule over us in wisdom
And that God may give grace to us each and all,
That we all may sound forth to the praise of the Lord
Our Alleluia.

APPENDIX TO CHAPTER XIII

On the Crucifixion

Triodion, for Friday of Third Week in Lent

'Twas a skull the name had given
To the place where they crucified thee, Christ,
The Jews, their heads they wagged at thee
In laughter and in contumely.
Thou didst endure it,
To deliver us all.

On the Cross they wrote a title,
And the tongues of the superscription three ;
On Thee, one of the Trinity.
And Thou must suffer, Pilate said,
As thou wert willing,
To deliver us, Christ.

Of the Trinity in glory
The triple light the faithful shall adore.
As Light the Father worshipping,
As Light the Son they glorify,
As Light the Spirit
They proclaim in their song.

Hymn for Sexagesima Sunday (*from the Triodion*)

Part of a Canon

Day of terror, I behold
Now Thine appearance, glory unuttered,
Fearfully I look for the judgment to come,
Now Thou art enthroned
Quick and dead will now be judged,
Lord God who art omnipotent.

When Thou comest, O my God,
There will be thousands, there will be myriads,
Princes of the Heavens in attendance on Thee ;
And me wilt Thou summon.
I must come before Thy face
O Christ in all my wretchedness.

Come and take to thee, my soul,
Take all the terror, think of the judgment,
When we all shall see that the Lord is at hand,
Lament in thy mourning;
Thus in purity be found,
And bear the test appointed thee.

Now the fear doth quell my soul
Of fires of Hell that never are quenched,
Worm that doth not die, and the gnashing of teeth.
But save and deliver
And appoint to me, O Christ,
A place with Thine elected ones.

'Tis Thy voice, ever adored,
Which doth Thy saints to their glory summon
Joyfully; that voice shall I hear, even I,
The feeble one, finding
Of the Kingdom in the Heavens
The blessedness unspeakable.

Enter not, I would beseech,
In judgment, reckoning my transgressions,
Searching all my words, taking count of intents;
But remembering mercy,
Overlooking all my faults
Save me, O Thou Omnipotent.

CHAPTER XIV

FINAL RESULTS OF THEODORE'S CONFLICTS

THE story of Theodore's life and activity would be left incomplete if it were not followed by some account, however brief, of the subsequent fortunes of those causes for which he laboured and suffered. To some it may seem that the man was greater than his causes, or rather, that it were unjust to his reputation to regard him merely as the representative of a particular party in the Church or of one particular aspect of Christian doctrine. Like most great men, Theodore exercised an influence upon his contemporaries, and through them on succeeding generations, which far exceeded in weight the effects of his conscious efforts to achieve definite results. Yet he so identified his mission in life with the restoration of the icons, the promotion of ecclesiastical unity, and the well-being of the "fathers and brothers" of Studium, that it seems fitting to conclude our narrative with a slight sketch of the vicissitudes of each of these causes during the period which followed Theodore's death.

I. As we have already seen, Theodore died without having seen the icons restored to what he regarded as their rightful position in the popular cult. But if he had lived a few years longer, he would have had to suffer worse things, in witnessing a revival of the iconoclastic persecution. Theophilus, son of

Michael the Stammerer, who succeeded his father in the year 829, had been a pupil of John the Grammarian, and seems to have followed his teacher in opposing image-worship in a thorough-going and logical way. In 833, John became Patriarch, and the two worked together for the suppression of the cult of icons, a suppression which involved the punishment, by exile and incarceration, of many devoted monks, among whom, as we should expect, the most conspicuous were Studites. There were two brothers belonging to Studium, Theodore and Theophanes, who, after repeated attempts on the part of the Emperor to induce them to conform, were punished for their obstinacy by having certain verses branded on their faces.[1] We read once more of the destruction of an image over the Gate Chalce, apparently in the same situation as that which had been removed at the very beginning of the iconoclastic movement and had witnessed the first shedding of blood in the controversy. Possibly Theophilus was the sterner in his persecution for being a persecutor on principle. It is not easy to discern clearly what manner of man he actually was, but from the record of the orthodox chroniclers who loved him not, he was distinguished by a great love of justice, a sense of public duty, especially in matters of state finance, courage and enterprise in war, and strong domestic affections. One is inclined to suspect some exaggeration in the stories of cruel punishments, though cruelty, or at least a callous content in inflicting pain, marks the whole public life of the time, and some of those stories rest on the testimony of the victims themselves, who continued to bear the marks of their sufferings.

[1] Hence they obtained the surname *Graptoi*.

RESULT OF HIS LIFE AND CONFLICTS 255

Whatever allowances we may make, we cannot doubt that the persecution of the iconodules under Theophilus was severe. He had a policy. But there were two tendencies acting against his will and preparing the way for a reaction to come as soon as he should be withdrawn. These were his want of success in war, and his orthodox wife.

Theophilus was five times engaged in war with the Saracens, at first with success, later with failure and ignominy. It is a curious fact with regard to the Emperor and the Caliph Motassem that in these wars each took and destroyed the town which was the ancestral home of the other—Sozopetra in Syria and Amorium in Phrygia. Theophilus came to be distinguished as the "Unfortunate." And every blow to the imperial forces was a gain to the cause of the recalcitrant monks.

The Empress Theodora was, as we have said, a favourer of the images. She was the daughter of a pious lady, Theoctista, who had obtained the dignity of *patrician*, and dwelt in a house close by the monastery of Gastriæ. We have already shown our [1] grounds for supposing that the influence of Studium was strong in this religious house, which was situated in its immediate neighbourhood, and in some associated monasteries. In any case, Theoctista herself possessed and venerated images, though in general she kept her practices from public view. When, however, her little grand-daughters went to visit her, she ventured to show them her icons. Probably she did so with a word of caution, as the elder ones did not mention the matter at home, but little Pulcheria let out the secret by telling how Grandmamma kept some dolls in a chest and took

[1] Page 196.

them out to kiss. The Emperor is said to have been very indignant, yet he took no measures against Theoctista, except the mild precaution of diminishing the frequency of her grand-daughters' visits. Against Theodora herself stories were told by a spy but rejected by the Emperor on the mere pretence of an explanation on her part. His lenity in this respect is all the more remarkable if we accept a story which illustrates his severity towards her on another occasion. Theodora had indulged in a mercantile venture, without the knowledge of her husband, but when the ship arrived at Constantinople, and he learned to whom the cargo belonged, he ruthlessly ordered it all to be consumed by fire, saying: "Who has ever seen an Emperor of the Romans or his Consort become a trader?"

It would seem then that though by no means an uxorious husband, Theophilus, in his own household, practised a religious toleration which had no place in his public policy. Herein he may remind us of Constantine Caballinus. And in both cases icon-worship among some members of the Court led to its restoration in the Church and the nation.

When Theophilus died of dysentery in 842, his widow was associated in the government with their son Michael, a child three years old. Theodora was, of course, anxious to bring about a reaction in favour of the icons, but she was willing to bide her time, dreading the influence of the Patriarch, and not, at first, quite certain as to the mind of her colleagues. The chief of these, appointed by Theophilus, were the secretary and household officer Theoctistus, Bardas, the Empress's brother, and Manuel, her uncle. Of these, Theoctistus was in favour of the change. Of the intentions of Bardas at this time we are uncertain. He did not, in the sequel, show much deference to his sister's judgment, but it is not likely that he cherished many religious scruples, and he was probably already planning certain educational reforms which, when he was able to carry them out, established a centre of intellectual culture in the Palace of Magnauria, independent of any monastic foundation. The heated air of religious controversy and the exile of many men capable of educational work must have seemed to him less favourable to culture than that unity in orthodoxy would be at which the Empress was aiming. In any case, he was willing to agree to her project. The other tutor, Manuel, was won over by some Studite monks, who, it was said, visited him in sickness and promised him recovery on condition that he used his influence and authority against iconoclasm. When once the rulers were agreed, the ecclesiastical authorities could, as on previous occasions, offer but a futile resistance. An imperial officer was sent to the Patriarch John to demand his submission, which was naturally refused. When, afterwards, John was found to have received a wound, his enemies declared that he had attempted suicide, and a specious excuse for his degradation was supplied. The world will never know what actually happened, nor be in a position to estimate accurately the character and career of this remarkable man, the most intellectual—it would seem to us—of the iconoclastic clergy. He was replaced by Methodius, a monk of undoubted orthodoxy, who had been imprisoned for his opinions, but released by Theophilus, in respect for his abilities.

Though it was the Court rather than the Church that had taken the lead in the matter, it received, as soon as possible, the authorisation of a synod. Meantime the piety of the Empress was set on a more private object, the absolution and rehabilitation of her deceased husband. She consulted on this question an assembly of orthodox clergy, who were unable to give her satisfaction. She then had recourse to pious fraud, and declared that on his death-bed Theophilus had expressed to her his penitence for the sin of persecuting the faithful. The clergy accepted her statement and promised to pray for the soul of the departed.

The great day of triumph for the party of the icons was the first Sunday in Lent, 842, still kept as a festival in the Eastern Church. On Orthodoxy Sunday, pious Greeks listen to the rehearsal of all the heresies against which the Studites wrote, and to other opinions, many of which have a strange sound to modern ears, and condemn them with a thrice-repeated anathema. At the same service, the names of many confessors of the faith are read, that of Theodore being prominent, and the people in each case answer thrice: "May his memory endure for ever."

History seemed to be repeating itself, and Theodora with her child to be taking the place assumed by Irene and her son two generations before. Had Theodore lived, he would doubtless have bestowed on this Empress the same eulogies that his party had lavished on Irene, and his biographer would again have had to regret that an act demanded by reason and justice should have been carried out by violent and irresponsible hands. Yet there seems to be a difference between the two cases. The work of Irene was speedily reversed, but after the first Orthodoxy Sunday iconoclasm, in the Greek Church, never revived. Many other differences of theology and of ceremony helped, as we shall see, to widen the chasm between the East and the West, but this particular point does not recur.

RESULT OF HIS LIFE AND CONFLICTS

True, the manner in which reverence should be paid to artistic representations of the objects of Christian worship, and the kind of representation commended, came to be distinguished and specified later on.[1] But the one doctrine which the recognition of the icons set forth in the clearest way possible retained its place. The Church acknowledged Christ circumscribed in the flesh. Whether or no some other doctrines, to which Theodore could not have subscribed, came to be inseparably associated with the cult, need not concern us here. He had, by his words and his sufferings, weakened the opposite party beyond hope of revival. In the great conflict of his life, he, though no longer alive, was conqueror.

II. Far otherwise was it with the other great idea of Theodore's, that of the unity of the Church under the spiritual authority of Rome. We have seen something of the forces that made for discord between both the spiritual and the secular authorities of East and West during the whole of Theodore's lifetime. These forces became aggravated in intensity and more complicated in their interaction through the succeeding two centuries, till the final breach between the Churches came in 1054.

If, however, we would cease to think of impersonal forces, and single out one man who more than any other availed himself of the conditions of his age in order to assert and maintain the independence—and consequently the isolation—of the Eastern Church and the Eastern Empire, we should point to Photius, the second Patriarch of Constantinople after Methodius. The great learning of Photius, and the careful record

---

[1] The process by which statues in the round (ἀγάλματα), came to be prohibited, while pictures (εἰκόνες) were approved, seems to have been gradual. See Tozer's note to Finlay's "History of Greece," vol. ii. p. 165.

which he kept of his very extensive reading, have made him a benefactor of modern scholarship. In relation to the parties and conflicts of his own times, he appears in a less attractive character. He was made Patriarch by the machinations of Bardas, who, on trumped-up charges, secured the deposition of the existing Patriarch, Ignatius. Photius notified his appointment at Rome, but Ignatius sent a complaint to Pope Nicolas I., who sent legates to inquire into the case. These legates were won over by Photius and Bardas. Pope Nicolas, dissatisfied with the issue, held a synod at the Lateran, by which Photius was declared to be deposed and excommunicated. Nicolas also wrote a long letter to the Emperor Michael, in which a good many old causes of quarrel were recapitulated. The whole Eastern system of Cæsaro-Papism was attacked, and the supremacy of Rome strongly asserted. The tension of feeling in Italy is shown in the expression of resentment against the Emperor's contempt for the Latin language. If the tongue of the Romans is barbarous, why is Michael so anxious to be called Roman Emperor? Of course these threats did not prevent Photius from retaining his seat, so long as he possessed the confidence of the Court and Emperor. Meantime, he went so far as to accuse the Latin Church of heresy, in that it asserted the Procession of the Holy Ghost "from the Father and the Son." This is the one doctrinal point at issue in the last struggle between the Churches. It is not one which comes home to the mind and feelings of the laity as do any questions affecting the popular cult. It served as a party cry for many centuries, but the "Filioque" clause in the Creed would not alone have stirred up mortal strife. Another ground of much dispute related to the rival missions of Eastern and Western Churches to the Bulgarians, who had decided to adopt Christianity, and found that in doing so they must range themselves under one or other hopelessly hostile system of discipline and jurisdiction. Photius was an artful diplomatist, and in the affairs of Western Europe he found forces at work which he might turn to account in his opposition to the See of Rome.

The Carolingian Emperors, in spite of the strained relations in which they commonly stood towards those who ruled at Constantinople, had kept up intercourse of various kinds with the East. When Theophilus was hard bestead in his wars with the Saracens, he sent a distinguished emissary, the patrician Theodosius, to suggest an offensive league between the two chief rulers of Christendom against the Moslems. This early project of a crusade was blighted by the death of the ambassador, followed by that of the Emperor Lewis the Pious, and two years later, by that of Theophilus. The various members of the Frankish royal house were too much engaged in domestic disputes to attend to the affairs of the East. Before long, however, it became evident that some of them had a foe in common with the Byzantine authorities in the person of Pope Nicolas I. We need not relate in detail the efforts of Nicolas to maintain the supremacy of Roman jurisdiction in the Western Church and also to uphold his own moral and spiritual authority over princes whose matrimonial relations would make those of Constantine VI. seem respectable in comparison. His actions brought him into conflict with the power of the great metropolitans of the West, —notably Hincmar of Rheims—and also with the energetic efforts of the Emperor Lewis II. to make the imperial power in Italy really effective. The point to be noticed is that Photius and his supporters had the cunning to utilise to their own ends the disaffection caused by the uncompromising independence of Nicolas. Thus we find that Photius entered into negotiations with Lewis II. and promised to secure the recognition of his right to the title *Basileus* (instead of the barbarous one of *riga*) if he would support Constantinople against Rome. But the course of events was checked by a revolution at Byzantium and a change in the Papacy at Rome. Michael was assassinated by Basil the Macedonian, who had already caused the death of Bardas, and who began a new and strong dynasty in Constantinople. One of his first acts was to degrade Photius and reinstate Ignatius in the Patriarchate. Meantime, Pope Nicolas I. was succeeded by Hadrian II., a friend to the interests of the Frankish Emperor, and generally a lover of peace. Accordingly legates from Rome attended the Council held in Constantinople in 869, which ranks as the eighth œcumenical, and in which decrees were passed favourable, in general, to the Roman views. Next year the forces of Eastern and Western Empires were combined against the Saracens, who were ravaging the coasts of Illyria and Dalmatia, and had gained a footing in Southern Italy. But in both cases the reconciliation was hollow. Before the legates left Constantinople, they had been subjected to many unpleasant experiences, and the Emperor Basil made an attempt to rob them of their reports of the Council on their way home. And before the united military forces had obtained more than one marked success,— the conquest of Bari—the Emperors were again at variance. A few years later, when the Frankish

RESULT OF HIS LIFE AND CONFLICTS

Empire had sunk into hopeless decrepitude, and Italy was in a state of anarchy and wild confusion, another Pope, John VIII., made overtures to Constantinople. But Photius, who had been restored to the Patriarchate, was in no mood for compromise, and he now had the Emperor Basil on his side. There were again wretched exhibitions of duplicity and acrimony, and the breach was made wider than before.

Meantime, the matters of ritual and of custom in which the Churches differed were becoming crystallised, and they called forth much bitter controversy. The Latin Church had adopted the use of unleavened bread for the Eucharist. It kept Saturday as a vigil, a practice unknown to the Greeks. The Greeks allowed married priests to officiate without repudiating their wives. They also postponed baptism till the eighth day, even in the case of delicate children. Again, the Greek priests commonly wore beards. The theological question of the *Filioque* and the ecclesio-political question as to the ultimate resort of spiritual authority might appeal more forcibly to thinkers and statesmen, but the visible signs of the inward divergence could be better realised by the people at large.

When the final breach was made, never to be closed up except for a brief and doubtful period, we see the collapse of Theodore's ecclesiastical policy. Yet that very occasion marks his personal ascendency as a distinguished confessor of his church. The events, briefly stated, were as follows:—

The year 1053 was marked by the victory of the Normans over the Papal forces at the battle of Civitella, in which Leo IX. was taken captive. This catastrophe put an end to the last project for a combined resistance of Greeks and Italians to save Italy from Western barbarians. The Western Empire had passed from the family of Charlemagne and become German in character and aims. The Emperor of the East was at this time Constantine X. (Monomachus), and the Patriarch of Constantinople, a cleverer or at least a more persistent man than the Emperor, was Michael Cerularius. It seems that the Byzantine Patriarch hated the Roman See, and made use of the calamities of Pope Leo and the failure of his alliance with Constantine, to adopt a more definitely anti-Roman policy than before. Closely associated with him was a Studite monk, Nicetas Pectoratus, who wrote a pamphlet against the Roman heresies, especially as to unleavened bread and the Saturday fast. Leo remonstrated, but without effect. Meantime the Emperor, who seems to have been more pacific in his intentions than the Patriarch,[1] invited the Pope to send delegates to a Conference at Constantinople, with a view to reconciliation and peace. These legates—all men of some standing—arrived early in 1054. They were armed with complaints of old and new grievances, and the Patriarch did not receive them with too much courtesy. They were, however, allowed to take measures against Nicetas. In company with some imperial officials, they visited Studium and demanded the submission of Nicetas, whose book was solemnly burned. We might naturally regard this episode as marking both a change in sentiments and a decline in vigour on the part of the Studite monks. We shall see, however, that Nicetas did not represent the views of the abbot and the community generally, though if the abbot

[1] Gfroerer thinks that Constantine favoured the monks of Mount Athos as a counterpoise to the influence of Cerularius.

RESULT OF HIS LIFE AND CONFLICTS 265

had had much of the spirit of Theodore, he would hardly have allowed an anti-Roman monk to remain in the monastery. Be this as it may, the legates were not allowed to proceed further in securing the satisfaction they required, and were reduced to taking the matter into their own hands. They solemnly published a ban on the Greek heresies and all who favoured them, and deposited the document on the altar of the Church of the Divine Wisdom. They then withdrew from the city. The Emperor in vain endeavoured to persuade them to return. The Patriarch held a Synod, at which he feigned that the legates had not been acting with full Papal authority. But the Pope was willing to accept responsibility for what had been done. The Emperor was now practically compelled to throw in his lot with the Patriarch. The Papal Bull was burned, and the heads of Eastern and Western Churches were each by the other declared excommunicate.

Now, as we have said, the Emperor had not felt cordially towards the Patriarch, and at some time during the conflict he seems to have asserted authority over him in a matter which only bore indirectly on the main issue.[1] In his zeal against all favourers of Rome, Cerularius had erased the name of Theodore the Studite from the diptycha. The abbot of Studium, Mermentulus, who was opposed to the policy of the Patriarch, complained to the Emperor. Constantine accordingly contrived a dramatic scene for humbling the pride of Cerularius. In a solemn assembly,[2] when

---

[1] I take this story from Gfroerer: *Byzantinische Geschichte*, vol. iii. It must, however, be noted that it seems only to rest on a manuscript commentary on the text of Cedren.

[2] On Orthodoxy Sunday?

the list of saints was proclaimed to the people for their veneration, the reader paused at the name which the Patriarch had desired to erase. Thereupon the Patriarch, having received instruction from Constantine, arose from his throne, and pronounced the name of Theodore the Studite. If this story is true, it serves to mark a notable fact: that the Eastern Church, while repudiating the policy towards Rome which Theodore had constantly upheld, felt, nevertheless, that it could not spare so great a saint from its calendar. It might depart from his counsels, but to this day it venerates his memory.

III. If Theodore could have foreseen the future, he would doubtless have rejoiced at the restoration of the icons, by whatever means it might be accomplished. The permanent schism in the Church would have grieved his soul, even if accompanied by an emphatic recognition of his own dignity as a confessor of the faith. How would he have felt as to his third object of solicitude, the future of his monastery? We may well believe that, on the whole, he would have been gratified. For though there are obscure passages in its history, Studium remained generally true to the character impressed upon it by his example, exhortations, and never ceasing labours.

We do not know much about the Studites during the reign of Theophilus,[1] except that many of them suffered severe persecution. Orthodoxy Sunday was, of course, a grand day for Studium. The first abbot after the times of distress was Naucratius, the trusted "son" to whom a large number of Theodore's letters

---

[1] For this part of the history, I follow almost entirely the account of Marin (*De Studio*, specially chapters v. and viii.) who has most diligently collected many scattered notices in chronicles and biographies.

were addressed. It was early in the time of his government that the great ceremony was held to which reference has already been made, the translation of the bones of Theodore, under the care of the monks of Studium and Saccudio, from the Island of Princeps to their final resting place at Studium, where they were deposited, in the presence of the Empress Theodora and a large concourse of citizens.

Naucratius and his monks had some differences with the Patriarch Methodius. The origin and the course of the dispute are obscure,[1] but it seems to have resulted from the jealousy felt by Methodius for the memory of his predecessors, Tarasius and Nicephorus, who had, as we know, been several times opposed by Theodore. Methodius felt it necessary to read a discourse to the Studite monks on the duty of subordination to superiors. But if there was a slight storm, it speedily blew over. Naucratius was succeeded in 848 by Nicolas, the companion of Theodore in his adversities and captivity. After three years Nicolas renounced his office to retire into a hermitage, but he was recalled to his post and induced to take a leading part in the conflicts respecting the Patriarchate. As might naturally be expected, Nicolas and the Studites were strong supporters of Ignatius against Photius, who, when his authority was established, sent Nicolas into banishment and tried, by the appointment of successive supporters of his own cause, to break the spirit of the refractory monks. In the second Patriarchate of Photius and during the following period, Studium seems to have grown and prospered. We have already seen how one of its members, Nicetas Pectoratus, entered the lists on

[1] See anonymous extract, *De schismate Studitarum,* at the end of the Migne edition of Theodore's works.

behalf of Cerularius against the Latin Church, and thus brought upon his monastery a visit from the Roman legates.[1]

The imperial family for several centuries showed respect in many ways for the greatest of Byzantine monasteries. We have an elaborate description by Porphyrogennetus of the imposing ceremony held there on St. John the Baptist's Day, when the Emperor and his officials went to Studium in state, and venerated the head of the Precursor,[2] which was kept there as the most precious of relics. Two emperors, Isaac Comnenus and Michael VII. (Ducas), sought a refuge there and adopted the monastic habit, and two young princes of the house of Comnenus were entrusted to the monks for education. In the Fourth Crusade, as has been already stated, great part of the buildings were destroyed by fire, but on the restoration of the Palæologi, Studium arose again to a position of influence and honour. In 1381, the head of the monastery (now called Archimandrite) had confirmed to him the precedence over all other abbots at synods and all ecclesiastical functions.

But it would certainly have been a greater satisfaction to Theodore to know that his monastery flourished in earnest and efficient labours, not only in wealth and glory. We have already mentioned the literary services of the Studite monks to their own and to succeeding generations, both in their own literary products, especially religious poetry, and still more in their invaluable work as careful copyists of ancient writings. It is not only the

[1] Marin makes Symeon abbot at this crisis and does not acknowledge Mermentulus.
[2] When did it come there?

Studites strictly so called that perpetuated the moral and intellectual influences which we primarily attribute to Theodore. Many monasteries looked to Studium as their model. Thence men could go forth skilled in various manual arts, trained to severe and regulated labour, accustomed to regard their meanest as their most exalted efforts in the light of a religious service. The Studite rule was copied in many details by those who, from the tenth century onwards, created a system of monastic rule on the promontory of Mount Athos. And our debt to the monks of Mount Athos is one that scholars are coming more and more to appreciate.[1] The influence of Studium spread over to Russia and helped in the development of monasticism there. "It is no exaggeration," says one of the best authorities on the subject,[2] "if the Studites say, in the Introduction to the *Hypotyposis*, that their rule has been adopted by many of the most important monasteries. In any case, the fact is beyond doubt that Studium had a powerful influence on Greek Monasticism, and that by means of this monastery, the development of the monasteries of Athos comes to be closely associated with that of Greek monasticism generally."

The modern world looks elsewhere than to the cloister for the springs of intellectual energy by which our present life is kept in touch with the past while reaching forward into the future. Still less do we look to that quarter for guidance in social

---

[1] The monks of Athos still maintain something of Theodore's spirit. A lady in society, speaking to a traveller who had visited them, remarked: "I suppose they lead very idle, useless lives." "Yes, Madam," was the reply, "they *only* work and pray."

[2] Ph. Meyer: *Die Haupturkunden für die Geschichte der Athosklöster*, p. 19.

organisation and for light on the complicated relations of present-day civilisation. Yet, after all, most of the knowledge we possess, and much of our power of social co-operation, have come down to our secular life from the religious institutions of the past. And the importance of those institutions, their influence for good and evil, is a profitless study apart from that of the great characters that stood at their foundation. Eastern monasticism, always a very powerful element in the Eastern Church, can only be rightly interpreted if we study the life and character of the greatest Eastern monks. Those who have followed the career and entered into the mind of Theodore the Studite will be able in some measure to estimate both the strength and the weakness of Greek monasticism during a critical period of the world's history. They may also increase their sympathy with the past and gather hope for the future as they discover how, amid political intrigues and religious controversies, when the ancient nations seem to have become effete, and the young and vigorous to be given up to violence and anarchy, there always remain some centres of moral illumination and of vigorous activity. For whatever else in national and social life may prove impotent and fleeting, fearless devotion to duty and strenuous effort towards a spiritual goal, must, in the long run, appear as the greatest of the powers that build up the history of mankind.

APPENDIX

THE PUBLISHED WORKS OF THEODORE

ALTHOUGH the works of Theodore have been copiously cited in these chapters, it may be desirable, for the sake of those students who wish to make a closer acquaintance with them, to indicate briefly where these works can most easily be found. This sketch will be confined to what exists in print. A good deal written by Theodore is still in manuscript form, and a certain amount has been lost altogether. In Omont's Catalogue of the Greek Manuscripts in the National Library in Paris, we find the titles of some works ascribed to Theodore which do not appear in our editions; and in the Catalogues of the Libraries of the Mount Athos monasteries, there appear a good many MSS. which might yield fresh matter. On the whole, however, what is mostly needed now is not so much a larger and completer as a more critical edition of Theodore's works, both in poetry and prose. The reader cannot help feeling that some of the orations, poems, and epistles are more than doubtful as to authorship and very uncertain as to date. The work of re-editing the whole requires a historian, a theologian, and a liturgicist. The fabric is as yet incomplete, but the foundations are well laid.

The books to which the English student can have access in any first-rate library are mainly seven :—

I. Chief of all is the great edition by Migne, which forms vol. xcix. of the *Patrologiæ Cursus Completus, Series Græca*, and was published at Paris in 1860. It is based upon the earlier edition of the learned Jesuit Sirmond, confessor to Louis XIII., and contains additional matter from the publications of Cardinal Angelo Mai (see No. ii.). This edition is, of course, a monument of care and erudition, if not without minor errors. The chief defect is that it is not complete, in that it lacks a very large number of Theodore's letters, and is deficient in the most characteristic of all his compositions, the Catechetical Discourses. Of these there are only a hundred and thirty-four (constituting the *Parva Catechesis*), and these mostly in a Latin translation only.

To give summarily the contents of the book:—

We have first (pp. 9–113), valuable excerpts from Introductions to earlier editions, with the testimony of ancient writers to the character and life of Theodore, and a very useful chronological summary by Sirmond. Then follow the two Lives, both of which were attributed to Michael the Monk (pp. 114–327), the first one, as appears, erroneously. Something is said about these Lives above (in chapter ii. and note at the end).

Next follow the *Antirrhetici tres contra Iconomachos* (pp. 327–436), of which an account is given above in chapter ix.

Another controversial work (pp. 436-478), following the above, is in the curious form of a refutation of certain iconoclastic poems, which had been written, in very artificial style, with acrostics, by John, Ignatius, Sergius, and Stephen. I am not sure whether these persons have been identified. *John* seems likely to be John the Grammarian, of whom there is frequent mention above. The acrostic verses are answered in others of the same kind, and followed by a commentary in prose.

The next work (pp. 478–486), is also controversial: " Certain questions propounded to the Iconomachi who deny that our Lord Jesus Christ is circumscribed (or depicted: $\dot{\epsilon}\gamma\gamma\rho\acute{a}\phi\epsilon\sigma\theta\alpha\iota$) as to His bodily form." It is an endeavour to make a kind of *reductio ad absurdum* of the iconoclastic position, by throwing into the form of a dilemma the ordinary arguments based on the Two Natures, and the cognate doctrines accepted by both parties.

The "Seven Chapters ($\kappa\epsilon\phi\acute{a}\lambda\alpha\iota\alpha$) against the Iconomachi" (pp. 486–498), are directed against the objections made to the icons on the score of idolatry, absence of icons from the Gospel, false analogy of the cross, and so forth.

We next have mention in Migne (p. 499), of the " Epistle to Theophilus concerning the holy Images," which conditions of time would prevent us from attributing to Theodore, unless it were written very near the end of his life, while Theophilus was interesting himself in public affairs, under his father's government. The general opinion of scholars seems to be against the attribution of this work to Theodore himself. It is published in the works of John of Damascus, who, of course, cannot possibly be the author.

APPENDIX

Then follows (pp. 499-506) what is called "An Epistle to his Father, Plato, concerning the worship of the Images." This is a brief statement, drawn up by the desire of Plato, of the chief arguments for proving the unity of worship in the cult of the images, in order to repel the charge of idolatry.

The "Catechetical Discourses" which follow (pp. 506-688) have been described in the text, especially in chapter v., and frequently referred to. As already stated, they are very imperfectly given in Migne, who has only the one hundred and thirty-four sermons of the *Parva Catechesis,* and, with the exception of sermon forty-one and some fragments, has these only in a Latin version.

The "Thirteen Orations" (pp. 687-902) (of which Migne gives the Greek text) are generally much longer, and far more pretentious and rhetorical in character. They comprise two (xii. and xiii.) which are of the highest interest and have been very much referred to in the text: the funeral orations on the Abbot Plato and on Theodore's mother Theoctista, both to a large extent biographical. The First Oration—on Abstinence and Temperance—is very much like the general run of the *Catecheses.* The Second—very rhetorical in style—is on the Adoration of the Cross. The Third, for the "Vigil of Lights,"[1] on baptism, fasting, and the human life of Christ, is especially Studite in character, since the symbolism connected with light was always much in vogue at Studium. The Fourth, for Easter Day, has incorporated a homily of St. John Chrysostom. Of course the debt is acknowledged, and we can see how homilies addressed to one congregation — like Theodore's own — might easily be read to another. The Fifth, on the death of the Virgin, has sometimes been attributed to John of Damascus, but it seems now to be generally assigned to Theodore. It acknowledges Mary as Queen of the Universe, and gives the legend of her death with the twelve-fold eulogy of the Apostles. The Sixth, on Angels, though there is a good deal of symbolism in it, is disappointing to any reader who is on the look-out for the ideas of Dionysius the Areopagite. The inferiority of most of the Orations to the Catechetical Discourses is very marked. It is, however, possible that some of them, if the work of Theodore, belong to his early days, and were composed as a kind of rhetorical exercise to be submitted to Abbot Plato.

[1] From the *Catechesis Chronica.* I should suppose this to be held on the eve of the Epiphany.

This suggestion applies also to the next four: "On the Birth and on the Beheading of John the Baptist," "On St. John the Evangelist," and "On St. Bartholomew." In the case of the last-mentioned saint, our meagre information about him is eked out by reflections on his coming last of the first six or first of the second six of the Apostles. The Twelfth—on the hermit Arsenius, is a more congenial subject for Theodore; one anecdote in it is worth repeating. A pious lady found out the hermit in his solitude and said: "Pray for me and always remember me." The hermit replied: "I will pray that the remembrance of you may be blotted from my mind."

The Letters of Theodore, of which two books follow in the Migne Collection, have been the chief sources for this biography. The first book (pp. 903-1116) consists mainly of a selection made from those written during Theodore's first and second exile, and are fifty-seven in number. The second book (pp. 1115-1670) of two hundred and twenty-one, is chiefly of those belonging to the third exile (pp. 1670-1679). In a few cases we have only the names of the persons to whom the letters were addressed. The names of correspondents and first lines of two hundred and seventy-seven more letters follow from the collection made by Montfauçon in the Coislin Library. The rest of the volume has chiefly to do with Theodore's disciplinary works. There is a very short treatise (pp. 1682-1684) called "The Four Chapters on the Ascetic Life" (taken by Migne from the *Thesaurus Asceticus* of Petr. Possin), very much like a catechetical discourse.

What is called the "Scholium of Theodore Studites on the Ascetic Life of Basil" (pp. 1684-1688), is a fragment defending the Basilian authorship of that work,—chiefly by critical argument, though with the suggestion that to hold the contrary opinion is impious; even as it is to doubt the Pauline authorship of the Epistle to the Hebrews or the Petrine of the Second Epistle of St. Peter. Theodore could argue as a critic, but the days of free criticism had gone—or were not yet come.

"The Explanation of the Liturgy of the Præsanctified (pp. 1687-1690), is a short description of the ceremonial followed in the Feast of Consecrated Bread—a survival, apparently, of the Agape, which seems not to have quite died out either in the Eastern or in the Western Church.

After a note on the unedited *Typicum* of Studium (pp. 1691-1692), Migne gives what is called the *Catechesis Chronica* of Studium, a marking out of the Christian Year with feasts and fasts (pp. 1693–1703).

The *Constitutiones Studitianæ* (pp. 1703–1720) have furnished material for our chapter v., as also have the *De Confessione et pro Peccatis Satisfactione Canones* (pp. 1722–1730). A few answers to sundry questions as to various observances follow (pp. 1734–1758), and then the *Pœnæ Monasteriales*.

Next come some metrical productions (pp. 1758–1768): first the "Canon for the Adoration of the Cross"; then that for the "Restoration of the Images," which, as we have said, cannot possibly be Theodore's.

The various Iambi (pp. 1780–1811), including those addressed to the various functionaries of Studium, follow. With these are a good many addresses to various saints.

A sermon (lxviii.) on keeping Lent (in a Latin version), follows here (pp. 1811–1812), though out of place.

The "Testament" of Theodore (pp. 1813–1824), his confession of faith, and last directions to his followers, is a document of considerable interest, though it does not seem certain that we have it in its original form.

In an Appendix (pp. 1824–1850), we have the account given by Naucratius of the last days and death of Theodore, and a note on the "Schism," or separation from the Patriarchs, of the Studites under Theodore. Among the Indices there are useful lists of the correspondents of Theodore, and the attempt of Baronius to arrange the Letters in chronological order (pp. 1857–1858).

It is thus evident that the Migne Edition, though fairly comprehensive, is deficient in three different departments of Theodore's works, the Letters, the Catechetical Discourses, and the Church Hymns.

II. In the first two of these departments, however, we are able to supplement Migne from the *Nova Patrum Bibliotheca* of Cardinal Angelo Mai. In the volume viii. of this work, published 1871, there are two hundred and ninety-six more letters edited by G. Cozza-Luzi. In volume ix., published 1888, the same editor gives us, in addition to the Greek edition of the *Parva Catechesis*, seventy-seven discourses from the *Magna Catechesis*. These do not differ greatly from the discourses of the *Parva* in form and tone. Perhaps on the average they are a little longer. The very great interest of the Catechetical Discourses in enabling the reader to understand the mind of Theodore and to discern the secret of his influence, has already been sufficiently set forth above.

III. There has since appeared (Paris, 1891) another Greek edition by Auvray of the *Parva Catechesis*, with an appreciative Introduction by Tougard. This forms a very attractive volume. The historical and critical notes are very helpful to the student.

IV. For the Church Hymns of Theodore, the student should go, first to the great work of Cardinal J. B. Pitra: "*Analecta Sacra Spicilegio Solesmensi*," vol. i., in which he will find (pp. 336–380) eighteen poems by Theodore. In the interesting and helpful Introduction and the account of manuscripts at the end, the author gives us some impression of the Herculean labour required to find out, identify, and put into legible form the hymns of this collection.

V. Another collection of Greek Hymns, the *Analecta* of Christ and Paranikos, contains a few by Theodore, and (on p. 264) a list of the hymns, or rather of a certain number of hymns, in the Service-Books, which are to be regarded as Theodore's.

VI. The reader naturally turns, if he can, to the Service-Books themselves, but here he is met by difficulties. The books themselves are not easily procured in England. They are (so far as I have seen) not indexed, the text has not been kept pure from additions or alterations, and the attributions of the poems to a particular author are not always to be trusted, even if there. There is a peculiar difficulty with regard to the poems of Theodore. His name is a very common one, and his works, both in prose and verse, are often confounded with those of other Theodores. The book which contains the largest number of his *canons* or other hymns, is the *Triodion*, a Service-Book for Lent with the preceding Sundays. The books of the *Menæa* are arranged in months with lessons and hymns appropriate to the various saints' days. The hymns include *Canons* as well as *Idiomela* and other types of verse. Several of the shorter, detached poems, especially in the *Triodion*, are attributed to Theodore, but, as Pitra shows, the Studite influence was in general favourable to the *Canons* rather than to other types of hymnody. There is a fine edition published in Venice: The *Triodion* in 1839, the *Menæa* in 1848, the *Paracletica* in 1843.

VII. It would seem ungrateful to conclude without mentioning the one Englishman who has endeavoured to put Theodore into English dress, and to present a few of his poems in a form suitable for modern readers and even for congregational singing. Dr. Neale, in his "Hymns of the Eastern Church," gives a translation of several odes of the *Canon*, which we have called the Studite *Dies Iræ*, as well as the hymn—of very doubtful authorship—for the restoration of images on Orthodoxy Sunday. This little book, with its introduction on Greek sacred poetry, may not be quite adequate to the student's needs, but it is written with enthusiastic devotion to the subject, and it has had considerable influence in making the English public familiar with at least some phases of religious thought and feeling in the Eastern Church.

The result of this brief survey would seem to be that a complete edition of Theodore's works is still wanting. It would also suggest that such an edition would require the labours either of a many-sided scholar, or of a group of scholars severally devoted to various lines of literary activity, so various were the paths followed by Theodore, successively or simultaneously, in the course of his full and strenuous life.

INDEX

ABGARUS, King, 126.
Academy, The, of Constantinople, 7, 18.
Acoemeti, The, 68 *seq.*
Acrita, Promontory of, 200, 219.
Adelchis the Lombard, 38.
Adelperga of Beneventum, 38.
Adrianople, Battle of, with Bulgarians, 137.
Aetius, minister of Irene, 102, 103.
Albeneca, wife of the Protospatharius, 212.
Alexander, founder of the Acoemeti, 68.
Alexius Moslem, 54, 63.
Anastasius made Patriarch, 8.
Anastasius, official under Leo V., 17.
Anna the Nun, 214.
Antirrhetici of Theodore, 160 *seq.*
Antonius, Bishop of Syllacum, later Patriarch of Constantinople, 141 *seq.*, 242.
Apollonia, Lake of, 145.
Arichis, Duke of Beneventum, 38, 47, 48.
Arsafius, 132 *seq.*
Athos, Monasteries of, 231 *seq.*, 240, 269.

BARDAS, kinsman of Leo V., 175.
Bardas, brother of Empress Theodora, 19, 256, 260.
Basil, Abbot, 125.
Basil, St., his rule followed in Eastern monasteries, 32 *seq.*; respected and quoted by Theodore, 32, 76, 127, 155, 163, 166, 217.

Basil, son of Leo V., 196 *seq.*
Basil, the Macedonian Emperor, 262.
Bithynia, Plato in, 25; connection with Theodore and his family, 25, 27, 171, 191.
Boneta in Anatolian Theme, 172.
Boscytium, Theodore in, 31, 34.
Bouvy, Edmond, 240.
Bulgarians, Wars of Greeks with, 6, 54, 128, 135 *seq.*
Bury, Professor J. B. quoted, 6, 9, 13.
Byzantium. See *Constantinople*.

CALLIGRAPHY at Studium, 77; Theodore's services to, 231-234.
Canon in the Greek Church, 239.
Casia (Icasia), the Poetess, 218, 226 *seq.*
Catecheses (addresses of Theodore to his monks), 82 *seq.*; translation of two, 89-92, 273, 274.
Chalcita, Island of, 197.
Charles, King of the Franks (Charlemagne), his relation to Italy and the Papacy, 37, 38, 46-48; events which led to his coronation as Emperor, 94 *seq.*; his coronation and its motives, 97; his negotiations with Irene, 99 *seq.*; his wars and negotiations with Nicephorus, 107, 108; receives embassy from Michael I., 132 *seq.*; his death, 135.
Claudius, Bishop of Turin, 206.
Clugny compared to Studium, 2.

Constantine V. (Caballinus) reigning at birth of Theodore, 6; his wars, *ib.*; his iconoclastic policy, 9 *seq.*, 24; his death, 26; exile of Studites by, 69; invoked by people, 137.
Constantine VI.: his accession, 26; betrothal to Rothrud, 39; marriage to Maria, 40; at Council in Constantinople, 42; signs decrees of Nicæa, 45; rivalry with his mother, 52 *seq.*; marriage with Theodote, 55; military disasters and blinding, 63; his character, 64; dealings of Nicephorus with, 108; his death, 109; note on date of his death, 113 *seq.*
Constantine X., Emperor, 264 *seq.*
Constantinople, position of Studium in, 1; Theodore born in, 3; repulse of Saracens from, 6; Synod in, 9; civilisation of, 12, 13; first meeting of Seventh Council in, 42; besieged by Thomas, 198 *seq.*; another Council in, 262; final embassy from Pope to, 264
Crescentius, Monastery of, 190, 200.
Crumn, King of the Bulgarians, 128, 130, 135, 138, 139.

DEMETRIUS the Consul, 212.
Dionysius the Areopagite, 157, 158, 163, 184, 206, 207.

ECLOGA published, 6.
Eginhard quoted, 98.
Eleutherium, Palace of, 103, 104, 122.
Eliseus, Greek tutor to Rothrud, 39.
Epiphanius the Studite, 126.
Eugenius, Pope, 203.
Eulogius of Alexandria, 127.
Euphrosyne, daughter of Constantine VI., takes the veil, 109; married to Michael II. 195; seeks a bride for Theophilus, 218, 228.
Euphrosyne, Abbess, 215 *seq.*

Euthymius, Bishop of Sardis, 143.
Euthymius, brother of Theodore, 17; forced retirement, 28.

FRANKFORT, Council of, 47.

GERMANUS, Patriarch of Constantinople, opposes Leo III., 7, and is deposed, 8.
Gnosimachi, 124.
Gregory the Great, 157, 204.
Gregory II., Pope, protests against Iconoclasm, 8.
Gregory III., Pope: his opposition to Emperor Leo III., 9.
Gregory Pterotes, 198, 199.
Grimwald of Beneventum, 47, 48.

HADRIAN I., Pope, 37, 41, 46.
Hadrian II., Pope, 262.
Haroun al Rashid, 98, 107, 130.
Hefele, History of Church Councils, 13.
Hirmus and *Troparia*, 238 *seq.*
Hodgkin, Dr. T. quoted, 5, 13, 153.

ICASIA. See under *Casia*.
Iconoclasm, policy of, begun, 7 *seq.* (see also Iconoduly); arguments against, 149–168; revived by Leo V., 140 *seq.*; by Theophilus, 254; abandoned, 258 *seq.*
Iconoduly (or image-worship), approved at Nicæa, 43 *seq.*
Irene, Abbess, 215 *seq.*
Irene, Empress, wife of Leo IV., favourable to Images, 26; power and policy after her husband's death, 27 *seq.*; her marriage project for her son, 39; changed policy, 40; rivalry with her son, 52 *seq.*; forced to retire, 54; her triumph and sole reign, 63 *seq.*; her negotiations with Charles the Great, 99 *seq.*; dethroned, 103 *seq.*
Isaurian Dynasty. See under *Leo III., Constantine V.*, &c.
Italy, Affairs of, 8, 38, 107, 262 *seq.*

INDEX

JOHN of Damascus, 21, 124, 153.
John the Grammarian, his influence over Leo V., 140; his life and character, 142 *seq.*; Theodore and, 166, 242; policy as Patriarch, 254 *seq.*; deposed, 257.
John VIII., Pope, 263.
Joseph the Steward marries Constantine VI. to Theodote, 56; degraded, 64; restored, 117; conflict concerning him, 117 *seq.*; degraded again, 129.
Joseph, brother of Theodore, 17; retirement, 28; with Theodore, 61; perhaps suggested for Patriarchate, 112; made Bishop of Thessalonica, 118; on Theodore's side against Leo V., 181; meets Theodore, 190; death of, 200; correspondence with Theodore, 208; translation to Studium, 221; poetry, 242.
Justinian, his legislation as to monasteries, 33, 52.

KRUMBACHER, Karl, 226 *seq.*, 234, 235.

Λατρεία distinguished from προσκύνησις, 44, 47, 162.
Leo III., Emperor, first of the Isaurians, 5; his wars, 6.
Leo IV., Emperor (Khazar), his reign and policy, 26.
Leo, son of Constantine VI., 56, 63, 109.
Leo V., his accession and character, 138 *seq.*; iconoclastic policy, 140 *seq.*; character of his persecution, 170 *seq.*; murdered in chapel, 185.
Leo III., Pope; his accession and troubles in Rome, 96; his restoration by Charles, 96; crowns Charles, 97; Theodore's correspondence with, 124 *seq.* sanctions treaty between Charles and Michael, 133.

Leo IX., Pope, 263.
Leontius, made head of Studium and Saccudio, 175.
Lewis the Pious, Emperor, 182, 202 *seq.*, 206, 261.
Libri Carolini, The, 46.

MAGNAURIA, palace of, 257.
Manichæism, 106, 153, 164, 206.
Manuel, uncle of Empress Theodora, 256 *seq.*
Maria, first wife of Constantine VI., 40, 55, 109, 114.
Marianus the Spatharius, 211.
Maunde-Thompson, Sir E., 233 *seq.*
Mermentulus, Abbot of Studium, 265 *seq.*
Methodius, Patriarch, 257, 267.
Metopa in North Phrygia, 145, 171.
Meyer, Ph., on the Monasteries of Mount Athos, 33.
Michael the Monk, biographer of Theodore, 29.
Michael I., Emperor (Rhangabe), crowned, 128; character of his government, 130 *seq.*; negotiations with Charles, 134 *seq.*; disastrous war, 137; deposition, 138.
Michael II., the Amorian, or the Stammerer, Emperor, 109; his accession, 185; liberates the monks, 187; his attempts at compromise, 189 *seq.*; marries Euphrosyne, 194; successful against Thomas, 198 *seq.*; his unsuccessful wars, 201; his letter to Lewis the Pious, 202 *seq.*; death, 254.
Michael III. (the Drunken), 256.
Michael, Ambassador, 99.
Michael Celularius, Patriarch of Constantinople, 264.
Minuscule hand, Studite development of, 232.
Mœchianic heresy, 124.
Monophysitism, 10, 69, 154.
Mortogon, King of Bulgarians, 139.

T

NAUCRATIUS, disciple and friend of Theodore, 175, 176, 220, 221, 266 seq.
Nestorianism, 10, 69, 154.
Nicæa, Second Council of, 43 seq., 150, 203.
Nicephorus, Emperor, circumstances of his accession, 103 seq.; negotiations with Charles, 107 seq.; befriends Constantine VI., 108; consults Studites about Patriarchate, 110; appoints Nicephorus, 112; his general ecclesiastical policy, 115 seq.; his death, 128.
Nicephorus, Patriarch; his appointment and earlier career, 112; resistance to Emperor in controversy regarding Joseph, 116 seq.; distrusted by Theodore, 121; crowns Michael I., 128; makes peace with Studites, 129; relation to Rome, 134; urges peace with Bulgarians, 135; Crowns Leo V., 138; opposes Iconoclasm of Leo. V., 140 seq.; deposed, 144; Theodore's letter to, 146; visited by Theodore, 190; Theodore's influence over, 193.
Nicephorus, kinsman of Theodore, 57 seq.
Nicetas, minister of Irene, 102.
Nicetas Pectoratus, Studite, 264.
Nicetas, Præfect of Sicily, 100.
Nicetas, Theodore in custody of, 172.
Nicolas, pupil of Theodore, 71, 170 seq., 231, 267 seq.
Nicolas I., Pope, 260 seq.
Nissen on Eastern Monasticism, 33.

OFFA of Mercia, alive at birth of Theodore, 4.
Orthodoxy Sunday, 258.

PARIS Council (or Collatio) of, 204.
Paschal I., Pope, 182 seq., 203 seq.

Paul the Patriarch, 26, 27.
Photinus, father of Theodore, 15, 22; his brothers, 30.
Photius, Patriarch, 19, 259 seq., 267.
Pippin I., King of the Franks, his career, 5.
Pippin, son of Charles the Great, 132.
Pitra, Cardinal, 236 seq.
Plato, uncle of Theodore, his early career, 16; forsakes the world, 25, 26; returns to Constantinople, 27; life as Abbot of Saccudio, 31 seq.; attitude to Tarasius after Council of Nicæa, 45; causes Theodore's ordination and election as Abbot of Saccudio, 48, 51; consulted as to Constantine's second marriage, 57; persecuted, 58 seq.; letter to him from Theodore, 59–62; at Studium, 66; his hand-writing, 77, 230; consulted as to Patriarchate, 110; subsequent sufferings, 113; imprisoned and exiled, 122; his return to Studium, death, and burial, 129, 221.
Princes, Island of, 104, 123, 194, 196, 221.
Procopia, wife of Michael I., 135, 137.
Προσκύνησις distinguished from Λατρεία, 44, 47, 162.
Prota Island of, 196.
Pulcheria, daughter of Theophilus, 255 seq.

RAVENNA taken by Lombards and then by Franks, 5.
Romanus, hymnographer, 240.
Rothrud, daughter of Charles the Great, betrothed to Constantine VI., 39.

SABAS of Studium, 45, 60, 69.
Saccudio, 31, 51, 58, 64, 66.

INDEX

Saracens repelled from Constantinople by Leo III., 6; wars with, 54, 63, 66, 118, 136, 201, 255.
Sicily, affairs of, 100, 107, 201.
Simeon the Abbot, 121.
Simeon the Monk, 121.
Sissinius, 99, 103.
Smyrna, 173.
Stauracius, Emperor, 109, 114, 128.
Stauracius, correspondent of Theodore, 210.
Stauracius, Patrician and Logothete, 43, 53 *seq*., 66, 102.
Stephen, Imperial Secretary, 57 *seq*.
Studium, Monastery of, its extant ruins, 1; its position in Church History, 2; Theodore made Abbot of, 66; its early history, 67 *seq*.; reformed rule under Theodore, 70 *seq*.; seized by forces of Nicephorus, 122; Theodore's return to, 197; service in copying of manuscripts, 231 *seq*.; after Theodore's death, 257; visited by Papal Legates, 264; character and influence, 266 *seq*.
Studius, founder of Studium, 67 *seq*.

TARASIUS, made Patriarch of Constantinople, 27; correspondence with Hadrian I., 40 *seq*.; his part in Council of Nicæa, 42 *seq*.; ordains Theodore, 48; behaviour as to Emperor's second marriage, 55 *seq*.; his friendly relations with Emperor Nicephorus, 105; death of, 109; his tomb visited by Michael I., 137.
Thaddæus, Studite martyr, 176.
Themes, 171 *seq*.
Theoctista, mother of Theodore, her character and early life, 15 *seq*.; her household rule, 16, 17; freedom from superstition, 25; adopts monastic life, 27 *seq*., 34; meets exiles, 60; her death, 129.

Theoctista, mother-in-law of Emperor Theophilus, 196, 255 *seq*.
Theoctistus, Abbot of Symboli, 25
Theoctistus (Abbot), recalcitrant after Nicæa, 45.
Theoctistus *Magister*, 121.
Theoctistus the Hermit, 219.
Theodora, Empress, wife of Theophilus, 218, 255 *seq*.
Theodore of Studium, his birth, 3; his biographies, 14, 29; his parents, 15 *seq*.; his literary education, 17 *seq*.; early life in Constantinople, 23 *seq*.; life in or near Saccudio, 31 *seq*.; ordained priest, 48; Abbot of Saccudio, 51; conduct as to Emperor's second marriage: negotiations and first exile, 57 *seq*.; persecution: letter to Plato, 58 *seq*.; his recall, 64; his attitude to Irene, 65; migrates from Saccudio to Studium, 66; his reforms at Studium and order of life he established there, 70 *seq*.; writes panegyrical letter to Irene, 105; consulted by Emperor Nicephorus on Patriarchate, 110; writes to Nicephorus on Church and State, 110 *seq*.; imprisoned and released, 113; part in controversy respecting Joseph, 117 *seq*.; exiled a second time, 123; correspondence with Pope Leo III., 124 *seq*.; return, 128; his influence under Michael I., opposes treaty with Bulgarians, 135 *seq*.; takes the lead against Iconoclasm, 143 *seq*.; his Palm Sunday procession and consequent exile, 145; his letters of encouragement, 145 *seq*.; his writings against Iconoclasm, 148–168; sufferings and activity during his Third Exile, 170 *seq*.; letters, 174–184; rejoicings at death of Leo V., 185; efforts for reinstatement of monks, 188 *seq*.;

returns to neighbourhood of Constantinople, 190; rejects compromise, 192; in Studium again, 197 *seq.*; writes to Emperors, 200; retires to Crescentius and Acrita, 200; reference to decision of Synod of Paris, 205; his private correspondence, 208–220; makes his Testament, 220; his death, 221; translation, 221; general estimate of his character and work, 221 *seq.*; his correspondence with Casia, 226 *seq.*; his services to calligraphy, 230–234; his poetry, 234–252; his posthumous influence, 253 *seq.*; commemorated on Orthodoxy Sunday, 258; his Commemoration in 1054, 266; his published works, 271–277.

Theodore, the Hospitalarius, 212.
Theodosia, wife of Leo V., 196.
Theodosius of Alexandria, 238.

Theodote, second wife of Constantine VI., 55.
Theodotus Cassiteras, Patriarch, 141, 144.
Theophanes the Chronicler, 13, 19, 51, 55, 65, 106, 124.
Theophilus, Ambassador, 99.
Theophilus, Emperor, 200, 252 *seq.*, 256, 258, 261.
Theophylactus, son of Michael I., 132.
Thera, volcanic eruption in, 7.
Thessalonica, Theodore in, 61.
Thomas, Rebellion of, 197 *seq.*
Thrace, invasion of by Bulgarians, 6, 135.
Troparius and *Hirmus*, 238 *seq.*

VENICE, 107, 125, 132.

YEZID, Caliph, opposes images, 7.

ZENO, Emperor, 69.

THE END